African Memoirs and Cultural Representations

Narrating Traditions

Toyin Falola

ANTHEM PRESS

Anthem Press
An imprint of Wimbledon Publishing Company
www.anthempress.com

This edition first published in UK and USA 2023
by ANTHEM PRESS
75–76 Blackfriars Road, London SE1 8HA, UK
or PO Box 9779, London SW19 7ZG, UK
and
244 Madison Ave #116, New York, NY 10016, USA

British Library Cataloguing-in-Publication Data
A catalogue record for this book is available from the British Library.

Library of Congress Cataloging-in-Publication Data
A catalog record for this book has been requested.
2022919299

ISBN-13: 978-1-83998-774-8 (Pbk)
ISBN-10: 1-83998-774-X (Pbk)

This title is also available as an e-book.

CONTENTS

LIST OF FIGURES

DEDICATION

To Professors Ayo Salami and Amidu Sanni
Scholars and visionary leaders

ACKNOWLEDGMENTS

Without the scholars who wrote their memoirs, the idea for this book would probably not have been conceived, let alone published. Part of my motivation for writing this book is to highlight the significance of the analyzed memoirs, encourage others to write about their lives, and for us to compile them into materials that will help us better understand Africa through African voices.

Over the years that I have worked on this manuscript, I accumulated many debts to those who assisted in various capacities as readers, evaluators, and critics. Dr. Bola Dauda is the most wonderful friend anyone can have. He reads everything I send his way. Your contributions are highly valued and are never taken for granted. Wale Oyedeji Luqman, Segun Atolagbe, Aina Kaosarat, Miriam Omotoyosi (Iyawo Oke, omo won l'Ode Omu), and Michael Efionayi, I am filled with gratitude to you all. 'Tayo Keyede has become the pillar of my work, the mainframe of my recent productive career, for which I am thankful.

I owe a lot to colleagues and associates who supported this project. I appreciate the love and affection of my family, especially the new grandchildren who fill the space with love and magic.

To everyone whose names are not mentioned here, thank you very much for your kindness and encouragement in countless ways.

PREFACE

Regardless of their race and social-political orientation, African scholars, journalists, and other writers of African experience tend to portray the people of this region as a single entity, homogenized by cultural practices, social formation, and political development. In this light, many in the West—usually the half-informed population—think of Africa as a country. Yet, Africa is a continent located in the middle of world civilizations with multiple cultures and traditions, practices, and people, as well as tongues and governments cutting across fifty-five recognized modern sovereign states with different geographical features.

By implication, the complexity of understanding "Africa" lies in divergent, exciting features. Whereas the above points to multiple space factors in this complex web, another vital point is the time consideration. When we discuss African cultures and civilizations, from which epoch of their consistent evolution are we concerned? This takes us back to the matter of space. Africa is vastly divided between two regions: the Maghreb and sub-Saharan. As early as circa AD 622, Islam had been a dominant force in the Maghreb region of Africa, perforating the social fabrics and steering the political wheel of the civilizations founded in that area. It was not until around the twelfth century that Islam and its cultural assets infiltrated the sub-Saharan part of Africa, having a significant effect on the people's culture and organization.

Compared to the Maghreb region, Islam had a less, if not substantial, effect on sub-Saharan Africa. Islam did not thoroughly spread across the states of the area until the twentieth century. In fact, in many of these modern states in Central and Southern Africa, the proportion of the Muslim population is smaller. In addition, those in the northern part of the continent (the Maghreb), for several reasons like color, cultural mores, and geopolitical advantage, consider themselves more Arab than African. The region's government could even choose to identify with Africa on one occasion and Arab on another. Then comes the Europeans with a taxonomy of modernity embedded in religion and religious practices, and considering that religion is a culture, the foregoing becomes clearer.

Taking its place in the heart of Africans, Christianity began to shape and guide the evolution of many of the states in the continent from the nineteenth century. Like a liberating force, as seen in the example of Iya Ayinla in Emmanuel Babatunde's *An African Journey through Celibate Priesthood to Married Life* reviewed in Chapter Three of this study, many flocked around this new culture at the time, evolving another set of belief systems and practices that cannot be lumped with pre-nineteenth century society in this part of Africa (the sub-Saharan region). Like Islam, Christianity changed the face and structure of African society, primarily for its sociopolitical advantage. The transformational force of these cultures was so intense that they altered the consciousness of their converts and mischaracterized the people as "infidels," owing mainly to their sociopolitical dominance and socioeconomic implications. Advertently and otherwise, society adjusted to these changes.

Notwithstanding, these divergent features have always received a central meeting point that makes some generalizations possible and valid, even though they might not always be absolute. Despite the extreme elements of having foreign doses on African cultures, some core aspects of "organic" African cultures still exist. These organic remains are often adopted by anthropologists, historians, scholars of African literature, and other social archeologists of the African past to illustrate Africans' resilience and the durability of their cultures. While it will be correct, for instance, to talk about an Africa where family tradition is held paramount, marriage practices are not always the same as they are ethnically determined. The intrinsic capability of gender representation in a "traditional" African setting aligns with what one could call a coat of many colors. This is perhaps the most dangerous minefield to navigate in African studies.

Based on these divergent notions, it is noteworthy to highlight that traditions and cultures represent a set of persisting or prevailing beliefs, social practices, oral, linguistic, and values that define an individual's way of life. In other words, the emphasis in some memoirs is often to propagate a unilateral need or embrace of self-identity. However, the dominant narrative and method of analysis in this study holds the notion and privileges that tradition and cultures imbibed by these memoirists are sometimes subverted, refashioned, or reworked due to the strand of experiences or realities they encounter in different spaces as their narration develops. Thus, the memoirists embrace indifference and open-mindedness, which is also greatly explored in the context of autobiography.

Furthermore, another strand that prevails in this study of memoirs and memories in Africa elucidates the complexity of narrating firsthand experiences. Oral traditions and creative oratures have been celebrated in African studies over the years, precisely from the 1950s, as the leading and most viable correspondence, aside from material artifacts, between the social "archeologists" attempting to penetrate the African preliterate past and the social–political and economic productions of that same past. In relation, this book synthesizes the idea that most scholars on memoir writings believe that the construction and presentation of the autobiographical self is hinged on the categories of individualism and relationality. In their narratives, the memoirists present their personal identity as not only part of their society, but also one that has been greatly influenced by important personalities in their various lived spaces.

Recently, the need to clarify the potency of historical realities, as well as the social and spatial reconstruction attached to traditions, has been brought to the fore. This came as social anthropologists and life writing scholars began to put the efficacy of oral traditions in their right context. The concern is that the argument about the supremacy of authority between oral traditions and written texts, like memoirs, which some oral literature scholars have consciously and unconsciously attributed to the former to further validate these traditions, can be counterproductive. The memories interrogated in this study show that these two reinforce one another, especially in sub-Saharan African literature.

Though oral traditions form the basis of African literature, they have attained the category of written texts for many reasons related to their production process. As noted in this book, decolonial African literary scholars began to adopt indigenous ideas and African creative art orature in their works to resist the western frame of literature. For instance, Wole Soyinka personified Ogun in his works as he sliced this mythical character in his literary productions. In Toyin Falola's memoir, *Counting the Tiger's Teeth: An African Teenager's Story*, this same legendary figure played a significant role. In Chapter Five of this book, we see how Ogun, the Yoruba god of iron, symbolic with metal, shaped the idea of childhood and society in Michael Afolayan's *Fate of Our Mothers*. Tellingly, this mythical character, known through the verses of different Yoruba oratorical repositories, performs more than a fictional role in the evolution of traditional Yoruba communities and the people. To consider how the depth of knowledge of the African past uncovered through traditions is superior to a primary written text, one needs to think of laying hands on a memoir written by Ogun himself.

Although oral traditions can hardly be lost, unlike written texts, memory could fail, and the ability to reproduce knowledge could deteriorate the same way as badly archived written texts could lose pages or fade. What oral traditions, like praise poems of numerous forms and functions, proverbs, (folk)lores, sayings, riddles, superstitions, and the likes do is form the collective voice of the lived experiences of the people of Africa, which could have been otherwise lost to the abyss or at best, placed in the footnote of history before the advent of literacy. In the memoirs selected for inclusion in this book, oral traditions are weaved with personal experiences in the production of the self, forming the basis of some African literary productions and promoted as having the potential to engineer the African knowledge system in the global academe.

The memoirs discussed in this study are concrete repositories of the transition of African societies from the traditional to the modern, produced through the methodological prism of autoethnography, that is, exploring and illuminating a society's inner workings through oneself. Aside from the introductory pages, which capture the study's conceptual frame, each chapter depicts the dynamic workings of African cultures, civilizations, and peoples. While this work primarily focuses on West African memoirs, a quick read of similar works from other regions of Africa concludes this study with the overall nuances and intricacies of the everyday life experiences of the African people.

As shown in this study, the progression to modernity in Africa and the overlaid structure introduced in pursuit of the evolution consists of peculiarities based largely on the culture/state's geopolitical reality. Gender discourse dominates the entire text due to the certainty of motherhood in a child's life and growth. The point is accentuated through the methodological prism, insisting that there is a possibility of pursuing the goal of cultural and social identity rather than transforming their lived spaces and ultimately developing a kind of deliberate and self-developed self-consciousness. Most memoirs include a strand of evaluation as they try to avoid promoting social and cultural alienation or supporting views of an unstable condition of human existence.

In this context, what is more paramount is the priority given to family tradition in Africa. For instance, when the experience of Firdaus in Egypt, as highlighted in the concluding chapter discussing the regional peculiarities of African memoirs, is compared to that of Iya Ayinla in Babatunde's memoir in Chapter Three, or that of Mrs. Ogonnaya Ogbaa Ikpo (in Kalu Ogbaa's memoir in Chapter Six), it is evident that the road to motherhood in Africa has diverse paths, each with its own experiences, actions, and consequences. The extent to which this text feeds into the contradictions inherent in achieving a balance in gender discourse in Africa is the most important aspect of this path. As a result, and to blur the gender lines, the memoirists, who are all men, usually construct and portray themselves as sentient, self-directed, and sovereign instead of women, who are more of a constructed relational identity. However, this book seeks to move in a direction where women are portrayed as dominating figures who pushed the authors to a threshold and boundary of identity and genre.

In *An African Journey through Celibate Priesthood to Married Life*, Babatunde expresses his vexation with gender imbalances in a traditional African setting as he applauds what appears to be a progressive symbol brought to light by western civilization, while also describing how the death of this system in apartheid and postapartheid South Africa destroyed homes, leading to a porous society in which his wife was a victim. From here, the discussion concerning the postcolonial condition of Africa forms another critical theme in this study. Deeply informative in this paradigm is Cherno Njie's *Sweat Is Invisible in the Rain*, which is examined in Chapter Four. Njie, who is away in exile from the dictatorial Jammeh's regime, is a front actor in the postcolonial evolution of the Gambian state. The fact that the economic condition of a place has its implication on society's social construction is an irrefutable truth, as this study shows. From Yahya Jammeh's Gambian dictatorial democracy to that of successive Nigerian governments that kept people like Ogbaa in exile, one that took land from Blacks in South Africa, and the one in Egypt that kept women prey to male chauvinism, the effect of the postcolonial condition of African states pounds heavily on the vulnerable groups in these states.

Considering the careful selection of memoirs interrogated in this study, the book covers modernization, postcolonial political development, culture and traditions, diaspora experience, gender, motherhood, fatherhood, communitarianism, and many other core themes that depict the variance and similarities of African cultures. It follows a careful and deliberate scope of analysis of the narrative history of contemporary West African memoirs with varying references to language, tradition, and cultures. This is because the authors, who are autonomous individuals who have traversed different worlds, are central in the discourse on the nature of narrating traditions and cultures, as well as how the spaces they come from should be related to their stories. As a result, there is a conscious attempt to redirect the development of contemporary West African memoirs from a disregard for traditional, cultural, and spatial conceptions to critical and reconstructive engagements with the social, personal, and communal identities of home and abroad. Cultural heritages are celebrated in all the memoirs.

The chapters in this volume follow a dual perspective and another way to view the readings of the African memoirs. They show that neither traditional, cultural, or communal nationalism nor traditional, communal, or cultural submission are viable options in the search for varying expressions with which to come to grips with the West African memoirist experiences, whether at home or abroad. Finally, the chapters discuss an approach that enables West African memoirs to review their cultural backgrounds in the light of living in other spaces and acquiring different experiences.

Chapter One

MIRROR EFFECT: NARRATING THE SELF THROUGH TRADITIONS AND CULTURES

Introduction

African memoirs are read not just as works of critical literary writing but also understood as writings that inspire achievements. African memoirists often use the concepts of the self, the other, and the community. These three are interwoven to the point that in telling the stories of the other and a specific community, the authors recount their own stories. Therefore, in reading an African memoir, one cannot grasp all the goals set by the author for the audience without examining the interrelation of the self and the other. African memoirs are sites to display the ontological, moral, and communal interrelations of the self and the other, which are central to this book. The narratives in the memoirs examined in this book highlight the essence of the relationship between the writers and their communities. These accounts share the experiences of the writers and those of others, as well as the influence of others on the writers. As explained in this work, each narration in an African memoir is told for different purposes, and at the center is the self (writer), who is greatly influenced by the other (community of others). Important to each memoir is the writer's identity, as he/she is the focal point, the one who is reminiscing, recollecting the memories from the past, and reflecting on the general implications of lessons from the past. This work aims to thoroughly analyze the experiences shared in memoirs written by Africans, particularly the various psychological, sociological, and sociopolitical underpinnings of the writers' narrations.

Therefore, it is important to lay the foundation of this work on theoretical frameworks, as one must conceptually analyze key concepts and theories such as the other, the self, personal identity, and social identity. By doing so, readers will understand the basis of many of the arguments, explications, and statements in this work. Issues about politics, activism, communitarianism, and so on should not be read in the seclusion of the self, the other, personal identity, and social identity. This is because the essence of this work can only be fully grasped through a critical understanding of how the writers are looking at societies to frame their experiences.

The Self and the Other

Understanding the self and its relationship to the community shapes the identities of writers, including those discussed here. The theories of personal and social identity are crucial to the theoretical underpinnings of this work. In many cases, the experiences of the writer within the surrounding culture or the interaction between the writer, their culture, and others shape the philosophical and existential leanings of these writers, including the cultures of the surrounding people and their traditions. As these writers narrate the cultures and traditions of their people, they relate their own identities examined through others, and others through the self, since others are a collection of selves.

The African notion of the self is a negation of the Western concept of the self in the West, as analyzed by the French philosopher Rene Descartes' famous aphorism "cogito ergo sum,"[1] which translates to *I think, therefore I exist,* as a depiction of early modern Western understanding of the self. This dictum focuses on the "I," and a very solipsistic definition of the self is presented through it; that is, in contrast to African ideals, the existence of the self is affirmed based on the self alone. Perhaps this laid the foundation for the solipsistic individualism of Western phenomenology and sociopolitical affairs. The central presentation of the individual as the most important unit is established and reaffirmed by the proliferation of the idea that one's personhood as a Westerner is affirmed through the submission that they exist.

However, the progress of phenomenology by Edmund Husserl has made it possible to shift from the Cartesian self-foundationalism upon which individualistic principles are built. According to Edmund Husserl, the self is subjective, and while it can affirm itself, it can only achieve its definition by seeing other "selves" with whom it shares qualities. In essence, to objectively define the self, the self must realize the existence of the other. Kolawole Owolabi describes this effort by Husserl as an attempt to rehabilitate Cartesian solipsism.[2] The solipsistic tendencies have not been completely jettisoned as attitudes and cultures, and the Cartesian analysis of the self is only stated here to give an insight into one of the many western conceptions of the self.

Existentialism has greatly influenced the way the self is conceptualized and thought of. For example, Jean-Paul Sartre declares that:

> I cannot obtain any truth about myself except through the mediation of another. The other is indispensable to my existence and equally so to any knowledge I can have of myself. Under these conditions, the intimate discovery of myself is at the same time the revelation of the other as a freedom which confronts me...we find ourselves in a world of intersubjectivity. It is in this world that man has to decide what he is and what others are.[3]

Sartre's position, like Husserl's, suggests an alternate way to perceive the self. He further claims that "I need the other to realize fully the structures of my being. The 'for-itself' refers to the 'for-others.'"[4] The existentialist definition of the self is synonymous with the African definition as explained by John Mbiti: "I am, because we are; and since we are, therefore I am."[5] The assumption in Mbiti's pronouncement is that individuals only exist because they have others to relate with and realize their essence from. The most unifying similarity in the African sense is the humanity between the self and others. The other forms the community in which the self may recognize and understand its own humanity through others and the humanity of others through interaction with other persons. According to Desmond Tutu:

> In our African weltanschauung, our worldview, we have something called ubuntu. In Xhosa, we say "Umntu ngumtu ngabantu." This expression is very difficult to render in English, but we could translate it by saying, "A person is a person through other persons." We need other human beings for us to learn how to be human, for none of us comes fully formed into the world. We would not know how to talk, to walk, to think, to eat as human beings unless we learn how to do these things from other human beings. For us, the solitary human being is a contradiction in terms. Ubuntu is the essence of being human. It speaks of how my humanity is caught up and bound up inextricably with yours. It says, not as Descartes did, "I think, therefore I am" but rather, "I am because I belong". I need other human beings in order to be human.[6]

Tutu explains that the essence of being a person is to exist in a community of others. Symbiotically, the person (self) is a product of the community, and the community is influenced by its people. Cultures and traditions are formed through constant interaction and intersubjective relations. By coming together, customs, laws, traditions, and linguistic rules are agreed upon, and a community of people with commonalities is formed. Through this, members of this community are socialized, and their identities are defined and realized.

The interrelation of the self and the other enables the development of linguistic standards, societal norms, mores, and behaviors. Through these paradigms, each person is influenced by their community's culture and traditions. For instance, in the *Fate of Our Mothers* and *Carrying my Father's Torch*, Michael Afolayan and Kalu Ogbaa respectively narrated the notions of community, cooperation, and unity by giving instances of the lives of others and community practices. Their narrations are a presentation of what informed many of their beliefs, demonstrating that we cannot understand the actions and ideas of the narrators in isolation from their communities. This relationship explores how and why writers inherited certain traits and why they are often affected by the plights of their people.

These memoirists' political involvement and intellectual contributions are born out of the effect and concern for the other, an attribute they learned through socialization in the communities in which they were raised. The alliance between these concepts is especially significant when the voices of underrepresented groups are brought forth, such as when African memoirists like Leila Abouzeid and Buchi Emecheta write extensively on the plights and travails of African women. They do not just tell us about their own pains but also those of other women, representing the collective predicaments of women in Africa. In this manner, the self may, in fact, mirror the reality of its community.

While this book presents different cultures and traditions, it is apposite to recognize that these cultures and traditions also tell us about the authors. When the authors narrate and present us with pictures such as polygamy, politics, and communal cohesion, they invariably present the experiences that defined them as a person and

Figure 1.1 Leila Abouzeid

what they have learned from those experiences. This is the case with the memoirists examined in this work, who express their feelings about the cultural practices (traditions) of their people. Due to the changing relationship between the writers and their communities, and because the self is not static, one may see some of these authors constantly juxtaposing their cultures and traditions with new cultures and traditions of the African diaspora.

One notable thing about African memoirists in the diaspora, and even continental, is the understanding of placing the shared bond of brotherliness, African identity, and blackness above the other commonalities of humanity, demonstrating that the self and the other are multidimensional. As will be discussed in this work, two of the features and qualities of an African memoir are the specificity of space and time. With this in mind, when the memoirists' critical analysis of the idea of the self in the West and Africa are contrasted, this grounding of the dialectic of the self and the other within a time and space gives the reader a foreknowledge of what informs the memoirists' comparison and juxtaposition. So that while the notion of individualism is frowned upon in Africa, as presented in some memoirs analyzed in this work, individualism in the West lays the foundation for the capitalistic nature of affairs in socioeconomic and sociopolitical spheres; therefore, the self must adapt and acclimatize.

Withal, the authors reminisce about the memories of home to point out the divergence between cultures and traditions at home and abroad while also suggesting the extrapolation of the self and the other, without which the goal of each memoir cannot be achieved and/or understood.

Personal and Social Identity

For writers to convey their experiences as influenced by their surroundings, they must develop a social identity to facilitate this interdependence. It is through this identity that they can narrate their cultures and traditions. Social identity within the context of this work is understood as:

> A person's knowledge that he or she belongs to a social category or group. A social group is a set of individuals who hold a common social identification or view themselves as members of the same social category. Through a social comparison process, persons who are similar to the self are categorized with the self and are labeled the in-group; persons who differ from the self are categorized as the out-group. [...] Social identity theorists regard the group as a collective of similar persons whom identify with each other, see themselves and each other in similar ways and hold similar views, all in contrast to members of outgroups. Identity theorists regard the group as a set of interrelated individuals, each of whom performs unique but integrated activities, see things from his or her own perspective, and negotiates the terms of interactions.[7]

Personal identity, the subjective peculiarities that activate what a person is, must also be recognized as essential to the writer's development and style. The recognition of the self is also influenced by ideas of the community and other identities held by the author. For instance, Cartesian philosophy suggests a relationship between consciousness and awareness of the self, whereas Thomas Nagel, in his paper "What it is Like to be a Bat," claims that there is a subjective "qualia" that defines the identity of an object.[8] He argues that a subjective domain determines what it is like to be a bat. Each object, therefore, exhibits its/his/her qualities that allow it to be classified. Nagel asserts that:

> There is a sense in which phenomenological facts are perfectly objective: one person can know or say of another what the quality of the other's experience is. They are subjective, however, in the sense that even this objective ascription of experience is possible only for someone sufficiently similar to the object of ascription in the first person as well as the third, so to speak.[9]

Social identity is the central thesis by which a writer can truly say he belongs to a group and then tell his readers about the cultures and traditions of the group. Gender, race, religion, and many other qualities serve as the basis for understanding the group to which they belong. Social identity is germane to understanding the goals and aims that narrations of traditions and cultures are set to achieve. However, because each person is born into an already structured society, social identity precedes and supersedes personal identity. In relation to the self, this means that the qualities by which a person is identified can only be fully grasped by those who share similar qualities. For example, a Yoruba man shares qualities with other Yoruba people, and he can only know he is Yoruba because of the qualities he shares with others who are recognized as Yoruba, reiterating that personal identity cannot be defined without social or group identity. According to Stets and Burke:

> Once in society, people derive their identities or sense of self largely from the social categories to which they belong. Each person, however, over the course of his or her personal history, is a member of a unique combination of social categories; therefore, the set of social identities making up that person's self-concept is unique.[10]

In this way, an African personal identity is largely related to their strong connection to society. In one of the memoirs analyzed in this work, *The Fate of our Mothers* by Oladejo Afolayan, a character is named "Dalemo," which means *to build a house alone* because he did not invite the community to help him. He is identified as a loner and has an individualistic personality, exemplifying how a person's identity is defined by his/her relations with the community of others and, in return, what others make of him/her. This is not to say that personal identity is inconsequential, but social identity allows a person to self-categorize themselves within the group, while inheriting the cultures and traditions of the said group.

   Within the context of a group, a single person is not considered more important than others. It may be the case that the group shares similar views, and there is a uniformity of perceptions among them. In this instance, the views of the self are ruled out but added to the collective views of the group. Whatever the nomenclature is (e.g., "tribe," political class, etc.), the group houses beliefs, traditions, cultures, and opinions:

> In general, one's identities are composed of self-views that emerge from reflexive activity of self-categorization or identification in terms of membership in particular groups or roles [...] that is, how people come to see themselves as members of one group/category (the in-group) in comparison with another (out-group), and the consequences of their categorization, such as ethnocentrism.[11]

To illustrate, when a European observer in nineteenth-century Africa wrote about Africa, he had the tendency to be Eurocentric because he belonged to a group that had socialized him into seeing being a European as the essence of his life. Therefore, his evaluation of other cultures was done with the notion of an "out-grouper," and there were possibilities that his presuppositions (gained from his social identity) would affect his objectivity. In consideration, African memoirists are not free from this. They also belong to a group, and they tell their stories from the point of view of insiders. At the center of a memoir is memory, and though this memory is housed by the self, it can be the memory of the self and the other, and it is influenced by the impact of the group(s) to which they belong.

The Self and Narrating Traditions and Cultures

The theoretical grounding of this book posits that the seat of subjectivity, upon which narrations are constructed, is the self. Truth and objectivity amongst groups are intersubjectively agreed upon by members of the group. Groups are not presented as ultimately objective entities. They come together as a people to agree on what is acceptable, what is true, what is praiseworthy, and what is beneficial to the group. Through these processes, they store their mores, beliefs, and worldviews, which become their traditions and cultures. Cultural behaviors are not natural or divine; they are collectively agreed upon based on history, time, space, and the unwavering desire for self-preservation.

Africans face dual conflicts as the narration of their cultures in the past have been mostly preserved in orality and must now be documented. To tackle these two problems, African writers and intellectuals have reformed how memoirs are written, and it is nearly impossible to see an African memoir that does not contain several narrations of Africans' cultural and intellectual traditions. African cultures and traditions have been erroneously (purposefully) told by others outside the continent. They have also continuously emphasized orality as the first point of contact in their experiences and searches into Africa's past. Indeed, the place of the self in narrating traditions and cultures cannot be jettisoned because the self interprets how cultures and traditions have influenced one's life, beliefs, and decisions.

The traditions live through the narrator and their narration, though this may not always be positive as experiences of corruption, nepotism, ritual killings, and other milieus present to us the ills of African history and traditions. Specifically, Leila Abouzeid's memoir tackles the subjugation of women, while Emmanuel Babatunde's presents a diacritical evaluation of the political decadence in Nigeria vis-a-vis the recurring development in Botswana. The narration of these traditions is not to dogmatically accept the experiences, mores, and norms but are attempts to reevaluate each writer's experiences and memories and present to us their positions. From these positions, the goals of each memoir can then be set out. Essentially, by narrating their traditions, the African memoirists in this work inform the readers of their identities, their affiliation with the stories they share, and how cultures and traditions shaped whom they have become.

Narration and Tradition: The Politics of Memory in African Memoirs

Each memoir has a goal. Some memoirs are written for political reasons, some to highlight the achievements of great men and women, and some to reminisce on the past and its influence on the present. There are also geographical, sociopolitical, and sociocultural issues that determine the nature of a memoir. For instance, the memoir of a German who lived during the Second World War is expected to reflect genocide, war, and international politics. Memoirs are shaped by personal and group experiences narrated in such a way that the memoir illuminates a particular story. This is the case with African memoirs. African history is defined by colonialism, imperialism, military coups, genocide, civil wars, and other existential crises. Memoirs help to jettison the idea that African cultures are inferior to those in the West.

One of the most common themes in many African memoirs is the exposition of African traditions. African memoirs debunk the idea that Africa is culturally homogenous, as memoirs from different regions show that Africans are culturally diverse. African memoirs elucidate culture, philosophy, politics, and African norms and mores. Intrinsically, in African memoirs, narration and traditions are inseparable. Narratives written by Africans in the diaspora are aimed at juxtaposing African cultures and traditions with those of the author's current context. Most importantly, the politics of narration examine the importance and bonds among people, the devices of language, and the philosophical underpinnings that distinguish a memoir written by an African in the diaspora from one that is not. The narrations of such memoirs play into the politics of finding convergence and divergence between African and Western traditions. In many cases, they narrate their cultures to disprove some Western parochial assumptions about African traditions.

African memoirists write for specific and defined purposes and have mastered the art of using narrative to showcase the sociocultural and sociopolitical background in which they grew up. Narratives are not created in a vacuum; they are constructed with the intent of achieving a sociopolitical or moral goal. Thus, the memories shared in narratives are philosophically and politically inclined because the ideologies and socialization with which memoirists were raised shape their understanding of the world. The sampled memoirists in this volume seem to interrogate these methods in their memoirs in a unique way worthy of scholarship for diaspora studies.

Also, in their narration of the different memoirs, the authors seem to draw on wide resources from their numerous realities to create a particularistic consciousness in telling their stories. African memoirs are incomplete without the narrator's cultural traditions. Cultural philosophy and ideologies are demonstrated in the narration of traditions, which are more than recapturing memories and reminiscing about the past. As a result, this volume reveals how the sampled works have helped illuminate cultures and traditions within African diaspora memoir writing and ultimately restructure how African culture is viewed globally.

Narrations of traditions should be considered for what they reveal about a people. Hence, these narrations are inherently political, not merely telling the story of an individual but of the people, philosophies, ideologies, and traditions that produced them. Narrations of traditions also reveal the psychological and social traits that shaped the ideas and worldviews of memoirists as they present African cultures, placing them side-by-side with Western cultures to show that African cultures are not inferior. By narrating traditions, African philosophical worldviews are displayed and analyzed.

This work, *Narrating Traditions: African Memoirs and Cultural Representations*, is a critical evaluation of African traditions, how they are portrayed in African memoirs, and what these traditions from different cultures represent. The chapters in this volume examine the history, philosophy, and politics of African nations. The memoirs emphasize the importance of African oral traditions by using folklore, folktales, proverbs, and motifs to illuminate philosophical positions, ideologies, beliefs, and existential plights. Likewise, by narrating traditions, these memoirs communicate the indelibility of customs and norms on behavioral patterns, worldviews, and belief systems. Essentially, this work is an appraisal of the place of narrating traditions and (re)placing African intellectual systems. The essence of re-placement is correcting the erroneous beliefs about Africa and its people, but more significantly, investigating the foundations of worldviews, history, politics, and philosophies.

None of what has been mentioned could have been achieved without analyzing traditions, as seen in various memoirs from different regions of Africa. Also, as examined in this book, the politics of narration in memoirs are many, and narrating traditions present cultural identity, the representations of Africa, ethnicities, the exploration of gender, language, personhood, and the philosophy of the African people.

Narrating Africa and Its Regions

An African memoir is only a fragment of the whole. This book contradicts the presupposition that Africa is culturally and historically homogenous. By focusing on the memoirs from West Africa, this book shows its readers that you cannot holistically narrate a vast continent like Africa. When a memoir from West Africa is written, its reader should expect that it will capture the characteristics of West Africa and not necessarily of the entire continent. Though it is an African perspective of history and culture, it is not the view of most Africans.

Africa's modern history cannot be separated from the foreign infiltration of its space. Due to human exploration of the earth, it is understandable that people from a particular geographical location would want to explore other lands that are yet unknown to them, like the West, and the Arabs explored different corners of the world, including Africa. Yet the infiltration of Africa by the oriental and occidental world was not a mere exploration to seek knowledge but one accompanied by exploitation and dehumanization.[12] Africans were taken to the West, where they were treated as slaves and subjected to various kinds of cruelty. The Arabs, just like the westerners, introduced religion, language, and education as media of overpowering Africans mentally and physically. Despite what looks like a shared history, each region of Africa is plagued by its own particularities; that is, one cannot narrate its own region as the paradigm for what Africa represents.

One approach to narrating Africa is by narrating its regions; in doing so, facts about Africa can become diverse and complex. Thematically, African memoirs are differentiated by their regions. Each region has its themes, tones, and qualities, and they are responsible for what their authors present as an African memoir. By adding the prefix "African" to the title of a memoir, there is a linguistic underpinning with the reference that a memoir is just a collection of experiences of an author. Therefore, the author's experience of his/her community and region does not represent, in totality, the cultural identity and historicity of Africa as a whole.

By critically evaluating different memoirs from different places, this book admits the divergence of issues, themes, and characteristics of African memoirs based on differences as seen in regions. However, this is not to push forward the argument that there are no convergences in themes and characteristics. Each region's history, culture, politics, and philosophies can be identified despite some shared similarities. African memoirists narrate not just their regions but also the multifaceted dynamism of African identity, politics, worldviews, and cultures, through the narration of experiences and memories that are affected by the peculiarities of each region.

Narrating the Interdependence of Culture, History, Worldviews, and Politics

Thus far, the explications indicate an indelible connection between people, their culture, and history. It is this culture and history that determine their worldviews and politics. Therefore, there is an interdependent relationship between culture, history, philosophy, and politics. These are factors that are ever-present in African memoirs, no matter the region of the writer. African memoirs are not just historical sources; they also evaluate historical events, the practices and effects of cultures, the politics of the land, and the philosophical inclinations of stories from the past. The lives of writers, their experiences, and the experiences of their communities are sites of exploration for grasping the influence of history, culture, worldviews, and politics.

African memoirs are not just narrations but are initiated for purposes such as analyzing and bringing to the fore African cultures, the symbiotic relationship between culture and philosophy, the role of writers in the politics of their homelands, and the critical evaluation of historical events. More than just reminiscing, African memoirs lay bare the psychological, philosophical, and physical formation of a writer and their people. African philosophies, cultures, histories, and politics make up the value systems that influence the writers. Subsequently, these influences help memoirists choose the parts of their life stories they want to tell. They carefully select certain stories, cultural practices, and political history to achieve a specific goal. Therefore, each narration plays its own politics. The politics of narration is to address issues that the writers are interested in, whether to lament and demand correction or to praise their people's cultural politics and philosophy as defiance against the erroneous understanding of Africa.

Therefore, it is important to note that understanding African memoirs with the yardsticks of conventional literary theories like Formalism limits one's understanding of such work. Like the humans of Africa, African memoirs are not independent of their people and culture. The subject and the other characters in an African memoir are products of what happens around them, not just what happens within. In other words, the fabrics and elements that make up an African memoir are the events of the writer/subject's immediate environment.

A full grasp of African memoir takes into consideration the principles of Historicism to tease out the embedded meanings in such a memoir. As the name suggests, Historicism is the literary inquiry that considers the historical context—including social and political underpinnings—of a written work. Scholarship recognizes that there is old and new historicism, with a slight difference between them. However, what they have in common is their respect for the historical background or context of a text. The new historicist differs from the old by submitting that while it is germane to consider the historical context of a work in its analysis, it only helps to understand the present reality of the critic in question. For the old historicists, nothing is as true as the fact that texts do not exist in isolation from their historical contexts.

Consequently, the chapters in this book approach the memoirs under study from the angle of old and new historicism. However, what remains common to them is their obvious inability to properly explicate the events of a memoir without adequate reference to the sociopolitical and historical contexts of the subject. According to Greenblatt and as explained by D. G. Meyers, the following are the guiding principles behind the new historicism as a method of criticism:

> (1) Literature is historical, which means (in this exhibition) that a literary work is not primarily the record of one mind's attempt to solve certain formal problems and the need to find something to say; it is a social and cultural construct shaped by more than one consciousness. The proper way to understand it, therefore, is through the culture and society that produced it. (2) Literature, then, is not a distinct category of human activity. It must be assimilated to history, which means a particular vision of history. (3) Like works of literature, man himself is a social construct, the sloppy composition of social and political forces—there is no such thing as a human nature that transcends history [...] (4) As a consequence, the historian/critic is trapped in his own "historicity."[13]

Considering the influence of culture, the new historicism indirectly leaves room for the multiplicity or plurality of meaning. This is important when African memoir is viewed as a generic term for a wide range of works under this nomenclature. The cultural experiences of people from West Africa differ from those in the East, just as much as the differences in the cultural experiences of two ethnic groups in the same country, like Nigeria. For instance, as documented in this work, the culture of the Yoruba people in Babatunde Emmanuel's *Kelebogile—I Am Grateful: An African Journey Through Celibate Priesthood to Married Life*, which is subsequently analyzed in Chapter Three of this work, is different from the dynamics of the culture of the Igbo people recorded in Kalu Ogbaa's *Carrying My Father's Torch*. Take the case of the North African memoir, for example. This region has been influenced by the Islamic religion over time, and some have argued that the true and original essence of African culture in this region has been eroded. These peculiarities and uniqueness in cultures form the centrality of cultural relativism.

Perhaps the best analogy for explaining cultural relativism is found in the seminal work of Nancy Ann Silbergeld Jecker, Albert R. Jonsen, and Robert A. Pearlman. In their co-authored book on bioethics, they narrate the ancient history of a king who invites two different ethnic groups—the Greeks, who believe in cremating their dead fathers, and a group in India who would cook and eat their dead fathers. In trying to understand the diversity in cultural beliefs, the king asks the Indian group if they would be willing to cremate their dead fathers, to which they answer strongly in the negative. He gets the same response from the Greeks when he asks if they would be willing to cook and eat their dead fathers. This analogy shows how people from different cultures have different practices. The differences do not suggest the superiority of one over the other but show relativism in different cultural orientations, just as the name of the anthropological approach suggests.

Cultures are not static, and when the tools of historicism are applied to African memoirs, one can understand the inevitable evolution of culture. To establish the place of peculiarities and the uniqueness of African cultures and beliefs, a chapter of this book is dedicated to discussing regional particularities in the African memoir. Chapter Two emphasizes how cultures are influenced and how this shape cultures over time. Taking the argument a step further, it has been noted that the new historicism can also be within the borders of structuralism, poststructuralism, and deconstruction. As a method of inquiry, historicism places emphasis on history, culture, and sociopolitical contexts, and this scope makes it suitable for this study. However, a quick consideration of the structuralism/poststructuralism movements shows that historicism has something in common with these ideas.

As Ferdinand de Saussure noted, which became a foundational ideology for the major proponents of poststructuralism, there is an arbitrariness about the use of language. In simple terms, a word means what it means because it is culturally agreed that such a word would mean that. As advanced by the deconstructionists, the same word can possibly mean something else in a different cultural context, bringing the argument to the inevitability of plurality of meaning in a text. These agree with the idea that historicism accommodates the need to understand the cultural context of the African memoir because meaning resides in the ability of the critic or reader to grasp the essence of the contextual culture of the memoir. This also further points attention to the fact that meaning goes beyond the language of expression of the African memoir. Hence, language (the English language in this case) becomes a mere vehicle with which the message is conveyed. To do proper justice to a work, a critic should understand the cultural setting of the work.

> However, the texts are not self-explanatory; they do not contain their own meaning because language is subversive of meaning. Therefore, the reader must place meaning into the text by deconstructing it, by placing it into context, by reviving the hidden meanings that are not consciously articulated and are taken as given by the author.[14]

Perhaps a good way to understand the position of historicism and its relationship with the text is with the knowledge of intertextuality. For historicism, especially the new historicism, there is an intertextual relationship between a work's historical/cultural/sociopolitical context and the text itself. To use the language of the new historicist, there is the context and the text, both dependent on each other. As Veeser notes, "It is a relationship between two kinds of 'texts': 'literary' on the one side, 'cultural' on the other."[15] Historicism provides a textual approach to the study of culture or society, just as this book has attempted to do.

Through texts, the writers of different chapters have engaged in analyzing different African cultures and beliefs, as seen in Politics, Philosophical Representation, and Culture in Cherno Njie's *Sweat is Invisible in the Rain*. Njie captures the interdependence of culture, history, philosophy, and politics, and proposes that there are some common cultural practices that build up the people's value system. One commonality in African memoirs is the repeated evaluation and romanticization of communitarianism. Communitarianism and humanism in African societies are two essential principles that eradicate any sense of individualism, not at the expense of the individual, but a principle that the interest of the individual will not trump that of the community.

African humanism and communitarianism are utilitarian, elevating the happiness and well-being of the whole over the well-being and desires of a selected few. Njie captures the interdependence of humanity and communitarianism with his narration of the knitted life he lived with his extended family in Banjul.[16]

There can be a misguided notion that African societies before colonialism were utopian. This is not true. However, the suggestion is that African societies had their own philosophical and cultural principles by which they were guided, making it less impossible for people to be individualistic. Njie recognizes that despite communitarianism and humanism, some people are still individualistic, greedy, and power-hungry. His insistence on those who maintain individualism is reminiscent of the case of an individual nicknamed "Dalemo" (who built his house alone without asking for the help of others) in Michael Afolayan's *Fate of Our Mothers*.[17] Njie insists that the cause of tyranny, lust for power, and political instability is a result of the abandonment of indigenous African sociopolitical ideologies and philosophies. He believes that these ideologies and philosophies could have helped curb sociocultural and sociopolitical decadence in African countries. This is similar to Babatunde's observation in his memoir, *Kelebogile*, that Botswana could forge ahead and make great strides because of the nation's adherence to the Ubuntu principle.[18]

Postcolonial African history is seriously marred by corruption, civil war, bad leadership, and political instability. As members of an intellectual community, Africans have made sure they not only document each historical moment but have also taken it upon themselves to take an active part in the politics of their homelands. Whether at home or abroad, African writers do not take backseats on how their homelands are ruled. In the case of Njie, while in the United States, he contributed immensely to the ousting of Gambian dictator Yahya Jammeh.

One aspect of the relationship between culture, history, and philosophy is the deployment of oral tradition. Njie employs folklore, folktales, proverbs, and aphorisms to achieve the aims of his narrations. Oral traditions are embedded with cultural and philosophical innuendos, which writers often cite to emphasize the morals of their stories. There are several instances in this work where folktales, folklores, chants, and aphorisms are looked at just as the writers have used them to capture the culture, beliefs, and traditional sociopolitical settings of their people.

Njie also employs oral tradition to capture the cultural beliefs and philosophy of his people. He uses proverbs and folktales to clarify his claims on humanism and communitarianism. In addition, his narration of the high level of African religiosity and spirituality. Njie points to the fact that Africans are greatly conscious of the supernatural. He alludes that Banjul, where he grew up, was a society that reflected the belief in gnomes, wizards, and witches.[19] This is also a feature in Babatunde's memoir, where he talks about the dominance of witches and the resistance against them through the Atinga cult in Imeko City.[20]

Njie narrates that proselytization began with colonialism—the penetration of Islam and Christianity into African lives. People accepted the religions to which they felt inclined. Despite the differences in religion, there was unity because the people understood that family life and the unity of the community trumped religious affiliations. Njie believes that Africans, especially Gambians, should not have discarded these cultural and philosophical beliefs. He argues that with this interdependence between culture, history, and philosophy, the politics of postcolonial Gambia would have improved significantly and that there is still time to right the wrongs of the early years of postcolonial Africa.

In Praise of Womanhood

Storytelling is an art of selection. It is the art of choosing the voices to be heard and the ones to be silenced. If there is anything the memoirs show, it is that there is no narration that is not politicized. The most common concept in African memoirs is the idea of womanhood and motherhood. These two related concepts seem to transcend the lines of regions. The idea of womanhood in West Africa is not entirely different from womanhood in any other region, yet the plight of women in North Africa, for instance, is narrated differently through each region's memoirs. The subjugation of women in North Africa is a tradition that dates back to the introduction of Islam to the region. It is a tradition narrated in North African memoirs to emphasize the magnitude of the repression of women and their voices. Therefore, memoirs from this region are narrations in praise and demand of a sociocultural revolution that elevates the rights and freedoms of women, thereby giving women cultural representation as complementary to men and as beings on their own.

North African memoirists use their narrations to push for change. For example, Emmanuel Babatunde's memoir, *Kelebogile*, discusses womanhood through the eyes of his mother and his wife. The narration of the struggles of his mother and wife captures the difference between West African and South African conceptions of motherhood and the shifting understandings of womanhood in changing times.[21] In relation to this, North African memoirs capture womanhood as a fragile existence dictated not by women but by men. This is in the context of religion, where women are continually subjugated in a patriarchal society, leaving many women at the mercy of men. As demonstrated in the chapter examining the peculiarities of memoirs in a different region, Nawal El Saadawi's *Woman at Point Zero* and Tayeb Salih's *Season of Migration to the North* capture the predicaments of women in North Africa. These two North African memoirs explicate how women are silenced, domesticated, and subdued.

The idea of womanhood is reiterated in many of the memoirs analyzed in this book. Addressing the issue of womanhood is to correct erroneous notions about women in Africa while also telling the truth about women's relegation to domestic and communal affairs. However, many social commentators fail to recognize that women can truly be subjugated and that women have risen above these subjugations, just as we can see in history that some women were more valued than men. Women are often commended as "women like men" to connote their strength, tenacity, and achievements, yet the praise is riddled with irony.

This book critically emphasizes how womanhood is perceived through the narrations of the authors. Like many memoirs from North Africa, Leila Abouzeid's *Return to Childhood: The Memoir of a Modern Moroccan Woman* narrates how women's identity

Figure 1.2 Tayeb Salih

and existence are perceived. This perception helps to understand how the females of this region are treated. Abouzeid's memoir explicates the Northern African value system about womanhood. This is not so different from how women are valued, perceived, and treated in other regions. A chapter in this book captures the juxtaposition of narrations in the ever-changing conception of womanhood and motherhood.

Babatunde's memoir *Kelebogile—I Am Grateful: An African Journey Through Celibate Priesthood to Married Life* speaks to metaphysics, philosophy, culture, politics, and history. There is the presupposition that women in African societies belong to a lower social class than men; that is, women in African society are regarded as the "second sex."[22] They are regarded as subordinates, which is seen in how women are treated in African cultures, as well as their domestication and restriction to home chores. Babatunde centers his work on the concept of womanhood and narrates gender-based discrimination and subjugation perpetrated through the idea of witch-hunting. Witchcraft is associated with women, who are believed to use this power in malevolent ways. Sadly, infertility is associated with witchcraft. The idea is that a woman is naturally endowed to procreate, and only a witch is not able to do so because she has used witchcraft to lock her womb.

In Babatunde's hometown, there was a coordinated attack on women by the men who organized the Gelada and Atinga cult to hunt witches. This exemplifies the creation of patriarchal systems formed to suppress women's voices and being. However, witchcraft is a universal phenomenon. Womanhood in African culture is intrinsically linked to motherhood; a woman only becomes truly a woman when she becomes a mother. A woman's womb is regarded as the bodily feature responsible for preserving and continuing the existence of a family; without it, the family goes into extinction. So, by giving birth, a woman affirms her own womanhood and her husband's manhood, bringing honor and prestige to him. With this, the development of a woman starts from puberty, to learning the values that epitomize a good woman, to giving birth, and then menopause. The cycle of a woman's existence is at its peak at the stage of motherhood. It is the busiest stage of a woman's life because of the many roles of childrearing, nurturing, fulfilling sexual obligations, and taking care of the home front.

Additionally, Babatunde observes that a woman is also expected to master the oratory skills of rendering the panegyrics of her husband's ancestors. This reiterates the importance of orality to the people of West Africa. Also, it shows that historically and epistemologically, women are far more important than they are given credit for. The Oriki, which they are taught to master, is a repertoire of the history and valor of their husbands' ancestors. Without them, the generation to come may not have the consciousness of what their ancestors were like. So, they are oral historians with the ability to link the past with the future. In *Kelebogile*, womanhood is well captured through the lives of Iya Ayinla, Adunni Oluwole, and Kelebogile. Iya Ayinla represents the cultural defiant, Adunni Oluwole represents women's political consciousness of women, and Kelebogile is a modern woman. Iya Ayinla lives in a patriarchal society, but she serves as a statue of defiance and resistance, so much so that Babatunde tags her as a feminist.[23] Though feminism is a Western concept and ideology, there are certain feminist concerns in African cultures. Whether or not she is a feminist, she stands against repressive customs that relegate women to playing the role of the second sex.

The introduction of Western culture to Imeko City cannot be underestimated, as one would see how it influences Iya Ayinla's decisions. She exhibits the close relationship between motherhood and womanhood by jealously guiding herself from extraterrestrial forces and striving to protect her son. Iya Ayinla becomes the first woman in Imeko to name her son by herself. Adunni Oluwole is a political activist popularly known for her postulation that Nigeria was not ready for independence. She believes there was still disunity amongst the ethnic groups in Nigeria and states the developmental influence of the colonialists. However, her postulations are overturned and disregarded. But her claims are justified by the postcolonial history of Nigeria—military coups, civil war, and immense corruption. Kelebogile, in contrast, exemplifies a woman raised in the culture of the Tswana people.

Womanhood differs in the western and southern parts of Africa. According to Babatunde's juxtaposition, African womanhood entails that the women stay at home to tend to their children; however, in the southern part, because of white supremacy, South African women leave their children every day to tend to the white women for pay. Subsequently, African children are left to themselves, often turning to peers who influence them into making bad decisions such as doing drugs, violence, crime, and prostitution. This may well explain the high crime rate in a place like South Africa. Contrary to this method of motherhood or parenthood, Kelebogile is given the right amount of love, attention, and care, which is responsible for how she turns out to be a strong woman. She then goes on to break barriers and take on traditional roles that were gendered to men.

In summary, the women discussed in Babatunde's memoir are a model of women who rose above societal pressure and the custom of repressing women in their societies. Through them, the conception of womanhood is reshaped and points to the notion that, in many African cultures, the drive to kill the African spirit has always failed when the attempts are met by determined and strong-willed women such as Moremi Ajasoro, Funmilayo Ransome-Kuti, the Aba Women, and many others. The narration and evaluation of womanhood in Babatunde's memoir is a laudable attempt at reshaping and repositioning the place of women in a postmodern world.

Another chapter that reiterates the interconnectedness of culture, philosophy, and history is "The Yoruba World in *Fate of our Mothers*." This chapter evaluates the sociopolitical and sociocultural settings of the Yoruba world. In this memoir, the author asserts that being Yoruba means belonging to a culture with cultural wealth and heritage. The Yoruba world is rich in traditions that envisage deep moral values and knowledge systems. However, to be Yoruba is beyond language and ethnicity; it involves actions, beliefs, and adherence to the terrestrial and extraterrestrial functionalities of the Yoruba world. As depicted in Afolayan's memoir, what the Yoruba world entails is divided into four categories: religion, society, literature, arts and recreation, and the natural world.

This chapter emphasizes that Yoruba people are religious and spiritual. One of the considered features of Yoruba metaphysics and spirituality is the concept of Orí (inner head) and àdáyébá (destiny). In Yoruba metaphysics, one's head is the most important element of one's existence. The author indicates that there is a close relationship between Orí and àdáyébá. In the Yoruba traditional belief system, Orí is believed to be the custodian of one's destiny. The Yoruba people believe that only one deity can follow one through life's journey without giving up.[24] This is why Mama Kekere, in Afolayan's memoir, pleaded with his Orí to make him a farmer. Another important feature of the Yoruba world is the function of oríkì, the oral panegyrics of a family, town, or an individual. Oríkì, like other oral traditions, serves as a historical source and a link between a people and their ancestors. Yoruba people also have special oriki for food and animals. Afolayan, like Babatunde, argues that women are custodians of family panegyrics.

In addition, this chapter captures the essence of superstitions to the Yoruba. Taboos are traditional principles that guide people's actions and inactions. In Yoruba jurisprudence, taboos are laws set to keep people in check. When these taboos are broken, the gods are appeased so that the social order of the Yoruba world will not be disrupted. Afolayan emphasizes in his memoir that these taboos instill fear in people, which helps keep them in check with strict adherence to the community's rules. Taboos serve the purpose of steadying the sociocultural and sociopolitical structure of society and as a control mechanism to curb youthful exuberance.

This chapter also examines the veneration and celebration of twins, who are seen as blessings from the Supreme Being. Similar to this is the Yoruba belief in reincarnation, a cherished metaphysical phenomenon. They believe that the ancestors of a people or a dead relative can return in the body of a newborn. In this case, the new baby's name will reflect the return of a dead father or mother. Another superstition is the Abiku phenomenon, which is the Yorubas' belief in the return of a child who died in infancy. They believe that such a child has not finished his work on earth, so when a woman continues to have stillbirths, they believe the same child keeps "coming and going." Close to this is the belief in death as a debt. The Yoruba notion is that life is a harmony of opposites, such as joy and sadness and life and death. The Yoruba people believe everyone promised death from the moment they gained life and breath; therefore, we owe death our lives. This is well captured in Afolayan's memoir. The idea of death as debt is to remind us constantly, as humans, that no one can live forever, and people should live their lives with purpose and the determination to do good.

The Yoruba world, as represented in Afolayan's memoir, is incomplete without the explication of Yoruba gods and deities. The number of gods and deities in the Yoruba belief system is limitless. These Yoruba gods and deities were assigned roles by the Supreme Being—Ifa as the god of wisdom, Ogun as the god of iron, Sango as the god of thunder, and many more. They are revered and consulted from time to time to interfere in the affairs of humans. As a result, there are rules that guide how these gods and deities can be worshipped in Yoruba societies. Yoruba people can have a communal deity and a family deity; that is, the community to which a person belongs may be a town that worships Osun, and the family may worship Ogun. All these happen without persecution, and it explains the religious tolerance of the Yoruba world founded on the belief in magic, medicine, and healing. Magic is the mastery of the manipulation of the laws of physics. It defies physical explanation, and it is mostly used for protection. Traditional medicine and healing are essential to the Yoruba because healers have also mastered the science of using herbs to cure sicknesses and diseases long before colonialism.

In portraying the Yoruba world in his memoir, Afolayan narrates stories that capture the Yoruba society and its core institutions. The author analyzes the traditional gender roles of men and women and explores the varying positions women occupy in the Yoruba world. A similar concept to this is the idea of motherhood. Traditional gender roles make men the sole provider of the family, while the women take care of the home front. Afolayan explains that mothers are venerated like goddesses in the Yoruba world. He is inundated by the sacrifices of mothers and narrates that mothers are the custodians of the father's wisdom because they act as confidantes for the men and are their husbands' advisors. Afolayan constantly evaluates the treatment of Yoruba women, and he found both blameworthy and praiseworthy aspects of women's lives under the reign of patriarchy.

The author also narrates the importance of names and their meanings among the Yoruba, as well as facial marks and circumcision. The chapter analyzes Afolayan's conception of rustic living, collectivity, and communal living. This collectivity and communal living is further seen in the author's narration of Yoruba games and sports, which fostered communal interdependence and unity amongst relatives. He also established that literature and arts are indispensable aspects of the Yoruba world. The impact of oral tradition can be seen in the figures from the author's life, as well as the ones he used to pass his message across.

Overall, the Yoruba world, as presented in *The Fate of our Mothers*, is where identity lies beyond language and ethnicity but in deep cultural practices that inform the decisions and philosophies of the Yoruba people. Many features make up the Yoruba world, and this chapter examines these features to show how the Yoruba people cherish religion, society, literature, and arts and their great regard for the natural world. Furthermore, the traditional Yoruba world is distinct from the modern Yoruba world; that is, in a postmodern world, the idea of the Yoruba world being secluded from the rest of the world is close to impossible. However, the Yoruba world can still retain some of its peculiarities and embrace the new dimensions of the world.

In memoirs, authors reflect on events that have greatly influenced their lives; therefore, a memoir is a compendium of reflections, and the crux of the conceptualization of a memoir is memory. Reflections and Refractions in *A Matter of Sharing* examine A. B. Assensoh's reflections on his life, scholarship, history, and politics. His memoir is a reflection and reevaluation of important discourses on the African front. One pertinent characteristic is the importance of space and time. The author admits that traveling and living in foreign countries helped shape his perspectives on many issues.

A central theme of his memoir is also the idea of motherhood, connecting Assensoh's reflections to the previous chapters. In Assensoh's memoir, he recognizes his mother's sacrifices, and there are conscious narrations of the struggles of women and mothers in Africa. Though personal experiences determine how womanhood and motherhood are viewed, there is a deliberate attempt by the authors to show their readers the existential crisis of women and mothers in Africa.

Another phenomenon connected to womanhood and motherhood in Africa is polygamous marriages. In the case of many of the authors examined in this work, there is a strong connection between the affection they feel for their mothers and how they navigated polygamy. With Assensoh's mother, this is also the case, but significantly, his predicament was coupled with the negligence and absence of his father. However, his mother's decision to divorce his father is an experience that ushered in life-changing events in the author's life. His father neglected him after the divorce, as apparent in Assensoh's connection with his mother. In the memoir, he repeatedly credits his successes to his mother for the sacrifices she made to raise him.

In corroboration, Assensoh emphasizes the roles of wives in the lives of their husbands. He highlights the achievements of husbands in a way that credits the support and encouragement of their wives. To make his points, the author uses the stories of Mrs. Christine Achebe and Mrs. Coretta Scott King, who were married to Chinua Achebe and Dr. Martin Luther King, Jr., respectively. Assensoh argues that women possess resolute spirits that cannot be daunted. The support of these two women is noteworthy when their husbands' successes are highlighted. They were also successful in various ways by being their husbands' backbones.

Assensoh's evaluation is similar to Afolayan's conceptualization of women, not as the second sex but as complementary actors. In both autobiographies, the complementary roles of women and men are discussed. This is not to say that there is still no issue of women's subjugation, but the conception of womanhood as complementary to manhood helps to relegate and curb the suffering of women under the grip of patriarchy. The author's evaluation of his mother's sacrifices and the efforts of Mrs. Christine Achebe and Mrs. Coretta Scott King signify the importance of Black women in the world. Also, the author looks at the impact of divorce and remarriage on the child and psychologically evaluates the relationship between parents and their children. Lack of love, care, and attention from either parent can leave a psychological scar on a child, just as it left on the author.

The author's reflections examined in this chapter are not limited to marriage, motherhood, womanhood, and the influence of Black women. He also reflects on the place of West African literary giants in African and world literature. He bemoans the problem of politics in literature, as seen in the politicization of the Nobel Prize for Literature. The author believes that the works of West African literary scholars are worthy of the Nobel Prize, but they have been denied because of the deep-rooted racist politicization of the prize. He also reflects on his meetings with West African writers like Buchi Emecheta, Chinua Achebe, Wole Soyinka, and Kofi Awoonor and the vibrant discussions on Pan-African brotherhood, and analyses of historical and political events in Ghana. Postcolonial Africa is historically and politically flawed by the political maneuverings of power-drunk individuals who truncated the freedom of the people and the development of the region. This model of politics and its long history has caused disunity and strife amongst Africans in all regions. The author recommends intermarriages as a Pan-African tool for unity and peace.

Also, the author reflects on the senseless ritual killings across Africa and the ritual murder pandemic in Africa, where people are killed for power and wealth. The author opines that this attitude has no place in this century. In the author's conception of a new Africa, certain elements should be left in the past. He believes that, going forward, this is an aspect of African tradition that should be jettisoned alongside the politicization of public executions and killings. With examples, Assensoh reflects on the inhumanity and politicization of public execution and its barbarity. Public execution is used to create a fanfare atmosphere that takes attention away from the failures of a government. Public execution is an experience common under military rule, and the author painstakingly reflects on the troubles and struggles that come with military rule.

The early years of post-colonialism and self-governance were marred by military coups in nations like Nigeria, Ghana, and Togo. In Assensoh's memoir, this chapter situates the perception that political instability, killings, and terrorism are the bane of Africa's development. He reflects on the intentions of Kwame Nkrumah's political ideology and his contribution to Pan-Africanism. This chapter showcases the narration of culture, politics, and history in Assensoh's writing. More importantly, the chapter examines the sociopolitical dynamics of Ghana and Nigeria as a whole. *A Matter of Sharing* indicates that the narrations in the memoir are carefully selected for a purpose, and what is shared is a matter of the author's willingness to disclose certain aspects of his life.

From the preceding, Africans reflect on the failures of their leaders and the place of their cultures in their lives. For those who came to Africa to proselytize, they found some cultural beliefs that could never be completely erased. Most often, the selected memoirists are faced with the realities of their cultural background and the newly adopted Western lifestyle. African memoirs are reflections on history, culture, politics, identities, and beliefs, which are carried out comparatively. African memoirs, written by Africans in the diaspora, are even more about the nostalgic reflections of home. So, there is always a confluence of culture and the politics of home and at home in the memoirs.

As reiterated throughout this analysis, African memoirs are not mere fun time narrations. They serve a purpose according to the wish of the author. These purposes are then narrated through personal stories and the stories of the collective. Therefore, African memoirs are context-dependent on where the author wants to place the narrations. In relation to the regions from which they are produced, African memoirs reflect the culture and politics of a people. African memoirs are deliberate intellectual sites to evaluate African cultures in contrast to Eurocentric analyses.

In the history of many African nations, there is often a cultural clash between Western cultures and African cultures, which all the memoirs regarded as the political and economic invasions of Africa. Therefore, African memoirs serve as the site where Africans analyze the effects of the clash of culture and colonialism. These are some of the recurrent characteristics and qualities of Kalu Ogbaa's *Carrying my Father's Torch*. In "Culture and Politics in Kalu Ogbaa's *Carrying my Father's Torch*," the influence of culture, traditions, and politics is analyzed at length. The chapter illustrates the influence of Ogbaa's Igbo background. Igbo history, customs, and traditions shaped his experiences and had both positive and negative impacts on him.

The Igbo tradition that is most significant in Ogbaa's memoir and in this chapter is the idea of wrestling, a metaphor for the struggles that Ogbaa faced in life. From time to time, he wrestles with one existential crisis or the other. One of these is his knotted relationship with his parents. The memoir shows that motherhood is linked with fatherhood. Like other memoirs examined, motherhood and fatherhood are physically, biologically, and spiritually connected. Ogbaa's relationship with his mother is that of admiration and celebration. There are many events in the memoir that show the irony of the joys of motherhood. Ogbaa's mother suffers as a result of the terrible treatment from Ogbaa's father, which is responsible for the strained relationship between Ogbaa and his father. However, Ogbaa exhibits an understanding of imperfection in fatherhood. The centrality of Ogbaa's memoir is the concept of fatherhood, or it is centered on his father's influence on him.

There are similarities between how Ogbaa and Assensoh feel about their fathers. However, Ogbaa recounts that his father gave him all he could. Therefore, fatherhood is not always perfect, but some fathers, like Ogbaa's, still give the best life to their children. The flaws and feats of a father can be ingrained and engraved into the psychology of his child. This claim is evident in Ogbaa's failures in his marriage, but his father's strength and determination (a character trait he inherited) influenced him to strive for the best and inspired him to reach the peak of his career. As stated in Ogbaa's work, the culture of the Igbo people is that of communal living and the elevation of the family system. This communitarian spirit is well displayed in Ogbaa's friendships and how his community rallies around its people when they are in need. This same spirit follows him to the United States and is exemplified in how he seeks out Igbo and Nigerian brothers everywhere in the United States. The culture of the Igbo people, as illustrated in the memoir, is seen in clashes in religion, education, and medicine. Despite these clashes and differences, Ogbaa's memoir shows the tolerant culture of the Igbo.

Concerning politics, African memoirs are incomplete without the evaluation of politics. Politics in Ogbaa's memoir is represented in the Nigerian civil war. The history of postcolonial Africa is muddled by political instability, military intervention, ethnicity, and corruption. Ogbaa traces the problem of the political history of Nigeria to the amalgamation of the northern and southern protectorates of the British colony. He further notes that the issue is more problematized by the first military coup carried out by the soldiers of southeastern extraction with the execution of northern leaders. This resulted in a countercoup that further disintegrated the fragile unity between the ethnicities in Nigeria and led to the secession of the eastern region from Nigeria and the creation of Biafra.

The Nigerian civil war was marked by the devastation of the Eastern region both physically and psychologically. By the end of the war, millions of Biafrans were left dead, and it caused a great chasm in the relationship between the people of the Eastern part of Nigeria and the rest of the country. However, the war also showed the level of cooperation and the spirit of industry among the Igbo. Ogbaa emphasizes that the Igbo displayed their sense of brotherhood during the war. The author captures that even after the war ended, the Igbo still lived in fear, and the federal government of Nigeria continued to marginalize and ignore the Igbo people many years after.

All of these made the author active in the politics and development of Igboland when he was called upon. After his Ph.D. abroad, he returned to Nigeria to be one of the founding lecturers at Imo State University. Ogbaa also negotiated with people at different levels of government to develop his community. He believes that to contribute to society, you do not have to be actively involved in politics. After moving back to the United States, he pioneered the formation of the Association of Igbo People in Connecticut. The Biafran experience prepared him for racial segregation and social injustice in the United States of America, and the sociopolitical dynamics of the Igbo people prepared him for the sociopolitical dynamics in America. This chapter also explicates the culture of parenting and the place of a man in society, which influenced his choices, and the wrestling matches Ogbaa had to fight with some existential crises. As explored in this chapter, the centrality of the memoir is an apt display of the relationship between culture and politics.

Conclusion

The authors' narrations are tied to their identities as members of the groups depicted. An important aspect of understanding the analyses of the memoirs in this work is understanding where each author is coming from and the themes examined in their memoirs. For instance, some of the memoirists studied here grew up in West Africa during the colonial era and have also witnessed the postcolonial era in Africa. The colonial period presented racial injustice, sociopolitical subjugation, and the adulteration and demonization of African cultures through the systemic forcing of Christianity on

Africans. Therefore, some of these authors reminisce repeatedly about the traditions that preexisted colonialism and the need to revisit these traditions and implement them in governmental principles and legislations.

In other cases, the memoirists evaluate the plights of women in a patriarchal society where they are subject to being domesticated, abused, and dehumanized. In similar cases, certain memoirists narrate the valor of women who disagreed with the status quo and how these women contributed immensely to reshaping the conceptualization of womanhood. Whether the narrations of traditions and cultures are done to argue for or against these practices, these cultures and traditions are cardinal points that tell of the writers themselves. Lucidly, each memoirist bears the flag and badge of his/her culture, and while they narrate their traditions to us, we see the traditions through them. To theoretically situate this work and the reader's perspective, the notion of the self and the interrelation between the self and its community cannot be underestimated.

The central core of the selected memoirs examined in this book is the narrations of culture, history, politics, traditions, and philosophies, all of which are subjective to the authors' regions and personal experiences. Therefore, when a memoir is examined, it is pertinent to remember that memoirs are a compilation of carefully selected stories that influence the authors' journeys. In return, they choose specific stories to fulfill specific purposes. A political memoirist would choose political events and tell either negative or positive stories, depending on their intended outcome. A memoirist can be a social commentator who reflects on people's sociopolitical and sociocultural problems. With African memoirs, they take on the task of elevating the cultural past of African communities—a dissection of historical events, failures, successes, and the impact of political history on African development.

This work is an explication of the cultural representations in African memoirs. Cultural misrepresentation of Africa is common in scholarly works, literature, and arts, but African memoirs can be the site where adequate cultural representations are presented. However, cultural representations ought to be fair when being evaluated, and African memoirists have used memoirs as the site for lucid expositions of African cultures just as they are. As stated, African cultures have never been holistically blissful. African cultures have their failures as much as they have their praiseworthy attributes. This book undertakes the essence of narrating traditions and the politics they play in presenting a culture just the way some of its members see it. The different chapters will show readers the intricacies of cultures and the interdependent relationship between cultural representation and the politics of everything—language, space, and philosophy.

Therefore, the basis of this attempt can be found in a consideration spread across theoretical, cultural, traditional, and socio-experiential perspectives. This is hinged on the urgent awareness of the need to redevelop, rethink, and reconstruct the African memoir as a tradition and spatial inquiry that can equip Africans and other races with the conceptual and narratology requirements with which to confront and grapple with the challenges of spatial and relational identities and social experiences. The central idea is to follow a tradition of inquiry, which, according to the memoirists and the evident attempt in the critical analysis of the essays in this volume, need not hinge or owe any special allegiance to established conceptions about traditions, cultures, or experiences. Hence, its theoretical framing is to reconstruct and employ these concepts as a guide to ensure their redirection to meet contemporary dealings in different geographical spaces.

Notes

1 Rene Descartes, *Meditations on First Philosophy*, trans. and ed. John Cottingham (Cambridge: Cambridge University Press, 2013), 137.
2 Kolawole Owolabi, "Edmund Husserl's Rehabilitation of Cartesian Foundationalism: A Critical Analysis," *Indian Philosophical Quarterly* 22, no. 1 (1995): 13–24.
3 J. P. Sartre, *Existentialism Is a Humanism* (New Haven: Yale University Press, 2007), 155.
4 J. P. Sartre, *Being and Nothingness: An Essay in Phenomenological Ontology*, trans. Sarah Richmond (Abingdon: Routledge, 2018), 222.
5 J. S. Mbiti, *African Religion and Philosophy* (Nairobi: East African Educational Publishers, 1969), 108.
6 Desmond Tutu, *God Is Not a Christian: Speaking Truth in Times of Crisis* (London: Rider Books, 2011), 21–24.
7 J. Stets and P. Burke, "Identity Theory and Social Identity Theory," *Social Psychology Quarterly* 63, no. 3 (2000): 225.
8 Thomas Nagel, "What It Is Like to Be a Bat," *The Philosophical Review* 83, no. 4 (1974): 435–450.
9 Nagel, "What It Is Like to Be a Bat," 442.
10 Stets and Burke, "Identity Theory," 225.
11 Stets and Burke, "Identity Theory," 225–226.
12 Walter Rodney, *How Europe Underdeveloped Africa* (London: Verso Books, 2018).
13 David Myers, "The New Historicism in Literary Studies," *Academic Questions* 2, no. 1 (1989): 27–36.
14 Dwight W. Hoover, "The New Historicism," *The History Teacher* 25, no. 3 (1992): 357.
15 Hayden White, "New Historicism: A Comment," in *The New Historicism*, ed. Harold Veeser (New York: Routledge, 2013), 268.
16 Cherno M. Njie, *Sweat Is Invisible in the Rain* (Austin: Pan African University Press, 2020).
17 Michael O. Afolayan, *Fate of Our Mothers* (Austin: Pan African University Press, 2015).
18 Emmanuel Babatunde, *Kelebogile—I Am Grateful: An African Journey through Celibate Priesthood to Married Life* (Maitland: Xulon Press, 2018), 137.
19 Njie, *Sweat Is Invisible in the Rain*, 14.
20 Babatunde, *Kelebogile*, 3.
21 Babatunde, *Kelebogile*.
22 Simone De Beauvoir, *The Second Sex* (New York: Knopf, 1953).
23 Babatunde, *Kelebogile*, 16.
24 Wande Abimbola, *The Sixteen Great Poems of Ifa* (Ibadan: The University Press, 2014), 132–143.

Chapter Two

THE UNIVERSAL AND THE PARTICULAR IN AFRICAN MEMOIRS

Introduction

Varying day-to-day activities that humans experience at different times are important and pivotal to their existence, many of which are also valuable when shared with others. Advancing the course of society requires that people are intimated with the activities of individuals whose existence is especially rich with educative exploits from which others can learn. Therefore, storytelling by individuals or groups is essential because it foregrounds the experiences of the ones telling them and how their relationship with each story affects them and their society. The consequence is that people are enlightened about many of the steps they will eventually take, making it possible for them to predict the outcome of any decision to advance their individual or collective course. Although telling a story demands that the narrator has reliable memory that would not fail when regurgitating past experiences, this is usually cardinal to record-keeping because a story told without any regard for genuineness will lose its narratorial value. It is important that stories are told strictly by experts who understand the art of organizing historical events in ways that will appeal to the readers.

It is pertinent to state that the memoirs I engage with reveal a considerate attempt to explore autobiographical writing and theory regarding relational and autonomous lives in communal spaces. The memoirs discussed in this book demonstrate that the authors engage in an autonomous, singular, and unitary narration with themselves while simultaneously emphasizing their narratives as they interpenetrate and mutually cross with others to create a whole new dimension of experiences. The memoirs that will be investigated in this writing are authored by individuals who experienced the colonial power play and the eventual postcolonial realities that have continued to widely shape the lives of the African people.

Types of Stories

There are several types and forms of stories, having definitive qualities that separate them from the arrays of others. For example, there are biographies, autobiographies, fiction, and even memoirs, all of which have varying characteristics that differentiate them from others. In a memoir, there is a thin distinction that makes it different from an autobiography. While the latter is about the chronological experiences of the writer, the former dwells essentially on a part of the person's history, giving enough information about that particular experience. However, what remains essential is that these stories highlight interesting thematic concerns that provide the readers with information about time, philosophy, attitude, and the collective focus of the society that produces such work. Therefore, themes such as indigence, underdevelopment, and ecological degradation reverberate through their works.

Memoirs delight readers with captivating narratorial sequences expressed through make-believe, truth-to-life, and remarkable style. A memoir aspires to rearrange life experiences in ways that will both entertain and inspire. Practically, it is very difficult to recollect the actions and incidences of the past, both remote and immediate, with the exactitude expected of a piece of nonfiction work, and a memoir provides historical ideas that reveal events and show incidences. African memoirs are a special breed of an individual's personal history through writing with dexterous characteristics. Africans are a very distinct community of people in telling stories, histories, and legends, among others, long before the discovery of print media. They tell their stories with captivating styles, using various methods and narrative techniques to clothe their messages in adventure. While using all these in their storytelling, their memoirs address issues bordering on their collective struggle expressed through the lens of an individual. The writing of memoirs and biographical accounts is an exercise that thrives on impactful life adventures that have a bearing on the collective progress of the people. Individuals with minimal contributions to their environment would lose the popularity needed to attract a reading audience because such people would generally have little or nothing to relay to the people.

In this book, I look at five different contemporary West African memoirs to examine how these memoirists privilege the narrative of an engagement with imbibed traditions and cultures in the past in a historical manner. The book presents how the narratives shape their current experiences and engagement with future aspirations. Ultimately, these chosen West African memoirists view themselves and their past or current experiences in relation to the universal and particular others. In their various experiences, they see themselves as shaped and connected to a tradition and cultural node that they have directly experienced and which serves as a guide to navigating new lands with new experiences. Thus, there will be an attempt to demonstrate that these memoirists frequently are not only attached to the traditions and cultures they imbibed but are transmitted constructively to navigate experiences outside the space where they were learned.

To emphasize, these West African memoirists often focus less on their autonomous narrative of self and more on how they relate to others, helping to establish a new social identity and currency that is relational and about the people from the space they grew up. In the context of autobiography, memoirists prioritize and synthesize others' experiences, traditions, and cultures than the self in familiar and unfamiliar spaces. However, it is pertinent to note that the concepts of tradition and culture may be somewhat partial, even though they are influential elements that give people a sense of who they are and inform a strand of identity. Nevertheless, in this autobiographical context, this book will extract the dynamic nature of the concepts of traditions and cultures and how they respond to changes in human experiences. The attempt is to demonstrate a constructive and multicultural engagement despite the inherent qualities of the typical African memoirs.

Characteristics of African Memoirs

Unlike autobiographies, memoirs capture an important moment of an individual's transition to unimaginable greatness or from a boring lifestyle to a sudden life of sufficiency. Therefore, the primary intention of a memoirist is to offer this storyline in ways that the readers will essentially see their lives through the writing and how their day-to-day experiences are reflected through stories documented by another individual. It is not unlikely that similar experiences are available to all, and this is a reminder that everyone has identical circumstances that determine the direction of, and eventually shape, their lives generally.

Therefore, African memoirs are stories that resonate with the audience because of the compelling similarities that the writer shares with the teeming audience or readers. In African memoirs, there are instances of shared pains and turbulent childhoods that characterize the formative years of every individual in an environment governed by conflict. The writers' personal and intimate experiences place them at the center of the narrative, where the experiences captured in the works revolve around them. At a point in human history where an important event changes the course of their journey, usually from misery, despair, worries, and fears to something more historic and eventful, there are instructive cues deployed to portray the event as they actually are instrumental to their fortune.

Narrative devices, such as the use of first-person pronouns, immeasurably help in engaging readers' minds, causing them to imagine themselves in similar circumstances as the author. This is primarily because they face similar circumstances that shape their personhood, confront them generally, and eventually shape their views, opinions, and several other characteristics. The literariness of a memoir is therefore seen in the narrative style that animates the pathetic background and experiences of the writer, as this would appeal to the emotions of the readers who would have internalized a level of compassion for the writer and then identify with the unveiling triumph that comes as a result of their unbending determination. From the body of memoirs authored by Africans in the contemporary time, there is an apparent exposition of their worries, fears and conflict, and the political expedience that authoritatively antagonizes their growth collectively. The agonizing pains, stories of tormented childhood, and instances of deprived expressions culminating in a dormant, rigid, and unyielding personhood are shown in their works, and these are very subtle ways through which memoir writers connect themselves to the African readers. As a result, when readers are confronted with stories of deprivation, they instantly identify with them.

From the experience of Leila Abouzeid, an African memoirist, there are intimidating records of the political unfairness of French colonial rule in Morocco. At a time when the Europeans reigned supreme by controlling the resources of the African people, the level of media gagging and other punitive laws that were targeted to restrain the people from protesting or fighting for their rights ensured that certain individuals with the unbending spirit of activism were used as scapegoats and tortured, ridiculed, and inappropriately maltreated. This advertent desecration of the rights of different voices led to supplanting oppositional parties and silencing their voices.

Therefore, in Abouzeid's memoir, *Return to Childhood: The Memoir of a Modern Moroccan Woman*,[1] efforts are made to contextualize the experience of the author's father, who has been a victim of the highhandedness of the colonial brutes. In a way, the book is a direct interplay of personal struggles and collective freedom that highlight the extreme experiences of a confident activist whose uncompromising position against a despotic reign earned him successive arrest and detainment. Here, the memoir has been used primarily as an instrument to show the umbilical cord between personal or intimate experiences and the general institutions and systems in vogue at the time.

To educate the audience about the ongoing inequity that governed the Moroccan leadership, Abouzeid reveals, through her memoir, the overwhelming experience of her childhood, which shaped her current position and, at the same time, protested the unfairness. Notable in the qualities of an African memoir is the ability to paint the sociopolitical conditions of the environment that reminds everyone of the longstanding hegemony of European imperialism, which does not only fit into the dustbin of history, especially as there are European actors who are tirelessly trying to pull a media narrative aimed at ensuring its suspension from public discourse and also their memory.

However, through the use of the first pronoun by the author, we are reminded that the habit of flexing superior sophistication in intellect, technology, power, and advancement has been the primary factor that influenced the Euro-American world to consider themselves as Big Brother with an egoistic conviction, believing they are in the position to save Africans from their own selves. Therefore, each memoir of an African whose formative years were spent under colonial rule, or when its (colonial) consequences are ubiquitous, tends to especially foreground how these intrusive exploitations of the past have informed their current status quo.

Memoirs are a resplendent indicator of the writer's directions, showing the interconnectedness of the various unrelated events and how they combine to form who the individual is. It thus helps in projecting the muted aspect of the author's life, the unsaid agony, and the obviously recognized fears and pains, among many other things. The writing genre enables the writer to remain as truthful as they can be, even when they splash their experiences with fictional characters who are adequately imbued with the make-believe qualities that help to project the messages in the narrative. Another shining benefit of the historicity and the liminality of the writer's exposition to society and the eventual attitude of society to the author (memoirist) is that memoirs always reveal how their relationship is indispensably determinant of the psychological structure of the individuals. For example, when we consider the experience of the young man in *A Long Way Gone: Memoirs of a Boy Soldier*[2] by Ishmael Beah, we imagine the despondencies rampant in the environment and how these have reconfigured the moral, mental, social, and psychological conditions of the people.

In a crystal-clear memoir, Beah, the character around whose figure the document centers, reveals the extremely daunting atmosphere that propels an underage youth to resort to taking up arms in defense of his land and identity and in a rapid quest for survival. The author finds himself in an abysmally poor environment, unconcerned with the agonizing consequences of war on the innocent demographic who would become the spoils of war or inevitable casualties in their failure to take drastic measures. Set in Sierra Leone during their civil war, the book itemizes the growing challenges of the younger generation in an environment harsh to their safety and indifferent to their wellness. The story is worth telling because it is a revelation of the crude nature of war and a rhetorical question about the colonial activities of the past that contributed to the postcolonial outlook of the ex-colonies, one in which Sierra Leone occupied an important position.

At the age of 10, Beah began to experience various chaotic issues that appeared entirely alien to him, without any clue of their effects on shaping many things about himself and his life. For example, refugees would pass through his area after unrecognized attackers chased them. On one occasion, when describing how these warring activities have become the primary decider of his personal agenda and the sole factor for his crude actions, Beah recounts intensely that "these days I live in three worlds: my dreams, and the experiences of my new life, which trigger memories from the past."[3]

The use of first-person pronouns and the possessive form tells a lot about how the acidic atmosphere of war revolves around him and the people in the community. The challenge to divest themselves of any innocence percolates the narrative, animating the call for freedom and survival at the same time. Before he took up arms at the age of twelve, the valiant young man and his family imagined the war would be short-lived. However, when the issues escalated more than anticipated, he demanded that he take up drastic means while having it in mind to claim their freedom. As a teenager, the narrator spends much of his time wandering Sierra Leone, running away from the civil unrest that has claimed the lives of his family members. Unlike a conventional childhood, Beah's own is spontaneously weaned of necessary maturity because he must fight for his living since other available options cannot guarantee his survival. Hence, the young Beah resorts to taking critical survivalist tactics needed to rescue himself, stealing when needed and killing when his life is under threat.

Another important characteristic of African memoirs is that the narrator is usually the character around whom the narrative is structured. With this, the audience (or readers) easily tap into the unsaid experiences that include the emotional turbulence experienced, which cannot always be adequately represented in writing, and the dilatory justice they collectively fight for. The African case is different because their recent history is dotted with unwholesome activities of the predatory civilizations who have come to wean them of their development.

Africans will continue to feel the vestiges of colonialism and how this experience has greatly shaped, reshaped, and reconfigured their philosophy, politics, environment, and economies, among many other things. So, when we read about leadership failures and the philosophical emptiness that grips the people's political class, we would begin to imagine the various unspeakable ways community members felt this lack of ideas. For example, in Leila Abouzeid's memoir, as highlighted above, we see the postcolonial realizations of the European agenda, which were strictly set to see that Africans' postindependence period was marred by violence, the quest for economic survival, and a revitalized interest to exploit one another for the interests of their paymasters. And then we are reminded that arresting Abouzeid's family—her father especially— was a necessary step to quench voices that negate or challenge the obvious inequity, commodification of justice, and rape of fairness.

Thus, memoir helps in conveniently placing in perspective how the unruly attitude of the postcolonial African leaders is a subtle adaptation of the erstwhile colonial brutes' strategy of silent opposition due to their psychological distance from the majority, which has invariably punctured their understanding of representational leadership, purposeful governance, and productive leadership. We can have a better understating of the prevalent highhandedness when we are familiar with how the African family structural system operates. In Abouzeid's case, her father—who is naturally the provider for the household—is arrested by an oppressive regime, with no contrite deference to the man's family. Therefore, it is inescapable for her to be exposed to financial, emotional, and sociological pressures. This is not to mention the intractable consequences of the arrest on her mother, the woman sitting next in the hierarchy of their family structure. It has automatically conferred on her a round of responsibility, exposing her to various emotional challenges and compounding her woes. As Africans (or non-Africans), we feel the despair in Abouzeid's life and her other family members. However, if the lady cannot take up arms against the state, as Beah does, it does not underwrite the layers of discomfort that such treatment has exposed her to.

Additionally, the centrality of the narrative focuses on the protagonist (the memoirist) shows to the audience, in most cases, the unfurling scenarios due to the prevailing or dominating philosophy of their environment. During childhood, when Ishmael Beah was undergoing limitless pressure from the continuous invasion of his town, by the reference of that war, we see that the then leaders were specifically interested in war and not dialogue, so long as this allowed them to satisfy their predetermined goals, among which are "sit-tight syndrome," clinging to power as a survivalist tactic, amassing the society's treasure for personal interests or aggrandizement.

As already inferred, African memoirs, among many other things, are surveyors of history because they help illuminate the available intricacies prevalent in the area at the point of production. The two memoirs, as exemplified above, are a telling tale of the writers' personal struggles. On numerous occasions, the boys in *A Long Way Gone: Memoirs of a Boy Soldier*[4] by Ishmael Beah—including the narrator himself, along with Junior, Talloi, and Mohamed—are helpless as they are found stealing to survive. These extreme acts of survival are naturally not advisable for people within that age, not least in an African setting that is condemnatory of such outrageous indulgence. But then, humans always have the instinct to rise to the occasion, even if it means losing their moral values.

Qualities of an African Memoir

Memoir is a genre of writing with exclusive characteristics and features that single it out from other genres of writing. While these features are not always available in a given memoir, their inclusion gives the genre the needed structure of a good memoir. Observable differences are easily identified, as these qualities are usually unavailable or stylistically avoided in other genres. For example, while writing a fictional work, the writer operates within a circumference of freedom where they can introduce nonexistent activities to sustain the readers' and people's attention. Following this method wistfully usually determines the writer's success and how they are perceived in the public eye.

However, this method does not hold such power when writing a memoir. Rather than being interested in the fictional perfection of the writer, the readers are categorically interested in the writer's genuineness, crudeness, and originality. By doing this, they begin to see themselves through the author's lens, living all the experiences shared by the writer in his or her life journey documented in that piece. Therefore, this genre is essential because it relates to the people who pick and read them and because of the innocent way the issues in the work are handed down. The African memoir is not actually different from this, and its qualities are shown below.

Proximal Distance

Writing a memoir usually is hinged on an individual whose life experiences inspire documentation, owing to the uniqueness of these experiences and how they tend to contribute to readers' development when they digest the piece. Memoirs help to answer certain puzzling questions about human existence while showing the intricacies of human relationships. A memoir can reveal the ideological stance of a people when we interpret the proximal distance maintained by the major character, the memoirist, to people, society, or even the things of nature. Maintaining a proximal distance helps to reveal the mutual interdependence of these variables: the human and the environment, society, or other things of nature. When we pick an African memoir, we would see the acute connectivity between individuals or between the individual and society itself.

In fact, African ideology that centers on mutuality can be primarily seen in the writings of memoirists whose dedication or commitment to a common cause is borne out of the need to show a great sense of togetherness. From many of the examples, we have seen how individuals put their lives on the line in their quest to fight for the common good. There is no mistaking that these memoirists—who often show characteristics of an activist—are deeply connected to the people in one way or another. It is very easy for them to denounce their activism, pursue personal agendas and desist from fighting for the voiceless in society. Rather than do this, they realize their closeness to these people cannot be for mere decorations. They imagine themselves in this quagmire and decide to represent the voices because of the believed familial connection they share with them.

For example, Ngugi wa Thiong'o's detainment in his memoir, *Wrestling with the Devil*, comes because he sees himself as close to the Kenyan people who are dispossessed of their valuable possessions, in which case they are also denied any access to good living. Therefore, the memoir maintains a proximal distance, not to an individual, but to the community. In other instances, there are chances that the individual's relationship with himself or herself is more important, and this will eventually be seen in radical individualism, which would be the predominant focus of the writer. However, Africans share fond relationships with one another and exhibit the attitude when the occasion arises.

Another important example can be found in the work of Ken Saro-Wiwa, whose sense of activism shows the closeness between him and his people of Ogoni. Even at the expense of his freedom and privacy, he endured enormous hardships at the hands of the tyrannical authorities at the time. He conceived of himself as the conscience of the people and did not fail in his continuous engagement of the people in activities that would educate them further about the inherent danger in drilling their resources without replenishing them appropriately. Wole Soyinka depicts such a level of closeness to his people and ideology when he courageously engages the political stalwarts of the Nigerian state in his memoirs *You Must Set Forth at Dawn* and *Ibadan: The "Penkelemes" Years—A Memoir, 1946–67*, where he pays a very expensive personal sacrifice for the freedom of the people. This would, however, force him to go into exile because of his safety.

An important impression that this memoir leaves on the audience is that the subject of the work maintains a very strong relationship with the people. This is a common denomination in memoirs written by Africans. In other words, African memoirs are a compass to understanding the people and their relationships, giving away the predominant philosophy that they practice as a people.

Specificity of Time

Although sometimes interchangeably used, a memoir is different from an autobiography because it does not follow the chronological representation of events around the writer. While the latter is expected to maintain a balance in this method, the former recounts the experience of the one writing it in relation to a specific time in their history. One does not take a memoir with the aim of getting detailed information about the author from the beginning of time. There is the understanding that the events discussed in it are traceable to a point in their life story. The definiteness of a memoir when dealing with past events places the readers within the appropriate frame to understand the activities that happened within this referenced time.

Given that humans may spend considerable amounts of time before their autobiographical documentation may pique the readers' curiosity, this does not apply to memoirs because, regardless of age, there are events that dot human lives worth sharing and recounting. This takes us back to the work of Ishmael Beah, the child soldier who joined the government in fighting the rebels. This event occurred in his life when he was between the ages of ten and twelve. Naturally, one would think someone of that age would have nothing appealing to share with the reading public, but one is automatically puzzled at the rugged life led by such young people in a war-torn environment.

Therefore, African memoirs are indicators of historical realities, giving information about a specific time in history. By revealing those details attached to a time, the audience is intimated with the dominant philosophy, style, and primary concern of the period. Events that happen to individuals and their society can be the product of the predominant philosophy of the period. Whatever happens to people can be linked to the available system during their own experience.

For example, Wole Soyinka's treatment that led to his exile can be viewed within the context of an authoritarian regime that showed extreme hostility to antagonizing voices in Nigeria. To an average reader, Wole Soyinka had his life under serious threat because the prevailing political philosophy did not accommodate oppositional views. If people unfamiliar with the political behavior of the country are privileged to have read his memoir, they would have been educated sufficiently about the interplay of democracy and military government in the Nigerian environment. Therefore, by referring to his experience with the military government, the memoirist intimates to his readers the emerging political tension that gave rise to his arrest and detention, coupled with other dehumanizing encounters they experienced.

In addition, society's growth is patterned along the line of the dominant attitude that is in play at any given time. Like how the personal encounters of Wole Soyinka, Ngugi wa Thiong'o, and Ken Saro-Wiwa, among others, reveal the chronological pattern of their political evolution, memoirs can also be used to measure the people's attitudes at a given period. People's aversion to undemocratic ruling can be easily spotted in Ken Saro-Wiwa's memoir, whose case was interestingly followed by the mass majority, with no success, owing to the intransigence of the dictator. The point of interest is that by fixing the readers' attention to the time the unjust arrest was made, we are intimated with the people's attitude during the period, as well as the government of the day and the ones under them.

Beyond the arrest and the obvious violation of human rights, time specificity in these works enables us to understand the veiled interests of these leaders who pushed them to act in such a capacity. As a result, the memoirist has fixed our focus on the socioeconomic and sociopolitical expediencies that motivated outright perversions of justice without mentioning them. Therefore, the stylistic use of animating the time of events is to foreground unspoken information about the actual time.

Emotional Appeal

All stories try to appeal to human emotions in one way or another. Stories usually attract people more when they exhibit shared compassion, despair, and fears with the people. In other words, writers deliberately invest emotional energy in their attempt to drive messages to the appropriate destination and quarters. Making demarcations between the emotions felt in fictional writings and nonfiction, such as a memoir, is necessary because one involves the deliberate alteration of events to get the emotional advantage of the audience, while the other appeals to human emotions through their innocence, originality, and perceived imperfections. The audience's natural desire to imagine themselves living the subject's life, identifying with their struggles, and applauding their efforts to turn things around, explains why memoirs appeal to people's emotions.

When human experiences do not generally offer exhilarating thoughts about life, people distance themselves from reading or listening to such stories. In other words, writing memoirs becomes ideologically unnecessary when there are insufficient examples of lived struggles and trials. After all, events happen to everyone, but not every event is worth the reading attention. For a person's personal experience to deserve scribbling down, there must be a lot of interesting activities that will emotionally appeal to the audience.

For example, readers are drawn to her plight and begin to imagine themselves in her condition when Leila Abouzeid, the Moroccan creative memoirist, writes about the unlawful detention of her father in *Return to Childhood: The Memoir of a Modern Moroccan Woman*. Family is very important to its members in different ways; therefore, when family members are confronted with dumbfounding challenges, our relationship with them usually determines the level of our emotional turbulence and the battles we fight within. In the memoir, Abouzeid expressively highlights her challenges as a child when her father was forcefully taken away from them because of his uncompromising position against the oppressive government. While it is possible for an outsider to dismiss all arguments relating to the emotional dislocation of the memoir, the family members of this man cannot share a similar perspective. Therefore, through the memoir, we are constrained to identify with her for all the disastrous results that her father's maltreatment has personally caused her and her family structure. In fact, she would later exile herself from Morocco, probably to rescue herself from the emotional torture she suffered as a result of that particular incident.

Nowhere can the emotional appeal of a memoir be captured more compassionately than in the memoir of Ken Saro-Wiwa Jr., who recounts the horrible circumstances surrounding his father's death. The memoir, titled *The Day My Father Was Killed*,[5] chronicles the ideology of the great activist, his determined character, and his unbending spirit in the face of obvious injustices. Ken Saro-Wiwa underwent overwhelming degradation and survived countless times until the government decided to sentence him to a crude execution when it appeared that people were beginning to understand the gravity of his message. His son, Ken Saro-Wiwa Jr., gives details about what he personally went through to ensure his father's safety, including his appeal to the international community seeking their intervention against the imminent execution of his darling father.

By giving these details, the memoirist invites the audience to feel his pains and understand his embattled mindset. Even if the readers do not live in Nigerian society, they might understand the context of insouciance that the government operates around. Therefore, it is apparent that when African memoirists pen their personal experiences down, they seem to appeal to the emotions of their audience.

Common Themes in African Memoirs

Every memoir has its narrative nucleus on an individual whose life experiences are the subject of the writing expedition. While documenting their personal encounters in relation to how people within the same geographical, philosophical, or political environment influence what they experience and how they absorb them, there are lessons that the narrator intends to pass across to people consuming their works. These lessons are usually understood as the writer's thematic preoccupation, and they imbue people with the knowledge of things, particularly as these issues are the predominant activities during the time of producing them or before.

It is imperative to lay it bare that African memoirs are usually different thematically from many others owing to various factors, chief of which is their unidentical philosophical priorities. For example, many of the works of the European world are usually appreciative of nature, especially during the nineteenth century, celebrating abstractions and adoring environments. However, the African focus has been different even in the age of oral rendition, where morality occupied their central focus. This will later be expanded to concrete things affecting their lives after their contact with the European world. These are pragmatically highlighted below, citing examples from memoirs of notable intellectuals.

Colonialism

Indisputably, colonialism and its soporific consequences have punctuated the growth of African people with an indelible legacy that continues to antagonize their efforts to re-strategizing all to revive their lost glories. Despite the various methods adopted to ensure such a lofty dream comes to fruition, they are usually sabotaged by the massive havoc already wreaked on their environment and economy. For a long time, postindependence African societies have been struggling with various infractions occasioned by political witch-hunting or outright collision of ideologies, all of which, naturally, have unreliable tenacity to bring about the desired changes.

However, despite these emerging complexities, the fact remains that many individuals are directly hit by the unsettled atmosphere due to the reality that commoners are always the sufferers of political upheavals. So, the problem inherited from the vestiges of colonial rule continues to confront African leaders even in their postindependence environments, compounding the woes of the community as the masses bear painful circumstances to adjust to the harsh reality. Therefore, the pastness of erstwhile colonial brutes' activities does not matter as much as it continues to dictate the present realities.

As an example, we are constrained to investigate the colonial expeditions in Sierra Leone again, but not from the perspective of Ishmael Beah, the underage soldier who took up arms as his way of ensuring safety. Rather, we are looking at another interesting piece from a brilliant mind who has used her pen to educate the audience about the underlying devastating results of colonialism which are naturally not observable from the surface or from an emotional distance. *The Devil that Danced on Water*[6] by Aminatta Forna clears our understanding of how succeeding governments in most ex-colonies, especially in Africa, find it tasking to inspire a turnaround as envisioned previously by a community of Africans.

Mohammed Forna, the narrator's father, is a morally sound Sierra Leonean with admirable characteristics. His desire for freedom under colonial rule cannot be underestimated, and he continued to partake in various activities instrumental to the people's freedom under the colonial regime. Immediately after their independence, he was chosen as a finance minister under Siaka Stevens during the 1967[7] national election. However, this man, with his upright philosophy, resigned because of the obvious failure of the president to initiate programs that could provoke the desired changes. Unfettered by the likely reactions of the masses and even his employer, the president, his zeal for a better environment is transformed into maverick activism, where he offers his services to the benefit of the people.

It must be emphasized that the attitude of indistinct arrest grows from a desire to rule unchecked in the manner of their erstwhile colonial lords, with the intention to control the commonwealth of the people solely and covetously. What is different is that, although European leaders may be feared because of their tactics and skullduggery, African leaders would not be feared as much because of an understanding that they are all coming from the same angle where collective African success should be their priority. However, these activists are mistaken, and it is sadder because they could not understand this in a timely manner. Therefore, when they challenge the government to initiate movements and formulate policies that will enable them to achieve a greater height, they were indiscriminately rounded up by the same government with no reference to their social hierarchy or political importance. In fact, after the marathonic trials faced by Mohammed Forna and a host of others, among which were the previous administrator who handed over to Siaka Stevens, Brigadier John Bangura wept bitterly on the eleventh hour of his execution,[8] having been shocked by his successor's indiscriminate ruthlessness.

Discussing colonialism as a theme that reverberates through the preindependence and postindependence literary productions cannot be sustainably handled without making notable references to the experiences of the South African people under the colonial regimes. Contrary to what is obtainable in other parts of Africa, the relationship between these people and their colonial brutes is tied around topography and economic exploitations at the same time. Topography, because they have an accommodating landscape in South Africa with space that can conveniently harbor them, the colonizing Westerners, without losing much of the comfort of their country homes in Europe. And economy because harvesting these pieces of land for their parochial gains will be unendingly beneficial to them. Therefore, it is inevitable for South Africans who are brought up in this environment to experience the pangs of the ideologically destructive political system of the colonial power in South Africa. Apartheid readily comes to mind: the creation of a distance between the minority whites and the majority Blacks emotionally and economically. Finding themselves under these political uncertainties, people resorted to protests, demonstrations, and other forms of indulgence to show their discomfort.

Reminiscent of this is the case of the freedom fighter Nelson Mandela, who was jailed by the apartheid South African government for twenty-seven years. In their effort to satisfactorily deal with individuals or groups who were ambitious to challenge their authority, they sent Mandela into confinement, which debarred him from enjoying his basic rights to live. This, however, finds intertextuality in some happenings that dominated the South African people's lives and helps to place Malaika Wa Azania's memoir *Memoirs of a Born Free: Reflections on the Rainbow Nation* within the normal context. Malaika Azania was born some months before Nelson Mandela's release from the prison on Robben Island for his role as the leader of the then-outlawed ANC.[9]

Chronicling her childhood experience, Malaika, in her memoir, hints to the audience about the torturous effect of growing up in an environment where segregation was rife. The psychological shock with which they were compelled to cope, the denigration of their human dignity, the bold desecration of their values, and others were all factors that unavoidably created that alienation in their minds where they had to struggle to get back their lost glories.

Her story reflects a struggle to regain total independence that would enable them to achieve the true meaning of freedom. Although there is a general understanding that the previous world of South Africans was peopled by revolutionaries[10] who engaged the imperialists using all available means—protest, peaceful demonstrations, and others—to combat them until they abdicated power and handed over the political reins of the country to the rightful owners, the succeeding generation is also engrossed in another struggle, even though its nature does not allow for force, that will emancipate them from the shackles of economic problems.

Therefore, a central thematic concern of African memoirs is the concentration on colonialism and imperialism and their effect on the people's progress. In that spirit, when we see the magnitude of oppression in Aminatta Forna's memoir, where her father becomes the victim of a power tussle, we realize that there is intertextuality of this, as reflected in Malaika Wa Azania's documentation, that is expressly revealing the devastating results of colonialism, we would conclude that African writings are always saddled with depicting what is situationally affecting the people and not a mere adornment of nature or its celebration.

Poverty

Without subscribing to any form of prejudice, we are not necessarily employing hyperbole when we assert that the colonial exploitation of African natural resources and their economic talents has been the foundation of the people's continuous regression into subservience on the economic and political front. Africans are blessed with everything required to court advancement and development, but their bondage was premiered by the invasion of the Europeans, who plundered their resources, depleted their wealth, feasted on their environment, and eventually displaced their focus. Therefore, the agonizing effects remain that those at the lower rung of the economic and social ladder would scavenge for food or experience increased risk and difficulty ensuring their day-to-day sustenance. It is not a coincidence that this contemporary indigence can be directly linked to the ceaseless exploitations of these ex-colonies systematically, even in the current human society.

In economic and political matters, all the francophone African countries are directly tied to the apron strings of France, their erstwhile colonial brutes. The French made unilateral arrangements that disallowed these countries from making any diplomatic relationships with any civilization that stood to benefit them.[11] Does this strike anyone as a surprise when people under this severe condition battle poverty? Thus, poverty is one longstanding theme that reverberates through the writings of African countries, and it bears no exemption from their memoirs. Literature reflects the happenings in human society, which explains why many of the writings coming from Africa, not least the memoirs, dwell essentially on the poverty-ridden conditions of the people, and how it continues to shape their perception at various levels.

Hence, the African writer, being the conscience, the lens, and the people's mouthpiece, selectively picks relatable themes—the chief of which is poverty—that the primary audience can identify with and immediately see themselves within the frame of the depiction of the narrator. The moment there is a demonstration of an individual's life of indigence, the readers (listener, audience) fix themselves into the story and begin to imagine how these things discussed influence them. Even though poverty is not a celebrated condition that many people would want to identify with, the fact that it was the cornerstone of their childhood development makes it resonates with them and offers them that emotional balance needed to steer clear on the voyage of life.

One exemplary example of a memoir that reveals the poor status of the environment is the work by Mpho' M'atsepo Nthunya titled *Singing Away the Hunger: The Autobiography of an African Woman*,[12] where the author, a South African, recounts her childhood experiences laden with poverty-inspired plans. This piece of literary material is rich with the depiction of the conditions inhibiting women from maximizing their potential in the Basotho community. She expresses the complex effects of institutionalized poverty, which has reconfigured their mindset as a people. The narrator, Nthunya, dwells so much on the sociocultural condition of the people and their poor condition, and she draws the asymmetric line between them. In the memoir, the narrator is a victim of an unplanned society because she must carry the weight of more than ten people on her shoulders, despite her meager income. She specifically feeds eleven persons from her salary. As a child, she is deprived of basic amenities that could assist in giving her a beautiful childhood. Despite these swelling challenges, Nthunya struggles to keep her feet firm, negotiating her way through society, and making a name for herself. Facing all these alone adds to her woes because of the absence of a supportive husband.

What is particularly striking is the narrator's ability to manipulate the prevalent indigence without losing her face to the struggle. Although her survival comes with a heavy price, the interlocking of poverty and unsettled environment notwithstanding, she survives and comes out unscathed from her trials. Therefore, we are reminded of the revelation of self and the depiction of societal vice that give room for contemporary readers to connect very closely with the writer's hidden and unsaid agony. Through the animation of poverty as a resonating concern of the contemporary memoirist, playwright, author, or poet, including even the past ones, we get an impression that the lives of the common people are directly affected by the decisions made in the corridor of political might. Mpho' M'atsepo Nthunya concludes in an interview:

I am telling my stories in English for many months now, and it is a time for me to see my whole life. I see that things are always changing. I was born in 1930, so I remember many things which were happening in the old days in Lesotho and which happen no more. I lived in Benoni Location for more than ten years, and I saw the Boer policemen taking black people and beating them like dogs. They even took me once, and kept me in one of their jails for a while.[13]

Consequently, poverty becomes the foundation upon which the people's agony, injustice, and second-class treatment are hinged. In a society with sustainable financial institutions, people, even under severe punitive circumstances, would always strike a common ground with the development in ways that would preserve their dignity. Having substantial amounts of money to lead a decent life is a threat to any oppressive regime, which is why economic decapitation is the most reliable weapon that the ruling class always deploys when on an expedition to launch destructive attacks on the people.

Examples abound in such memoirs by Malaika Azania, Nelson Mandela, Mpho Nthunya, and even Ishmael Beah, each exposing the uncanny circumstances that precipitated their individual worries and fears, among many other things. Ishmael Beah is not forced because of the exclusive explosion of the rebellious struggles that have arrested their environment, but rather he is drawn to take the drastic survivalist tactic because all the people around him have been executed, leaving him no hope of continued existence. Therefore, the torment of poverty, which naturally becomes the inescapable condition, forces him to steal, kill, and maim when the situation demands it.

Having all these as the prevailing situation in most African countries makes many memoirists perfunctorily undertake the duty of sharing their personal stories with the hope that their resonation with the majority of the people will give them a shared identity, as well as energize them when facing daunting conditions. Even though these issues are sufficiently discussed in different genres to spotlight the agonizing conditions of the people within the continent, the contemporary happenings are not convincing indications that poverty is breaking the relationship it maintains with Africa in any proximal future. Most peoples and nations are still indebted to their erstwhile colonial brutes, revealing that their poverty index will not reduce soon. These nagging developments result in a nasty and uninteresting condition for the commoner, who is always afflicted by the policy statement that seeks to expropriate Africans from their collective economic values to the advantage and the advancement of their colonial invaders.

Class Suicide

Another important thematic focus common in African memoirs is the odd issue of class suicide. Immediately after attaining independence around the mid-twentieth century from their erstwhile imperialists, the expectation of the African masses all around the continent essentially borders on the resuscitation of their lost glories on the economic, cultural, political, and philosophical fronts. Many people believe that the emergence of African leaders in their political sphere would automatically inspire sporadic improvement and unprecedented advancement, thinking positively that their shared emotional experiences under the European powers would incur in them the necessary compassion to rule with fairness. Sadly, this would turn out to be a utopian chase.

Hardly had the new African leaders emerged that they began to rule with intense highhandedness. The effect of their hardhearted leadership style is that many people were shocked and began to develop psychological distance from their leaders, a movement that has had a daring effect on their political life. In a manner that shows them as victims of unsettled psychologic battles, African leaders began to lead a life of questionable opulence, where wastefulness became a common indexical indicator of these politicians, and this, in a short period, led to the forceful overtaking of power by men in uniform—soldiers and the military. Although there were instances of internal uprisings among people before the invasion by Europeans, the forceful nature of the military overtaking of political systems is unprecedented in the history of Africa. The consequences on people's mental health are unavoidably devastating.

It, therefore, serves as the beginning of the turbulence that people are bound to experience. Failed leadership can be very disastrous to the collective course of the people because of the difficulty involved when individuals are confronted with mountainous challenges that keep neutralizing all their efforts to advance or change the status quo. For example, when the political class fails to deliver more intensely in their duty, the economy of the people would be affected (either through international collaboration or internal coordination), basic amenities will suffer untold abandonment because of corruption, medical facilities will not be adequately provided, and infrastructure, which ordinarily would have been the driver of a stable economy, would be left to wallow in abject avoidance. When all these become normalized, it is not surprising that development becomes more difficult to attain because the available resources would have been the primary focus of the covetous representatives to feast on. Postindependence Africa battled with these issues during the early period of freedom, and how it affected and continues to affect individuals determined how they would be represented in their writings and memoirs.

Neocolonial servitude runs through many writings of African people who detail layers of their personal experiences, including Wole Soyinka. In his historic memoir, *Ibadan: The "Penkelemes" Years—A Memoir, 1946–65*,[14] which was stylistically fictionalized for security and safety reasons, Wole Soyinka talks about the increased level of corruption of the African leaders who are particularly concerned about ruling and not necessarily about making an observable impact. As a characteristic of memoir writing, the writer is always at the center of the work; thus, the whole material revolves around them. In Soyinka's memoir, we witness Maren, a fictional character, perform various contextual assignments, the most important of which is to lessen the gravity of Wole Soyinka's activism, displayed in reactions to electoral and political indiscretion in the then Western Region of Nigeria. There are pieces of historical evidence that detail the sordid engagements of Nigerian political leaders and their immoral quest for power at all costs, even if it means sacrificing the lives of the commoner to achieve their goals. Such an attitude forces people to interpret their interests as being parochial and self-serving.

Therefore, we should understand Wole Soyinka's actions in his interpretation of the obvious failure of the postindependence African political leaders when he decides to take a bold step and approach to bring the horrible conditions under redress. Wole Soyinka took a very daring move, though condemnable, it appears, to challenge them by holding the radio station to ransom in a planned shenanigan aimed at declaring the then Premier of the Western Region the winner of an election in which there were obvious manipulations, through Radio Nigeria. At gunpoint, he ordered the anchor of the ongoing program to annul the announcement of Chief Akintola and shortchange the tape with his own that contained a message asking for the immediate resignation of the man from public office.

Arrested later, it took the intervention of the international community and a bold and empathetic judge to rescue him from the claws of the venomous Nigerian dictatorial leadership. A keen observation of events would unveil the reality that the strained relationship between the Nigerian leaders and Wole Soyinka started from their intrusive meddling in university affairs, which naturally has its autonomy to be respected. Due to the government's persistent interference with their internal affairs, Soyinka left the University of Ibadan for the then University of Ife, Ile Ife.

Another theme of class suicide can be found in Binyavanga Wainaina's memoir, *One Day I Will Write About This Place*,[15] where he laments the undesirable conditions of the political system after their freedom. Postindependence disillusionment reverberates through the work, too, as we see the memoirist dilating the electoral violence that characterizes their environment despite their imagined maturity to manage the country decisively after being poorly cared for by the colonial powers. One of the persistent problems in choosing a leader after colonialism has been the issue of ethnic groupings. The ex-colonial Europeans merged people of different cultural, philosophical, and political concerns without regard for their compatibility and planted a potent seed of discord for their future realities.

Therefore, many African nations with internal political crises only strive for tribal relevance by using state resources to pursue their personal agenda. It is on record that the multiple ethnic groups that form Kenya have been heavily contesting the domination of their politics. While it is incontestable that the time after their independence will automatically lead to internal strives; however, we cannot dispute the reality that the existence of this would not provide the needed atmosphere for growth to happen. The more the people drag themselves into wars, the more they plunge their little resources and remain stagnant in terms of the development index.

Succinctly, class suicide becomes a compelling yardstick for understanding writings, especially those produced by Africans in the postcolonial environment. Neocolonialism, redefined as servitude and indentured slavery, is the continuous characteristic of postcolonial politics where the leaders display a high level of incapacity yet cling to power at all costs. The "sit-tight syndrome" affects many African leaders even in contemporary times, but their inability to throw in the towel and allow others to come into the system for their contribution continues to pose a challenge to the advancement of the African people.

Unlike the Europeans, the growing concern to feed themselves, enjoy basic medical care, and experience revolutionized infrastructure are nagging problems Africans face. This makes it unavoidable for them to experience agonizing situations when they are not in provision. Except for those benefiting from the scourge of unproductive leadership, these people (the masses) have a common challenge, which is the very reason their writings resonate with readers from the same area. By placing the writer within the same setting with them, they understand their shared pains and identify with the same struggles that threaten their lives daily.

Fluid Identity

In the contemporary world, the project of globalization has enhanced the animation of different things, one of which is the conceptualization of identity. The perception of people about human identity has unavoidably been influenced in modern times because of the multifarious nature of global advancement, in technology especially. In the distant past, people were pigeonholed to limited identity because of the restrictive nature of human relationships. However, this practice has drastically changed with the inception of the internet, technology, and the unprecedented economic dependence of one nation on another. With the help of all these, the project of uniting the globe into an indivisible entity has achieved a laudable accomplishment. Therefore, accessing other people's cultures, styles, and practices automatically creates an interest in finding a cultural family among people from far geographical distances.

In the case of Africa, however, the unique history of colonialism has enabled a multicultural space where ideologically mixing with other people is done without stress. Aided by the internet and powerful technologies, people begin to travel both physically and philosophically. In other words, Africans in the postcolonial period are more inclined to act, behave, and structure their life patterns following the design of the West. Therefore, one of the issues discussed in African memoirs is the idea of unstable identity. People are strictly becoming very difficult to fix into an identification method because of the fluid nature of human relationships in the twenty-first century.

African writers depict this condition with a mixture of despair and admiration. Despair, because of the likelihood of straying from the African identity that has been unconsciously guarded for centuries. There is a measure of admiration in their revelation because they celebrate that Africans now have access to multiple cultures and believe that such would enable them to widen their horizons indefinitely. However, it is particularly striking that exposure to these multiple cultures can become a challenge. This is inevitable because when various contrasting ideologies are fighting for a space in a person's mind, they would have the limitless tendency to exhibit certain condemnable behaviors. For example, it is common for many Africans to judge African cultures using the lens of any civilization they have a flair for. Most will never see this reality as an identity crisis because they also function within that capacity. Beyond this, contemporary African people are predominantly unstable compared to past generations, which can be illustrated in several African memoirs today.

Describing them as unstable is not meant in a negative way. However, we are influenced by the sort of personhood that we find in the memoir of Tanure Ojaide, a Nigerian memoirist. The title of his memoir is *At Home, Away from Home: A Memoir*,[16] which he uses to document his experiences outside his home country. Finding himself in a cultural habitat other than his original environment inspired him to view things entirely in a different light. In the book, we are reminded of how American society provides him with enough tenderness, especially those he has only imagined throughout his childhood. Being faced with this level of hospitality helped in his contrastive evaluation of the two environments he has experienced. In fact, this treatment is seen in the warm reception that inspires the title of the memoir, where the American home is conceived as one that is receptive to anyone, with unlimited capacity to make landmark achievements even in a foreign environment. This has been the predominant reason why the identity crisis is rife in contemporary African discussion.

People who have the chance to move away from their geographical habitat to developed societies tend to easily accept the available system because it often provides them with comfort.[17] However, these people are also filled with premature nostalgia. In the case of Tanure Ojaide, as demonstrated in his memoir, his longing for Nigerian cultural activities is a psychological void that needs to be filled despite the remoteness of his distance to his cultural home. From time to time, he is caught in the web of negotiating the American space with the cultural values known most to him. It explains

Figure 2.1 Tanure Ojaide

why he never dissociates himself from Nigerian cultural wear, food, and behaviors. This nostalgic feeling makes him miss Nigeria while he is in America, and he would act in a similar fashion of likeness for America when he is in Nigeria. Therefore, this confirms our assertion that the contemporary African is sandwiched between at least two identities or more. Continuously, he feels like a stranger, which further complicates the identity issue we take up in this writing. Despite how accommodating the American environment is, Ojaide feels the void of his ancestral beginning.

A similar experience percolates the memoir of Buchi Emecheta, whose exposure to different environments also reconfigures her perspective, at least about identity. Her memoir, *Head above Water*,[18] gives an account of the fierce battle encountered after her relationship with her husband became sour. The torridity of her experience is captured in the writing, where she finds greener pastures in North London, having the backlog of responsibility to cater for five young children after her divorce.

Although her writing highlights more of her struggles than the idea of dual identity, it remains ideologically difficult to separate the sense of identity from her experience in the foreign land. To keep her head above water, she is constrained to undertake arduous tasks just so that she would survive catering for her innocent children. Her condition evokes the quest to look into the overwhelming effects of poverty because she is exposed to dangerous atmospheres in her attempt to survive. Therefore, her financial identity as a poor (with middle-class privilege) person from Nigeria is reduced value in the United Kingdom. She suffers double jeopardy for being a female, African, and poor, necessitating that she must create an identity for herself that would give her access to the things she needs to survive.

Consequently, this provokes imaginable changes in her life because of her strive to sponsor herself to attain a degree in sociology, all of which contributed to the change in value and self in the diaspora environment. Therefore, this memoir celebrates her Africanness and again valorizes her character as an individual. She addresses her exposure to the Western environment as a stray individual whose chances of survival are slim and uncertain. But then she persisted, courageously well enough to turn the table around. However, what is fundamentally important is clinging to an identity that becomes more and more difficult in a multicultural environment. She tries without success to maintain her identity when she gets to the Western environment, but she is confronted with the need to become an individual with a fluid identity that is difficult to pin down to just one. This is a testament to the current sociocultural reality of the African people in today's society. Save for the fact that people are conditioned to function in predetermined directions, individuals of today are disposed to see themselves from different angles because of the multicultural dictates of the current world.

Through the representation of the emerging events, African writers, especially those in tune with the development of their society, factor into their writings those prevalent realities that affect them as individuals and collectively. Without so much doubt, identity politics has perforated modern intellectual discussions because of the consuming influence of the media, technology, and the accompaniment of the globalization project. Having people with the tendency to exhibit behaviors symptomatic of multiple identities is commonplace, as this is only a resultant effect of contemporary politics.

Therefore, when Ojaide becomes un-homed in his memoir by showing excessive attributes of an African person when in diaspora and immediately showing premature nostalgia when he is in Nigeria, it only points to the argument that maintaining a single identity is especially difficult in the current definition of a society. Apparently, Buchi Emecheta's experience does not contradict this, as she is stuck between her African identity and the other, more Western one.

Oppression

Oppression has been a constant thematic concern inevitably dominant in the writings of Africans. The primary reason why most of these writings are revolutionary in form is simply because the multitude of African people has been victims of emotionally numb leaders whose universal language is oppression. Oppression, in this sense, is multifaceted. Politically, people are oppressed, coupled with the fact that they face an array of oppressive treatments socially, mentally, ideologically, and emotionally. When Africans are not experiencing political oppression, they must be battling gender oppression, as well as social, economic, and tribal oppression.

While all these instances of oppression are longstanding impediments to development generally, the fact that the people can be exposed to more than one at a time draws attention to why African societies are still submerged by retrogressions of unimaginable proportions. Growing up in such a society can be extremely difficult because maximizing potential is helplessly difficult in an area where complex issues interlock to challenge people indiscriminately. That many dreams die unfulfilled in Africa points to this conclusion.

Oppression happens on the political front when oppositional views are not entertained by rulers at a given time. Oppressive political leaders usually invest heavily in censoring voices that challenge their political moves and activities or question the rationality behind some of their policy statements. In their attempt to shut the windows to criticism, they often arrest, maltreat, accuse, or restrict active voices who amplify their misgivings and shortcomings to the masses and an international audience.

On this basis, people who have the ambition to become the voices and conscience of society are tactically discouraged and disrobed of their valiant spirit. For example, most of the generation responsible for the fight for independence in Africa are witnesses to the agonizing consequences of inactive leadership, oppressive political regimes, and irresponsive representation. Without people who are irreversibly committed to calling them out, even though it will result in the denial of their freedom and dignity, Africa would probably have been in a worse state without their determination to challenge the authority for their obvious misgivings.

Economic oppression is unavoidable in an environment where the few political leaders are prone to living extravagant lives, despite the obvious fact that their economic system does not support such materialistic lifestyles. There have been cases of blatant mismanagement and unethical spending at the corridors of power by the people who swore to promote first the interests of the average citizens, but the provincial quest for material things, the hedonistic characteristics of man and their insatiable needs are always their primary concern. All the African countries have been guilty of this immediately after their independence, which is why many of them experienced military overtaking of power at one point or another.

Regrettably, the men in uniform do not come up with reliable solutions to the African people's myriad of problems. Instead, they are equally extending the worm in democratically elected leadership style by doubling their greed, increasing the rate of corruption and obvious mismanagement of the government resources. If we condoned Karl Marx's argument that economy is the primary decider of social activities and directions, we would understand the various angles where the masses are affected because of the poor management of the people in power.

Political oppression in Nigerian society propels many activists to spring into action, using their intellectual power to engage the power-drunk politicians for accountability. A very powerful and influential voice is Wole Soyinka, whose severance of ties with the political class has won him a mountain of torture. His uncompromising position to always challenge the politicians when straying from their statutory duties, which is done primarily to enhance true democracy, has brought him into perpetual conflict with many despotic Nigerian heads of state and has earned him a series of arrests, imprisonment, escaped death sentence, banishment from the country, and the outright violation of his human rights.

Soyinka combines literary expeditions with activism and straddles them successfully on both fronts. The fact that he has a number of memoir collections to his name confirms the assertion that he has lived to witness many experiences. Even when it is expected that his continued interest in the democratic behavior of the country and continent at the same time will wane considerably because of his age, he always comes up with surprising stunts, making efforts to challenge the authority when things are not right. Wole Soyinka's *You Must Set Forth at Dawn*[19] remains a shining memoir that tellingly explains the political expediencies of the Nigerian sociopolitical landscape. Banned by various dictatorial leaderships, the memoir recounts the writer's experience, whose courageous voice against oppression by the political leaders has been the foundation of his ugly experiences with them. Erstwhile military dictator, General Sanni Abacha, considered certain voices that condemned his iron leadership style as potential barricades to his personal interests and would stop at nothing to ensure that they were silenced. Top on Abacha's wish list was Wole Soyinka, who was compelled to smuggle himself out of the country for his safety; otherwise, he would have been in severe danger by the military dictator.

You Must Set Forth at Dawn chronicles Soyinka's exhilarating public life, the country's judicial system, and the oppressive nature of Nigerian political stalwarts. From the denial of MKO Abiola's electoral victory, the Nigerian government showed, with unmistakable definitiveness, their disinterest in any democratic process, as this would continue to deny them any opportunity to hold the public to ransom. In order that they may distort the electoral system, there were all kinds of arrests, intimidation, and glaring abuses of power that involved locking activists up without trials.

Ngugi wa Thiong'o, another vibrant African voice, has written an insightful memoir on the oppression prevalent in African society. For anyone familiar with the literary market of the African people, identifying the unmatched innocence and the uncompromising vigor of the duo of Wole Soyinka and Ngugi wa Thiong'o will never be a difficult exercise. For the whole of the twentieth century and counting, these two individuals, in addition to other vibrant people like Chinua Achebe, J. P. Clark, and Femi Osofisan, have been irreversibly committed to the cause of the African people, regardless of the eventual challenges.

Ngugi wa Thiong'o's memoir, titled *Wrestling with the Devil*,[20] chronicles his experience with the Kenyan police ordered to arrest him from his house over unsubstantiated allegations. Along with many other political prisoners, he was arrested and remanded in Kenya's Kamītī Maximum Security Prison, meant to undergo emotional and physical torture to break them or silence their voices. The men and others were targeted because of the respect they commanded among the Kenyan people and beyond. Their freedom of speech constituted a threat to the smooth running of their dictatorial agenda, forcing the Kenyan government to take these drastic measures against them. To the ruling power, oppression becomes a useful tool to enable them to have their way without dealing with much pressure from the unsatisfied majority.

One would think that restricting these people under heavily guarded confinement was the height of oppression that could be perpetrated against them, but shockingly, even though they were under the watch of the oppressive regime, they were further placed under intrusive surveillance. Therefore, *Wrestling with the Devil* highlights the unfolding drama of writing under such open privacy, as it is filled with experiences that are both amusing and infuriating. It can be amusing because one is bemused by the determination of the government to ensure the censorship of people against whom they are ruling disrespectfully. Also, it can be infuriating because the individuals faced with this reality would battle a psychic demolition without end. The memoir captures the agony of being separated from one's family, who naturally are expected to provide emotional succor in case of emergencies such as the one they are confronted with, and again talks about the unbroken spirit of political activists investing their energy into the course of the advancement of society generally. These people are molested, dragged out injudiciously, and are made to suffer untold pains because they choose to speak for the voiceless in their society.

Treatments such as the author's personal experiences culminate into the issues that form the foundation of the writing in the contemporary African space. As inferred in this thread that the focus of other people in their literary engagement could be different because of the centrality of their thematic concern, this attests that people have different priorities. African writings usually reflect their emerging sociopolitical, sociocultural, and economic conditions in relation to how it generally affects their growth. Therefore, one can begin to see through Wole Soyinka's personal experiences in his memoir, *You Must Set Forth at Dawn*, instances of oppression and dictatorship deliberately meant to silence antagonizing voices against unproductive leadership, and one would have no problem linking it to the similar experiences of Ngugi wa Thiong'o as also depicted in *Wrestling with the Devil*.

In all, these writers are mere victims of oppression from a government that has little or no interest in their well-being. However, in an environment where the government—either a democratically elected or a military one—is not challenged when they trample on the rights and freedom of the citizens, arriving at any growth would be difficult because the people would not have had meaningful contributions to make in the process.

Liberation

The theme of liberation technically goes hand-in-glove with oppression or aggression because the ones afflicted by the poisonous effects of venomous leadership would search for escape routes tirelessly. In other words, anywhere we have aggressors scheming their antics of oppression, there are always parties committed to liberation movements to emancipate the masses from the claws of despotic movements. There are always different opinions concerning the level of oppression that Africans face in their postcolonial environment.

Many people are convinced that the complexities of the current African challenges are a product of their experience with the European invaders. People give this opinion, placing their arguments on the forceful merging of various settlements and civilizations that stand to profit none of the countries, but as long as they served the interest of the European people, the welfare of the people became a secondary assignment. They are convinced that this enforced union set the very foundation for the tribal, ethnic, and religious challenges that consume these different African nations even today. When the incidences of oppression perpetrated against activists calling for the respect of the rule of law are examined, it will be discovered that there are always undertones of tribalism, sectionalism, or religious coloration to it.

The other angle to the unceasing oppression of the government on their citizens is the lack of creativity needed to drive these countries to the next level. Many postcolonial leaders are ideologically deficient and philosophically handicapped to lead the people to a desirous future. However, their quest to remain in power or be protected by it has been the major driving force of their ambition. Therefore, when these people come to power, they display a high level of incompetence that cannot escape the flagellating sword of criticism.

These leaders are always averse to innocent criticism devoid of malicious content because they are prisoners of conscience. And then, there is a team of revolutionary voices saddled with the responsibility to identify with the majority, speak for them, and give them a sense of belonging and direction. These people are always exposed to difficult challenges because the system does not entertain criticism or anything that will reveal their concealed incapability. Therefore, by writing about these horrible experiences that characterize their childhood, African memoirists are engaged in the fight for liberation by communicating their personal experiences to the audience.

Ken Saro-Wiwa's *A Month and A Day: A Detention Diary*[21] is a good example of a memoir that particularly talks about the people's liberation. Critical of the military dictator and the Nigerian government's parasitic relationship and the Ogoni people's natural resources, Ken Saro-Wiwa is exposed to successive denigration and dehumanizing treatment by the government because of his uncompromising stance in calling them out every time. During this time, it is very difficult for these minority groups to speak to the political gladiators about the obvious trampling of their basic human rights.

Being an outspoken critic of the then despotic and unyielding military officials, in addition to their international accomplices with their collective energy to plunder the resources of the people without worthwhile projects to cater to the people, sadistic judgment was meted on this conscience of society, including many others who shared his vision and concern for the Ogoni people of Nigeria. In his bid to liberate his people, Ken Saro-Wiwa was an advocate of peaceful protest as a demonstration of dissatisfaction with the unlawful and unjust exploitation of their natural resources. Before his arrest, which eventually led to his detention and execution in 1994, he was a victim of a similar tragedy preceding it, when the pressure from the international community was instrumental to his release without knowing that a more aggressive attack was in the offing.[22]

Liberation struggles are animated by the specific concerns of the courageous emancipator who is primarily preoccupied with the betterment of their people and not their selfish interests. When Ken Saro-Wiwa was documenting this classic piece, there were worrying developments about the Ogoni people—the people who are the central focus of the determined activist. Saro-Wiwa states that "since 1958, when the first oil companies started drilling on Ogoni lands, an estimated 30 billion dollars in oil has been pulled from the ground, yet Ogoni people were given nothing in return."[23] This sad reality propelled Ken Saro-Wiwa to commit his pen to educating the people on the unimaginable size of the harsh treatment they received from the government. He believed that when people are properly armed with the knowledge of the possible consequences that could happen from the unrequited benefit the government got from their land, it will influence their decision to stand against the oppressive government that was draining them of their land resources with nothing to show for it. However, this would not come without its attendant negative results from the government that would not allow an individual to armor the people against government actions, even when these actions are unjust.

As demonstrated so far, people always take it upon themselves to spearhead liberation movements, which do not necessarily have to begin with physical violence or disruptive demonstrations. Having enough instances of writers using their trade to combat oppression can be conveniently understood as a liberation movement. We have seen it in Ngugi wa Thiong'o of Kenya and Wole Soyinka of Nigeria, and here, we witness the liberation struggle of Ken Saro-Wiwa in his memoir written a few months before his final prosecution by the government against which his critical pen has been vibrant. Although they have experienced multiple denigrations from the government, the fact that their memory lingers on in the people's minds has been the only consolation for this set of people. What they encountered during their struggles for emancipation usually consumes many, so much that they are not presented with the opportunity to pen down their experiences. In whatever way, African memoirists could conveniently be categorized as unceasing voices of freedom who, despite the obvious pains and others, do not falter in their ambition for a better Africa.

Conclusion

So far, I have demonstrated how African memoirs are characteristically different from other genres of writing because of their nature, structure, and composition. Memoirs document the writers' experiences, primarily focusing on a time in the person's history. Unlike autobiography, the memoir does not provide elaborate information about the memoirist's background, among many other things. It foregrounds the circumstances the writer has witnessed, which have shaped their perception, understanding, and emotional sensibility. Memoirs of African origin are different because of the unique history of the people in relation to their contact with the West. While it is not uncommon to find memoirs written by others that center on the appreciation of the things of nature, it is not commonplace in Africa to find works that follow a similar focus. African stories are inseparable from their relationship with their colonial invaders, which has structurally re-engineered their development chart. Therefore, this underscores why memoirists always document their encounters to show how invirile leadership bequeathed by colonial actors shapes and continues to recalibrate their focus.

Having all these characteristics regardless, the thematic preoccupations of most African memoirs are always around poverty, colonialism, oppression, liberation, and class suicide, among many others. Their works revolve around poverty because the postcolonial reality opens the people to a sad side of an economic downtrend. Thus, people experience the aggravating effects of poverty firsthand, forcing many to be displaced from their cultural habitat, social net, and psychological abode. Also, one of their primary purposes for writing memoirs is to clearly state how colonization has been the sole reason for Africans' emerging challenges in modern times.

By giving them democracy, the postcolonial Africans battle political upheavals on end without solutions in sight because of the challenging process of adaptation to the political philosophy. Coupled with the docile mindset of African people, which has been submerged to think independently in ways that they would fashion out the appropriate political philosophies that would be contextually applicable to the African environment, the African people have been misapplying the philosophy, and this has been a suffocating disadvantage to the people generally.

A good African memoir must be time-specific, including its ability to appeal to the emotions of the audience and show a proximal distance between the writer and the audience in an attempt to make them view the events by placing themselves within the context of the experience. When people are emotionally entrapped in reading these memoirs, it indicates that the writer has factored in their emotions when documenting their personal experiences. Without such qualities, the memoir is not different from other genres of writing. By being about the time of actions and events in the memoir, writers have used this style to show the prevailing philosophy of the time when the work is gathered. In relation to society, memoirs inform the audience about those things that are especially important in human society. With all these, African memoirs are a market of history, a site of philosophy, and a ground for understanding why Africa is how it is and why Africans react in a similar fashion.

The book is hinged on the attempt to demonstrate that there is a third way in which African memoirs can be read and analyzed. This particular way the essays in the volume are explored transcends the traditional, cultural, and experiences strands to show that it is possible to honor an imbibed culture or traditions without being totally engulfed by them. In other words, we can develop an awareness of our trado-cultural elements while also recognizing their limitations and moving beyond them when encountering new experiences or realities.

Notes

1 Leila Abouzeid, *Return to Childhood: The Memoir of a Modern Moroccan Woman* (Austin: Center for Middle Eastern Studies, The University of Texas, 1998).

2 Ishmael Beah, *A Long Way Gone: Memoirs of a Boy Soldier* (New York: Sarah Crichton Books, 2007).

3 Beah, *A Long Way Gone*, 20.

4 Shmoop, "Study Guide: A Long Way Gone, Memoirs of a Boy Solider," *Shmoop*, accessed April 5, 2022, https://www.shmoop.com/study-guides/literature/a-long-way-gone/summary#chapter-20-summary.

5 Ken Saro-Wiwa Jr., "Memoir: The Day My Father Was Killed, by Ken Saro-Wiwa, Jr.," *The Cable*, October 18, 2016, https://www.thecable.ng/memoir-father-ken-saro-wiwa-jnr/amp.

6 Aminatta Forna, *The Devil That Danced on the Water: A Daughter's Quest* (New York: Grove Press, 2002).

7 Sekou Daouda, "34 Years after the Execution of Mohamed Sorie Fornah and 14 Others," *The Patriotic Vanguard*, July 21, 2009, http://www.thepatrioticvanguard.com/34-years-after-the-execution-of-mohamed-sorie-fornah-and-14-others.

8 Daouda, "34 Years."

9 Malaika Wa Azania, *Memoirs of a Born Free: Reflections on the Rainbow Nation* (Johannesburg: Jacana Media, 2014).

10 Nelson Mandela, *Long Walk to Freedom: The Autobiography of Nelson Mandela* (Randburg: Macdonald Purnell, 1994).

11 *Liberty Writers Africa*, "France Collects Over $500 Billion from Former African Colonies Yearly as Colonial Tax," *Liberty Writers Africa*, October 10, 2019, https://libertywritersafrica.com/france-collects-over-500-billion-from-former-african-colonies-yearly-as-colonial-tax-outrageous/.

12 Mpho Nthunya, *Singing Away the Hunger: The Autobiography of an African Woman* (Bloomington: Indiana University Press, 1997).

13 Nthunya, *Singing Away the Hunger*.

14 Wole Soyinka, *Ibadan: The "Penkelemes" Years—A Memoir: 1946–1965* (Ibadan: Spectrum Books, 1994).

15 Binyavanga Wainaina, *One Day I Will Write About This Place: A Memoir* (Minneapolis: Graywolf Press, 2012).

16 Tanure Ojaide, *At Home, Away from Home: A Memoir* (Milwaukee: Cissus World Press, 2017).

17 Of course, it is important to note, as an aside, that not all immigrants are treated kindly when they enter more developed societies. No two immigrants' experiences are exactly the same.

18 Buchi Emecheta, *Head above Water* (London and Nigeria: Ogwugwu Afor, 2018).

19 Wole Soyinka, *You Must Set Forth at Dawn* (New York: Random House, 2007).

20 Ngugi wa Thiong'o, *Wrestling with the Devil* (New York: The New Press, 2018).

21 Ken Saro-Wiwa, *A Month and a Day: A Detention Diary* (London: Penguin Books, 1996).

22 Epicfehlreader, "Review of A Month and a Day by Ken Saro-Wiwa," Epicfehlreader, December 19, 2016, http://epicfehlreader.booklikes.com/post/1506168/a-month-a-day-a-detention-diary-memoir-by-ken-saro-wiwa.

23 Epicfehlreader, "Review of A Month and a Day."

Chapter Three

THE PORTRAITURE OF WOMANHOOD IN EMMANUEL BABATUNDE'S *AN AFRICAN JOURNEY THROUGH CELIBATE PRIESTHOOD TO MARRIED LIFE*

Introduction

Womanhood has been widely discussed across disciplines and eras; however, an analysis of womanhood from an African writer's perspective is quite hard to come by due to the traditional African perception of women as belonging to a lower social class than males. While there have been times when women held positions that were considered barred only to them, women are still relegated in many African cultural settings to an inferior class status. This part of the book explores how Emmanuel Babatunde, the author of the memoir (*Kelebogile—I Am Grateful: An African Journey through Celibate Priesthood to Married Life*) being analyzed in this chapter, broadly embarks on documenting the lives and travails of women dominated by both isolated and collective acts of male chauvinism in African societies. It highlights key moments where each of these women, including the memoirist's wife and mother, challenged these traditions and attempted to shift the dominant understanding of womanhood in African societies.

The African Negative Perception of the Witch

In many African societies, the strict adherence to culture and traditional ways of doing things can specifically rub women unfavorably, indicating the need for such change.

The book, *Kelebogile*, perfectly captures the age-old tradition of relegating African women to a lesser social status. The title of the book takes the name of the author's wife, a Batswana woman he met during his academic sojourn to the United States. *Kelebogile* starts with a discussion about the prevalent conception of gender in the typical African communities yet to tap into the influence of European tenets and civilizations. Born to a Yoruba family, Babatunde focuses on the social status of the woman in the Yoruba cultural setting, such as the difference between the gendered use of the pejorative term "witch" in contrast to its more positive gender counterpart "wizard."

Like many other African cultures, the male-dominated Yoruba culture takes pride in validating the existence of covert women associations that operate in the extraterrestrial world, and these women are referred to as witches. Despite this denigration, the witch role is one of the earliest known roles in which women held a superior status to other women in traditional African societies relative to men. There are areas where women can claim to achieve more status through their involvement in transcendental spirit medium cults, such as covens[1] that act in quasi-political roles on issues that include women.

While the concept of witchcraft is a universal social and cultural phenomenon throughout Africa, the Yoruba and other African societies with strong male-dominated structures take it to a different level. Witchcraft is seen as the manifestation of malevolent spiritual powers within the female folk, some of whom are known to use these powers to affect the welfare and survival of their immediate community. A woman more disposed to using her spiritual powers for evil is known to be a witch seeking the means to garner dominance over society. The African witchwoman is a strong character imbued with powers that can manifest in an especially potent manner when channeled toward matters of utmost importance to the Yoruba people: birth and rebirth. This is beyond the perceptions of a woman's role as the vessel through which all living human beings emerge. The "woman-as-a-mother" is perceived as a peaceloving, good, and caring woman who nurtures the future of men through her acts of sustaining offspring.

As part of this role, she ensures that resources are managed effectively, no matter how small. These responsibilities, rooted in gender beliefs in African societies, confer gender-based roles to individuals and prompt the resultant gendered effects based on social constructs.[2] In Africa, motherhood is taken as the totality of feelings and behavior that originates from pregnancy, exists through childbirth and childrearing, and ultimately continues until such a woman leaves this material world. Africans believe that the motherhood role is a sacred and spiritual path that any female must take to validate her stature as a worthy woman, but it also represents an experience that is permanently shaped for women by the sociocultural stipulations of their society. It is considered a God-ordained role through which all human beings, by necessity, enter the world. As such, a barren woman is prevented from enjoying the stature of motherhood in African society. The dehumanizing position these women face is such that they may think it is better for them to have never been born rather than to be born and later be summarily categorized as barren.

The African negative perception of the witchwoman goes even further than that of a barren woman. While a barren woman is denigrated as failing in her socially assigned responsibility to bear and raise children, the witch attempts to debar other women and their male partners from having the capability to procreate effectively or cause miscarriages and is even believed to have the power to transform into a man and copulate with women in the spiritual realm to make these women barren. For the Yoruba society, the propagation of this threat against the "natural" procreation standard serves as an epitome of evil that must be forcibly addressed by its male-controlled structures and organs to prevent the witch's unnatural machinations.

Babatunde describes three methods by which the Yoruba society neutralized the malevolent powers of the witchwoman: through the priests of the Ifa Oracle, the Babalawo (diviner); through the Gelede cult; and, if ultimately deemed necessary, through acts of witchhunting done by other cults that allege that they have sufficient powers to finish the witches off. These three methods were used in order of progression, not interchangeably. When the Babalawo is ineffective in canceling out the power of a witch, then the Gelede cult is invoked to make an effort before the final escalation of employing a witch hunter. Babatunde gives an account of this progression—particularly the movement away from addressing witchcraft by the Gelede cult to the more aggressive Atinga cult—and its effects on the perception and social status of women in his hometown.

The African "Super" Woman

Additionally, Babatunde discusses how Imeko, his hometown, contained a gender-sensitive and female-empowering Yoruba subculture whose people did not see their women as second class within the social order. Women were celebrated and honored as the miracle workers of their families, who managed the results of the economic efforts of the man, no matter how meager, to feed the whole household. The understanding of a prototypical Imeko woman is that they are saviors, working tirelessly to carry their unborn children, who will transform their partner up to the elevated status of a father. In a society that upheld the belief that a man is not yet fully complete without having children, it became imperative for male residents of Imeko to proffer honor and respect to the woman who will go through the pain of childbirth to allow her husband to achieve this milestone. When a man becomes a father, his socially constructed role within Yoruba culture changes, as evidenced by how his identity shifts from being called by his name to being called by one that fuses his original name with that of his first child's name.

The relationship between procreation and change in identity is also seen among women in the Yoruba culture, as exhibited by Ketu Imeko. It is held that women are the major fulcrum of any society, understood by dividing a woman's life into four distinct phases. The first phase starts from birth to puberty, when female children are nurtured and taught the fundamentals of the Yoruba culture and the position of women in society. Upon reaching puberty, another phase begins where they are tutored on the attributes and characteristics that epitomize good women. These are done to prepare the female adolescent's mind to become a good wife. The third phase spans from the time they start giving birth to the time they enter menopause, where they are celebrated as the custodians of life because they have started to give birth to new human beings.

The last phase is from menopause onward when the right to give birth has been withheld by nature. At this stage, women are no longer perceived as a source of creativity but as dangerous entities. Since a woman in this phase cannot bear offspring again, she is perceived as having lost the good, nurturing aspects of womanhood and can no longer be trusted to do good all the time. The Ketu people believe that at this stage, the woman tends to acquire potent spiritual powers that can be used for good or bad, depending on how society treats her, so they are deemed vulnerable to corruption. The older woman may present herself to the Ketu people established by the Gelede cult because of this potential threat, and they will, in turn, appeal to her to use her powers for the good of society. By doing so, they hope the potential women witches will be appeased and will not bring doom and calamity to society.

Babatunde asserts that things took a different form in his hometown with the coming of the Atinga cult to displace the Gelede cult in confronting the witch problem. The men of Imeko Ketu did not feel at ease with the emergence of this witch-hunting cult in their enclaves—and that it was coming from the Dahomey side to the west did not help matters. The Imeko had felt the constant brunt of violent raids from people on the Dahomey side, and they understandably felt the need to be cautious of anything coming from the west. Imeko had experienced a significant portion of its women slaved off in raids by the Dahomey warriors until the British and French came to partition Imeko Ketu into two distinct zones.

Women developing in Yorubaland are also conferred with singing skills, as well as cooking and other practical domestic skills. The importance of this ability and its relationship to the social construction of womanhood is so strongly held that a woman is expected to be capable of a sound oratory rendition of her husband's *oriki*, tracing the husband's family back for many generations without missing any detail. In order to capture one of the major highlights of women emancipation in Yoruba land, Babatunde tells the story of his mother, Iya Ayinla, who resided in Imeko and whose story brought about more reverence for the womenfolk in Imeko. Iya Ayinla's exploits raised consciousness about female rights, especially as related to men in Imeko. She had continually suffered a series of miscarriages and, after successfully giving birth, ended up losing the son to a protracted illness.

Childbirth has profound implications for women in traditional African settings because the African culture and tradition perceive the woman primarily as a vessel for procreation. A woman is not considered to attain full womanhood if she has not gone through the process of successful childbirth, so Iya Ayinla was faced with all manners of taunts and abuses. Not relenting in the desire to procreate and have offspring, she soon got pregnant again, but the hostility directed at her by her husband's extended family and their wives entered top gear, and she had another miscarriage that almost took her life. Since the Yoruba culture attributed all deaths to the machinations of evil beings within a household, there were accusations that her predicament was the work of jealous women in her husband's extended family. When she became pregnant again, Iya Ayinla felt the need to safeguard herself by going far away from them. She believed that the more she stayed among this set of envious characters, the less her chances of finding the peace to overcome the stress associated with pregnancy and have a successful delivery. She found safety by staying with a nurse whose methods were seen by community midwives as going against their own tradition.

Traditions were still strictly adhered to in this era, extending to diets for Yoruba midwives. Traditional African culture believes certain foods to be unhealthy for an unborn child. Some of these beliefs are illogical and mere superstitions stipulating that pregnant women are not supposed to eat meat, eggs, or drink milk. Furthermore, pregnant women are supposed to limit their movements so as not to fall into the evil machinations of other jealous women. Yoruba traditional culture strictly forbids a pregnant woman from walking in the sun, believing that the pregnancy might fall under the influence of bad spirits. Instead, the woman is expected to stay indoors until later in the evening when she can have a little stroll around in the company of some other women.

This new nurse with whom Iya Ayinla was staying had just arrived in Imeko, and she encouraged her clients to move around as a form of exercise, while also feeding them plenty of the foods from the forbidden diets. The fact that she was educated in the white man's medicine seemed to emphasize how her procedures clashed with those of the traditional midwives in Imeko. This clash of culture and procedure was sure to set her against the community of midwives at Imeko.

Any society that truly wants to change will find individuals willing to consciously embrace such change to test it out and validate its advantages. Soon enough, people thronged to the nurse, much to the dismay of the community midwives. Starting with one pregnant woman, the new midwife in town increased her clientele, and although most of the pregnant women who patronized her were apprehensive of breaking alleged taboos, they still decided to give it a trial. Like Iya Ayinla, some women had made up their minds to embrace the newly introduced regimen, even though it was in total opposition to what they understood as the requisite procedure for pregnant women. While some returned home after their antenatal sessions, Iya Ayinla never returned to her husband's house because she had her mind made up to stay as far away as possible from the vultures lurking around her husband's extended family compound. This action was a serious break in tradition, but Iya Ayinla was not in the least perturbed. Whatever the consequences, she was ready for them.

In those days, the Yoruba culture ascribed the leader of the traditional midwives as the head witch of the community, and sometimes these women paraded themselves as objects of worship. They were the be-all and end-all of childbearing in the traditional Yoruba society, and no one who wanted a safe delivery would dare to offend these powerful covens of witches. In this case, as Babatunde depicts, the traditional midwife was quick to pronounce a curse on all those who patronized the new midwife in town. She also began singling out Iya Ayinla and proclaiming that she would not make it to childbirth, but Iya Ayinla never felt disconcerted. The emergence of the new culture brought about by the new nurse led to more women in Imeko becoming emancipated.

Despite the curses from the traditional midwife, the nurse began to deliver babies successfully. She also accorded the mothers the chance to bond, despite it being frowned upon within the traditions they had been living with, and this was a great eye-opener for these women. Later, they would be celebrated in the same way that revolutionaries receive. It also undercuts, as Babatunde puts it, how "men reduce the time, ways and means of keeping the women together," and "[t]his was possible because the men feared that women would realize the strength they wielded in the community as the gender validated their manhood."[3]

The exploits of the female nurse who used the white man's knowledge to start a successful midwifery practice brought a new definition to female power in Imeko. It arrived unexpectedly to dethrone the existing body of knowledge on childbirth in Imeko and the Yoruba society. While Iya Ayinla encountered minor problems before her successful delivery, the span of her labor was so short that she confessed to it being the least demanding of her experiences with labor. At the same time, a woman who had returned to the traditional midwife, fearful of curses, also entered labor and lost so much blood that the woman's family decided to transfer the woman back to the new midwife.

Babatunde recalls that the expectant mother was attended to as soon as she arrived at the new midwife's place. She then gave birth quickly and with lesser pain. The success of the new nurse resounded in all the corners of Imeko. This seemingly simple event was celebrated by women in Imeko as Iya Ayinla and her deviant group of women pitched their tent against a new force and won. Not stopping there, Iya Ayinla established another milestone for the womenfolk in Imeko by setting a precedent of naming her newborn herself, a practice that was not in existence before her battle against male chauvinism and the traditional structure of midwives.

The African Woman's Struggle for Emancipation

The African practice of placing women in a lesser social status gradually withered in Imeko because society was willing to embrace a system that accorded better status to the woman. This battle for emancipation also led to Iya Ayinla deciding against moving back to her husband's extended family enclave, despite pressures from her and her husband's families. She was determined not to allow anybody to hold her back from claiming what she felt was her right. The oppressive forces established by men to kill the spirit of the African woman have always failed when confronted with determined feminine folks because the rebellious African woman is not easily trampled upon.

The Aba Women's Riot will always be a case in point when discussing the nature of the rebellious African woman. Having felt humiliated when his wife left him with no one to cook, wash, or assist in house chores, a husband was forced to accept his wife's preconditions to come back, including building another house far away from his extended family. Baba Ayinla also could have gone the way of his fathers by marrying another woman in the absence of Iya Ayinla, but he was already deep within the Christian faith, which did not permit polygamy. The belief that monogamy results from a spell cast by a woman on her husband in order not to share him with any other woman is deeply rooted in African societies, but the specter of suspicion and coercion would not work on Iya Ayinla. Eventually, the family members had no choice but to accede to her demands before the wife returned to her husband's home.

From that moment, the Imeko woman became liberated, with Iya Ayinla as the hero of it all. She settled in a home where she wielded control over what happened and was not just an object to be controlled. Her newborn child was free from the evil eyes of jealous family members. Things began to take a new direction onward in Imeko with the triumph of Iya Ayinla over her husband. Iya Ayinla, with a bold and determined mind, had conquered the forces of a male-dominated society, albeit through grit and outright strongheadedness. She succeeded in changing the status quo, laying a new blueprint for fellow women in her society to emulate. Never again would Imeko women get trampled upon or be relegated to consider only mundane issues. She had decided to pave the way herself for the journey toward female emancipation. But rather than facing the punitive measures she had expected, all she could perceive was a victory for the female folk in Imeko. This is a perfect example of confronting a problem head-on. As Aduke Adebayo opines:

> [...] the woman to tear the veil of invisibility by breaking the barriers of patriarchy, the metaphor of the "veil" is vital especially in a predominantly patriarchal society, it is important the woman tears this veil because if she does not, it will mask her identity, it will muffle her voice and distort her vision.[4]

Yet, even with these successes, the legacy of the confined representation of gender did not fully erode out of Iya Ayinla's life.

Iya Ayinla epitomizes the motherhood concept of Yoruba culture by guarding her surviving child Babatunde, the author, with all her strength. She constantly drummed into his mind that he was a special boy who could achieve anything in the world, even if the world doubted his ability. The strength of her bond with her son amazed the whole community. Babatunde believed his father's misconceived acts of abuse and estrangement from his wife and son were aftereffects of his father's military mind, which he inherited from his warrior ancestors.

Within the Yoruba culture, there is a sentiment among men that the woman is a slave inside the home and should be treated as such. Women are physically abused for simple acts like not getting the food ready on time, and men are quick to use their strength on women to indicate they are in control. In response, the African woman will sing praise songs to calm the man's nerves rather than fight back, for this would often result in more anger being directed at the woman—and no one among the ever-present relatives will make any move to manage or alleviate the situation. Iya Ayinla, possessing such a dogged mind, occasionally tried—though feebly—to fight back, even with their child strapped to her back. At one point, Babatunde, at a tender age, was forced to stand up and condemn his father's actions toward his mother. This incident ate deeply into his father's consciousness, culminating in him never indulging in such brutal acts again.

Figure 3.1 Emmanuel Babatunde

Babatunde also notes the exploits of Aduni Oluwole, another woman who challenged strongly held sentiments about the expectations of her society and gender by vigorously campaigning against Nigeria's move for independence, citing the fact that the rush to become independent from British rule was not right and would eventually leave the country worse off. When African nations were scrambling for independence, Aduni believed that the Nigerian sociopolitical terrain was not yet ripe for it. She attributed the rush for independence as a selfish attempt by a few elites to grab hold of power—largely men who were lurking to pounce on the power vacuum created by the exit of the British colonial government.

The irony of the concept of a free and independent "Mother Africa" was that, although it was constantly promoted by various African political leaders as a reason for independence agitation, the women who took on the role of mothers in African communities were neither free nor were they promised freedom from gender roles promised as a part of the African independence movements. They were still being oppressed because of their gender, despite many notable attempts by women to break from the shackles of male chauvinism.

Visions of ideal womanhood in various African societies are centered on maternity, particularly reproductive and home-managing responsibilities, relegating the relevance of the African woman's political and social life to home affairs alone. Aduni organized rallies where she admonished the women who followed her to resist the purported rush for independence by some African men who had banded together from various regions to drive the white man away to take over the reins of the government and institutionalize their selfish desires. As Babatunde notes: "That prodigious female leader had gone against the political stalwarts of the day to campaign that the rush to independence was wrong and would eventually backfire on the poor citizens of Nigeria."[5]

One of Aduni's major arguments was that traditional Nigerian ethnic societies had yet to treat people—especially women—equally. Instead, these societies continued to offer preferential treatment to men, particularly in politics and governance. Women, she argued, felt the greater brunt of the hardships of Africans. She also claimed that the social importance of Nigerian women declined with the advent of colonialism, which provided an opportunity for a small group of elites, of whom the vast majority were men, to amass lands. Women with limited access to such endeavors automatically become more dependent on men who do not face these hurdles. Aduni believed that a short extension of the white man's stay would allow African women to become involved in wealth generation via land resource gathering and be placed on an equal footing with the men.

Before independence, colonial laws sharply restricted women in many rural African societies. Women received little education because the colonial patriarchs never saw it as important, and women were also restricted from rights to ownership of land—limiting the degree of autonomy available to women. Colonial regimes accorded women only the chance to engage in petty trading while their male counterparts engaged in profitable export businesses. It was not surprising to see how the available little national power was ceded to the wealthy and influential male elites. With African men expecting women to become magicians able to feed hundreds with what little resources the men brought home, Aduni was quick to tell women to understand that the inadequacies of the Black rule would increase children's mortality rates. She urged women to consider and learn from the hardships faced by the Oyo Empire in the nineteenth century due to wars propagated by men with selfish desires.

In her defense of the colonialists, Aduni pointed to the vast pool of economic opportunities they brought, coupled with the improved social status the European culture promoted, which she believed would put women on equal footing with men socially and politically. She thought that these opportunities under colonial rule would be more particularly beneficial to women, as women would have a greater ability to cater for their children while also being better positioned to acquire new skills over what was offered by the archaic methods that traditional knowledge promoted. All these opportunities were under threat of being lost by the rushed call for independence, as the independence agitators ignored such moves toward gender equality.

She also emphasized the substantial positive impact that the white man has brought to the country, highlighting improvements such as tarred roads funded by the proceeds of cash crop sales, which had provided easier means of conveying farm produce to various destinations. She also mentioned the benefits of constructing railway links across the country and hospitals being built by the colonial administration. Aduni believed that all these good deeds would not be managed well by the indigenous leaders and that the likely consequences of this would disproportionally fall on the shoulders of the womenfolk, worsening age-old hardships such as those related to childbearing.

Aduni did not campaign against the independence agitation in her native town of Ibadan alone. She campaigned around the country, pleading with women to resist the rush for independence. She encouraged women to put more pressure on their husbands to decelerate the independence charge so that individuals could take their time to imbibe the white man's ways, which she believed would be beneficial for all. Her advocacy of a cause that promoted the white man's stay and control over Nigeria for a longer period automatically united men from varying backgrounds and ethnic groups who plotted to silence her to advance their aim of forcing the British away from the country. Assisted by the power of numbers, the march toward independence yielded fruit, and Nigeria finally became independent in 1960. But all the consequences that Aduni highlighted came to haunt the country at far greater levels than even she might have expected.

The decay that accompanied various projects and parastatals established by the colonial administration lends credence to Aduni's argument. From the moment of the Independence Day celebration to more than four decades later, the country still struggles to achieve and maintain what the British administration left behind. From the beginning of Nigerian independence onward, unconscientious leaders have employed all available means to perpetuate their power to acquire more of the wealth and fame that has come to be associated with political leadership in Africa rather than act out of their love of the country. The improved lot, which should be the shared dividends of the collective liberation from the colonialists, has become a mirage. Aduni's beliefs that Black men were not democratically inclined enough to govern themselves seem prescient, given the fast pace by which the military intervened in politics and governance and how various countercoups followed this intervention. Additionally, these countercoups ushered in successive military governments with no blueprint for development other than to amass more wealth for themselves.

Babatunde highlights women's growing influence in traditional African settings outside the political realm. These women have seemingly decided to individually push for the emancipation of the womenfolk on their own through isolated acts to position themselves in ways that have allowed them the opportunity to control men. One example of this was the trend of women converting to Catholicism and moving to women's convents to be tutored by nuns from the white man's land. The appeal of these conversions to the Catholic faith was largely due to its strong stance against polygyny, as well as the availability of Western education for women, as Imeko indigenes were not fully in synchronization with these demands.

Kelebogile: The "Model" African Woman

The centerpiece of Babatunde's book is the titular, Kelebogile, whom he met in the academic environment. She was deeply introverted and gentle, but she possessed a strong survival instinct within an environment harsh on reserved and mild-mannered individuals. Kelebogile did not like the noise the students around her produced, but she refused to be cowered by their acts of boisterousness. People are often amazed that such a woman could survive in the highly competitive academic environment at the University of Lagos, even ignoring that she was a foreigner from far away South Africa. How such a creature possessing so many stereotypically feminine qualities could survive in that jungle-like environment, featuring a series of unethical conduct by both the lecturers and the students alike, raises the bar for survival.

Like Babatunde, the uncommon circumstances of Kelebogile's birth heralded a rare personality. Her mother was alleged to have felt the need to answer the call of nature, only to find out that it was the child within her forcing herself out. Kelebogile, christened by her father, grew up a loving child who was always available to assist her mother in various chores. At a very tender age, while her peers were still grappling with washing dishes, she had mastered the womanly art of cooking to such a degree that her mother would proudly leave her in the kitchen to cook the family delicacies. This was a great feat in an African society that upheld cooking as one of the most important talents that a woman could possess.

Kelebogile's father, Reverend Setiloane, never allowed Ouma (as she was nicknamed) and her siblings to embrace the Western culture as his indigenous African culture. He made sure they spoke their indigenous language fluently and tutored them in the ways of the Tswana people of the southern part of Africa. Ouma's father had a deep resentment for Africans who, as a result of their exposure to the West, felt the need to turn their backs on their own African culture because he believed that they were only projecting themselves as inferiors to the outside world. He upheld that his culture remained his culture, no matter how archaic or strange it may have seemed to outsiders and ascribed the largely middle-class Africans he saw abandoning their culture as just a small step above poverty. The Western tradition of hiring domestic workers to do most household chores particularly drew his ire as he believed those tasks were meant to be reserved for the African child.

As a Tswana wife, Kelebogile's mother considered herself first a mother before a wife. She believed that the motherly role accorded her the opportunity to get the whole family working together, while the wife's role was limited to only her husband. She agreed with her husband's belief that the African culture could not be substituted for the Western culture. She taught her children to see the English language as meant strictly for educational purposes and that it should not take the place of their indigenous language. During their stay in Switzerland, Kelebogile's parents were apprehensive that she and her one younger sibling were so used to learning in the English language that it would be hard for them to blend into learning in another language. This made the family decide to enroll them in a boarding house in Africa, though it was a decision that was made with a conflicted mind. Their intent was that, upon completing their General Certificate Exams, Kelebogile would be sent to Botswana for tertiary education and become enmeshed in traditional African culture.

Reverend Setiloane did not appreciate the possibility of European traditions and values being superimposed on his children. He would often meditate on his decision to continue residing in Europe rather than bring his resources to the shores of Africa to help build the continent. Kelebogile had already developed a sound grasp of the Tswana language, though, while in the United Kingdom, which would make her stay in Botswana less stressful. She adapted well to the African setting despite not being brought up there. She also never carried herself as superior to her peers, as expected of children who had returned to Africa after being brought up in Europe. There was never evidence that Kelebogile had the arrogant attitude often displayed by children brought up in affluent families.

It was remarkable that she and her younger brother retained the mannerisms expected from Africans despite growing up in England. This was perhaps attributable to the fact that they were born into a pastoral family and their father being a professor. As Babatunde alleges, the apartheid policy instituted in 1948 and the Bantu Education of 1953 to centralize Black African education had unintended positive consequences for the children of middle-class Africans from Swaziland, Botswana, Lesotho, Republic of South Africa, and Namibia. While the presence of the whites in West Africa improved education, the South African whites were also seemingly conscious of not giving too much education to the South African Blacks to limit their prospect of standing a chance to rule.

Under the apartheid regime, womanhood in the southern part of Africa was quite dissimilar to its West African counterpart; the Black South African woman had to leave her children daily to tend to the children of the white women for pay. Even the older women who were already grandmothers still had to deal with the overindulged children of the whites in South Africa. Such precarious situations left the unsupervised Black children to cater for themselves, forcing teenage children to be left to control the affairs of their younger siblings. In situations where the eldest is a male, it is probable for various forms of irresponsibility to be committed, such as leaving his younger ones at home, vulnerable to abuse, so that he might attend to his own escapades.

As Babatunde points out, when a mother leaves the house for many days, her home becomes chaotic. There is a high tendency for these children to become social cretins, moving about unsupervised to exploit the environment in ways that would have been governed if the mother were present. By the time the mothers realized what their absences had cost, it would be too late to salvage the situation. Both parents' absence results in the teenage males embarking on pleasurable acts without fear or forbearance. In a bid to find the means to support the family, the absent mother also leaves the children to fall under the preying eyes of other older children. In the absence of elders to guard them, teenage violence becomes the norm for getting what you want, and children begin to introduce other vulnerable children to drugs and alcohol abuse.

Conversely, Kelebogile exhibited the perfect nature every African parent wants to see in his or her child. She acceded to the pressure of her father by studying science at the university. She was introverted but attentive, closely observing her parents' behavior and how they responded to situations, which her parents found endearing. She would dedicate time to help her mother in the kitchen, learning the African traditional feminine duties of washing dishes and making delicious foods. During her years at the university, her mother would go on a break from cooking anytime Kelebogile was back on holiday. She also learned a great deal from her time with her father; she picked up his habit of waking up early to listen to the news on the BBC.

Kelebogile had hoped to earn a scholarship to complete her study before she finished her first graduate degree, but when she desperately needed aid from her immediate relatives, she did not receive one. She survived an assault that demeaned womanhood, and the incident led to her resolve to never put her security or hopes in the hands of anybody—save herself. The perpetrators were drawn from the pool of those who spent their immorally cultured childhood without parental monitoring and guidance. This incident typified the moral decadence in South Africa because women were physically absent from monitoring and observing their children's daily activities and habits. Kelebogile was able to hide the trauma she felt from the incident behind her introverted nature, but this led to the family leaving the enclave of South Africa to go back to the more decent Botswana environment.

Concerned that Kelebogile would experience psychological disorientation due to the assault, her family embarked on a campaign of overzealous acts of niceties. She had grown resilient, but to the outside world, she seemed to display acts of vulnerability. Though she had moved on mentally from the attack, her closest family was too concerned about her to understand this. She was determined to move on and treat her survival as a necessary education—a hard lesson to never allow the trauma to hold her life hostage. Kelebogile believed that she needed to reengage with life and become more attuned to the opportunities for success and happiness, affirming the maxim that whatever does not kill you only makes you stronger. Even as she got past the incident, she felt sorry for her father, who continually nursed guilt-burdened thoughts about the event. For her own sake, she decided that as much as she still held her parents in high esteem, she had to get past what had happened and became determined to pursue her heart's desire to strive for success.

Summoning up the courage in 1986 to return to South Africa and explore another aspect of life there, Kelebogile—in the company of her friend—went to the University of Pretoria to test the waters for attending it in the future. Their experiences only validated their belief in the decadence of the South African system and what to expect if Kelebogile furthered her education in Pretoria. With her friend, Sheila, she searched for meaningful living and confirmed her conviction that she needed some purification from her traumatic experience if she were to be able to truly move on. This was to come in three stages: separation, seclusion, and reentrance.

On completing her first degree, to the surprise of people around her, she opted to take a job outside the city. While many of her colleagues assumed that she was not thinking clearly, Sheila understood that Kelebogile had a reason for her decision. Along with another coursemate, she gained employment within the Botswana wildlife habitat, leaving the people in her life to speculate about her decision. No one understood that she was on a journey of purification after her attack. While out in the wild, she led teams of tourists deep into the woods for camping excursions. Being a woman and often the youngest person in these groups, establishing leadership was not easy for Kelebogile, but her position was always clearly established to the team before setting out, and it was communicated that she was to be accorded all the respect and benefits owed to a leader. This was not going to be an easy task in a male-dominated culture, where men with overbloated egos boasted about how subservient a woman should be to the menfolk. She controlled their means of livelihood, though, and they would have to bow to this young woman if they did not want to lose it.

Kelebogile's exploit in the Botswana wild is a perfect depiction of how money had the power to transform power relations in a gender-biased African setting. She took up habits that were traditionally attributed to men, such as driving cars and waking up to jog in the mornings. Her actions spurred the local village women to imitate her by joining her during her morning jogging routine, and she energized the community of women around the wildlife habitat. These women questioned how she came about these seemingly unfeminine-like routines—not to challenge her choices but because they earnestly wanted to be like her.

In an environment dominated by the power play between man and beast over who controlled the scarce resources available, the men asserted their dominance as the village protectors and, therefore, saw themselves as the natural leaders of the women. This reflected the strong patriarchal system in Africa that positions men at the head of society.[6] Some women wanted a life that was not based on perennial subservience to the menfolk, and though these beliefs were often perceived as deviant and tending toward witchcraft, Kelebogile was able to come into contact with a few women while working in the wildlife habitat who held these beliefs.

A particular woman named Mpho was a change agent who was tagged as rebellious due to her recalcitrant attitude. Kelebogile served as a model for her; she wanted to be in control of her life, much like the young, educated woman who was always seen leading groups of old men and tourists into the woods. Mpho wanted to become educated to break from the shackles of male domination, and she was amazed at how a great education had empowered a young female to lead men and earn more than they did, all the while giving them commands that they had no choice but to follow. Mpho's mother also represented the African women who longed for a female messiah to change the status quo despite existing in a male-controlled society. She welcomed that her daughter longed to be like Kelebogile because she knew that her daughter wanted to explore the jungles in a manner only men could.

Kelebogile's arrival into their village showed that her daughter might finally get a chance at the life she longed for. She continued to break barriers erected by village tradition, and while some of these traditions did not require adherence from white foreigners, Kelebogile was not a foreigner. Still, she was not a villager either, and her liminal position made her immune to the punishment meted out on village transgressors. She envisaged a time the female villagers would also be emancipated, so she began to tutor Mpho on various activities that were barred from female participation. One of these forbidden activities was driving a car, and Mpho was a keen learner who mastered it in a short time. Mpho had been an outsider in her village. Despite being born in the same village, she did not socialize with her peers and behaved in strange ways.

When an opportunity for another scholarship presented itself to Kelebogile, she initially felt reluctant to exploit it because of her deep resentment of the white supremacists of the South African apartheid government. She had applied for the scholarship but had never felt positive that anything would come from it until she received a letter congratulating her for being selected for further interviews. Kelebogile felt a strong desire to study and improve her status in life, much like the nineteenth-century English ladies described in *An Ideal Husband* who longed for higher knowledge to compete against males for significant positions in society.

After university in South Africa, Kelebogile experienced a different form of white supremacy in the United States, where she moved to study for her master's degree. But, as with the proverbial cat with nine lives, her determination to succeed rose to overcome whatever adversity she encountered. Her introverted nature endeared her to the small American community at Louisiana State University, where she was studying, and she found common ground with Black American students and their similar experiences of living in a society ruled and controlled by white supremacists.

Kelebogile moved to Nigeria for research work after her master's degree, where she met Professor Babatunde. During this time, she remained in the purification stage of her self-imposed rites, and she continued her journey of self-purification despite several barriers put up by her university roommates and other professors, and, on one occasion, Professor Babatunde himself. Not too far after the time they shared in Nigeria, the two of them met again in the United States.

Although Ayinla had wanted to become celibate to stay on the path of becoming a Catholic priest, this was not to be, and he later settled down with Kelebogile as his wife in the United States. Born and raised in strange and challenging circumstances, two individuals met by fate and were married in holy matrimony. Kelebogile made a startling demand of her husband, as Babatunde notes:

> Kelebogile expected her husband to perform his role perfectly to the best of his knowledge, with no apologies. She insisted she had a Priest for a father, but she did not want one for a husband. She expected her husband to make a clear move in two main areas. The first was to understand that he was no longer an individual worrying about every other person's problem and fussing to solve them while losing touch with the realities of his own family.[7]

The variance between their respective African cultures and traditions is worth noting. Kelebogile's culture permitted the woman to be responsible for her husband and children before she could think of assisting any other family member. Babatunde, a Yoruba, was culturally expected to use part of his resources to care for his wife's junior siblings, even as a priority over his own children. Fortunately, the couple dodged such issues since they stayed far beyond the reach of their African relatives and were not held back by the African cultural norms they grew up with. They remained committed to focusing on their offspring alone, unlike the African tradition of caring for extended families.

Kelebogile had been raised by parents that heavily emphasized the centrality of her African identity, despite having lived a significant part of her life in the Western world. She was certain that she would not raise her children the same way as the South African women she had observed, who would leave their children to care for the children of white women in order to financially support their families. As the children would later get to know, their parents were Africans who migrated to the Western world and were conflicted about whether to raise the children by the totality of African traditions or by embracing the African American model of raising a child. To accept the former could result in the children becoming cultural misfits, while fully embracing American culture would likely be alien to Kelebogile and Babatunde and could result in unforeseeable problems for both the parents and the children.

African migrants were more comfortable embracing American culture, and in the end, they settled for a fusion of both the African and the American cultural systems that still maintained various elements of African traditions, such as exclusively giving their children African names, which the children came to love since African names have meanings that reflect an African community's understanding of the nature or essence of a being, a plant, an animal, or a river,[8] unlike the white community's names.

Like Ayinla's mother, Kelebogile made sure she was strongly focused on her children's future, pushing her husband beyond the mediocre aim of seeking a good future for them. She would often remind Ayinla of their past and how they should make the right decisions for the future of the children. Unlike the traditional African woman, Kelebogile was educated enough to make an impact on her husband and could steer her way through excellent arguments. Just as in *Pygmalion*,[9] Kelebogile was not deterred by the influence of a man in her life. She never stopped pursuing her ambitions and dreams despite knowing that Babatunde was equally capable of taking the reins. Babatunde explains it thus: "As if to convince her husband that she meant business as to where her priorities lay when it comes to the success of their children, Kelebogile set in motion a second socializing effort for the main focus of what she calls the Babatunde/Setiloane marriage and family."[10]

Kelebogile showed a total commitment to her children, with her husband relegated to second in the order of her priorities. Babatunde knew Kelebogile's loyalty to him was second only to her passion and attempts to ensure that their children excelled in the United States, and he came to appreciate her viewpoints. By winning Ayinla in these arguments, she demonstrated her great intellect and showcased the Batswana culture of pragmatism and logic.

Kelebogile also cleared another hurdle widely believed to be too daunting to leap by finishing her doctoral thesis while nurturing three children. This led to her being hired as an Assistant Professor at the University of Delaware. She never failed to share the responsibilities of caring for the children with Ayinla, leaving him to occasionally take care of the children by himself—something an African man's ego would not easily accept. But Babatunde knew better than to allow his African ego to overtake him. He understood the essence of the arrangement and even promised not to let his work hinder him from his childcare responsibilities. At times when Babatunde got careless with babysitting, resulting in injuries to one of the children, Kelebogile cursed him for not being watchful enough. She quickly reminded Babatunde that he was now a father and no longer a loner responsible for his itineraries alone. They worked with a simple ideology: their children should take utmost priority in their respective affairs.

Conclusion

Society's intent on development and progress will always grant opportunities to embrace change, even if these opportunities might not look beneficial from the outset. It behooves the elements of such a society to understand that things cannot always remain the same, and a time will come when undertaking such a change will be imperative. Kelebogile represents a model of an African woman who defies her society's pressure on women and pushes forward for success. In doing so, she and these other remarkable women help reshape the depictions of African womanhood. Their accounts highlight the leadership roles of various women in the emancipation of their fellow women in their respective societies.[11] As a result, Kelebogile remained the central pillar of her household, and her husband, Ayinla, could look back at his mother's experiences and recognize the value of Kelebogile's strength. Therefore, he could accept her as an equal within their family. Rather than exhibiting the mode of the patriarchal dictator promoted by African culture, he encouraged her to take charge of many affairs and took cognizance of her decisions most times. He considered her an extremely sensitive person who put her sensitivity to good use, as well as a true partner in their family's leadership. Just like in Wole Soyinka's seminal play, *The Lion and the Jewel* (1959), *Kelebogile* brings to the fore the reality of African women under the domination of the male folk in their society when women's roles were limited to home chores like carrying, scrubbing, and procreation in large numbers for the benefit of their husbands who position themselves as small gods to be worshipped.

Notes

1 Flora Nwapa, *Efuru* (London: Heinemann, 1966).
2 Kwadwo Okrah, "The Dynamics of Gender Roles and Cultural Determinants of African Women's Desire to Participate in Modern Politics," *Journal of Global Engagement and Transformation* 2, no. 1 (2018): 1–15.
3 Babatunde, *Kelebogile*, 28.
4 Aduke Adebayo, "Tearing the Veil of Invisibility: The Roles of West African Female Writers in Contemporary Times," in *New Visions of Creation: Feminist Innovations in Literary Theory*, eds. María Elena de Valdés and Margaret R. Higonnet (Tokyo: University of Tokyo Press, 1993).
5 Babatunde, *Kelebogile*, 75.
6 Oseni Afisi, "Power and Womanhood in Africa: An Introductory Evaluation," *The Journal of Pan African Studies* 3, no. 6 (2010): 229–238.
7 Babatunde, *Kelebogile*, 283.
8 Babatunde, *Kelebogile*, 291.
9 George Bernard Shaw, *Pygmalion* (London: Penguin Books, 1906).
10 Babatunde, *Kelebogile*, 302.
11 Afisi, "Power and Womanhood in Africa."

Chapter Four

POLITICS, PHILOSOPHICAL REPRESENTATION, AND CULTURE IN CHERNO NJIE'S *SWEAT IS INVISIBLE IN THE RAIN*

Introduction

Human early life is characterized by experiences that shape ideation and principles that carve pathways that people tend to follow later in life. In essence, human outcome is a function of many factors, one of which is social interaction and conditioning. The continental African is a construct of ancient and modern cultures, belief systems, epistemologies, and philosophies that shape his or her opinion, interaction, and disposition toward life. Also, irrespective of the glaring diversities and complexities of the African continent, some philosophies and value systems constitute an area of commonality between nations. These philosophies, ideologies, and values have impacted various aspects of African society, and they should ideally influence systems and structures like politics and the economy extensively and positively.

However, concerning the underdeveloped status of the continent against the rest of the globe and the dreadful track record of politics and government in postcolonial Africa, this study propounds the idea that the continent's politics operate on a misrepresentation of ancient indigenous philosophies. This conception will be extensively explored in subsequent sections of this work. It will also analyze and provide textual evidence from Cherno Njie's memoir, *Sweat Is Invisible in the Rain*.

With reference to Njie's text, the need to explain or clarify complex aspects of self and actions has driven many into the art of writing. In other words, several literary genres have emanated from the single need for expression, the urge to tell one's story. In the memoir, Raab buttresses this notion by stating that "many memoir writers choose this genre as a way to find or reclaim their voice, share a family secret, or tell a story."[1] Cherno Njie's *Sweat is Invisible in the Rain* is one of those literary publications, a memoir at best, that tries to capture time and history in print, to explain motivations for actions not fully understood by many, and to clarify misconceptions that might have arisen from a singular act of patriotism. For the writer, the text is a product of introspection, a clarification, a tale of tyranny and bravery, and the unveiling of fallen and living heroes.

Figure 4.1 Cherno Njie

African Culture and Philosophy in *Sweat Is Invisible in the Rain*

The African principles of contentment, tolerance, humanity, honor, and communitarianism cut across several regions of the continent and are often reflected in the proverbs and sayings of the African people. The Ubuntu philosophy of African heritage reflects the African belief in community. The African spirit of humanity, compassion, hospitality, harmony, and justice for all is represented within this philosophy. The overall ideation of Ubuntu is essential to a universal African culture; however, the word "Ubuntu" emanates from the isiZulu language of South Africa, from the aphorism *Umuntu Ngumuntu Ngabantu,* which translates as "A person is a person because of or through other persons."[2] Desmond Tutu further elaborates by stating that within the concept, the African person is conditioned to see the following:

> A person is a person through other persons. None of us comes into the world fully formed. We would not know how to think, or walk, or speak, or behave as human beings unless we learned it from other human beings. We need other human beings in order to be human.[3]

The concept of community and humanism is echoed in the above excerpt, and Tutu goes on to reaffirm the claims of the universality and commonality of the idea within the continent by stating that the Ubuntu philosophy is integral to the daily lives of Africans and plays out in various societies of southern, eastern, western, and central

Africa.[4] The philosophy can be considered a holistic representation of the social ideals and consciousness of the African people regarding humanity and community. This is also adequately reflected in Njie's text and clearly surmised as follows:

> [...] in my family's compound at 2 New Street in Banjul [...] I was the third of six children by my mother, my father's second wife. My sister Mberry and my brother Baboucarr came before me. There were, in all, twelve children between our two mothers. My father was the eldest of his three brothers—Sulayman, Ousman, and Kebba—so he was the head of the extended family, and our home on New Street was a sort of base for the rest of the family. Around it the community of our family revolved. Two of my uncles and their families lived with us—our two mothers and all the kids. So, of course, we all lived very closely [...] We made no distinction of mothers, of half-brothers and half-sisters, of cousin or brother or sister, so that to me I had only mothers, brothers, and sisters, and there was much love, care, and respect in our compound. (For the Wolof, sisters of one's mother are regarded as mothers, and brothers of one's father as junior fathers; while sisters of one's father are regarded as aunts, and brothers of one's mother as uncles.) There were three different buildings in the compound, shared by different members of the family [...].[5]

From the above excerpt, the lifestyle and commitment to community and the welfare of others are reflected in the close-knit family of the writer. However, this sense of togetherness is not exclusive to the text; many African life stories echo a consciousness of community, humanity, and family. In Toyin Falola's memoir, *A Mouth Sweeter than Salt*, he also makes reference to the essentiality of community in Nigerian society: "A house or compound is not exclusive to a nuclear family, small in number, so small that one can count the members. A house can have a large number of occupants, a man, his many wives and children, visiting relatives, a fluid population of strangers."[6]

The above mirrors Njie's family and is equally reflected in many other life stories written by Africans, such as Mariama Ba and Chinua Achebe. Therefore, this single attribute of communitarianism instills in Africans a consciousness of humanity, the principle of care, and mutual support. It aims at eliminating selfishness and promoting oneness with its philosophy of strength in numbers. It also provides an ideal approach to leadership based on unity and overall representation, which is why, when it comes to leadership and African communitarianism values, Gbadegesin sees the philosophy as one that pledges that "every member is expected to consider him/herself an integral part of the whole and to play an appropriate role towards achieving the good of all."[7] In other words, it is expected that every African will play a role in the development of their immediate environment. Ideally, the African frowns at injustice, selfishness, greed, authoritarianism, and human suffering, which gives credence to the outcome of events in Njie's *Sweat is Invisible in the Rain*, as well as the writer's devotion to the welfare of The Gambian people. However, it does not account for the selfishness, greed, lust for power, and individualism reflected in the life of the Gambian dictator, Yahya Jammeh, around whom the text is woven.

Furthermore, peculiar to every African community are various concepts and ideologies contained in sayings, aphorisms, folktales, proverbs, and other forms of oral tradition. These distinct concepts and ideologies convey the principles and value system of the people and are usually passed down from generation to generation. For reference purposes, the writer's mother imparted and lived by three terms from Wolof tradition: the yarr, tegin, and ngor. The writer further attests that it is impossible to translate these terms with the precision they deserve as they contain a string of complex meanings and ideas. The writer attempts to explain the three traditional terms earlier identified:

> In the most basic sense, yarr refers to the value of a congenial comportment and openness to others based on mutual respect; tegin refers to a calm and pacific, almost stoic, temperament in relation to the world; and finally, the most important, ngor, is the commitment to morality and an unshakable integrity. (Jom, a somewhat similar concept, is what may be called honor). Wolof society, apart from these, also puts a high premium on cultivating a sense of shame (gache) and of scruples such that personal behavior conforms to societal values.[8]

With the above excerpt, the social expectations for acceptable and honorable behavior amongst the members of Njie's community become clear to the reader. The writer also examines the place of proverbs in conveying complex thought patterns and the philosophies and epistemologies of his community, which account for the writer's use of proverbs to substantiate ideas and convey meaning throughout the text.

Another aspect of culture encountered in the text is the role of folktales in the education of the younger generation. Folktales constitute an integral part of African oral tradition. In African communities, folktales perform social, educational, entertainment, and therapeutic functions. This, therefore, lends credence to Mphahele's opinion that the oral artist in Africa, which includes the folktale performer, is "the sensitive point in his/her community and the cultural impacts about him must, if he has the makeup of an artist, teach him to express his longings, failings and successes of his people."[9] As such, the cultural impacts of the folktale should serve as a template, one which the performer must use in expressing the peculiarities of his/her community. To top it off, Abraham considers the art of storytelling as a means of representing the cultural and traditional information of a people while providing the rationale behind these cultures.[10]

In the performance or telling of folktales, the setting, audience, and content can also be considered real expressions of community and kinship. The setting is usually within a compound in the moonlight, and in fact, there is a saying of Yoruba origin, "the mother of the storyteller will turn into a hen if he/she performs in the day,"[11] which emphasizes the timing associated with the narration of folktales. Folktales are usually narrated to children in large family compounds. These tales convey a wealth of knowledge of a people's history, traditions, spiritual education and training, philosophies, and culture. Realizing this, Njie notes that:

> But we also learned more than I can adequately remember from stories, folktales that she or the other women in the compound—Fatou Tunkara, one of my foster sisters, told stories in a particularly entrancing way—told us children gathered at home in the evening [...] These folktales provided us significant lessons in Wolof society. Historically, they have been important for maintaining the pillars of that society: honor and shame. The folktales were as much moral tales as they were stories for entertainment. But they were moral tales

that were as difficult to understand as her proverbs: walking down the street one day, much older, you might remember a bit of a story, and then a spark flits, and you finally understand what you did not as a child. Its meaning opens itself to you, as you grow older, as you are, that is, becoming a member of the community.[12]

In addition, the synchrony of the tale and response and the atmosphere of oneness created by young children huddled up to listen to these tales create a bond of familiarity that strengthens a community, which is handed down from one generation to the next.

Another aspect of African society reflected in the text is woven around a complex interaction of religiosity and spirituality. Like other aspects of culture, spirituality constitutes a binding force for the otherwise diverse African continent. Paris puts it best when he states that "the African people are united by their common spiritual strivings."[13] This opinion plays out in Njie's account of the collective prayers offered on his behalf by Gambians in the United States following his arrest for violating the Neutrality Act. This solicitation for supernatural intervention indicates and expresses the African perception of divinity as the controller of one's fate. Therefore, it is typical of the African to seek spiritual intervention in the writer's time of need.

> Gambians in Minneapolis organized a prayer session to seek divine intervention for lenient sentences. We wanted to attend, but there was already a prohibition against any contact among us defendants, and so we did not go. Imam Baba Leigh, another victim of the regime, then in exile, presided over the prayer session.[14]

Yet this is unsurprising given that Africans are inherently religious, while the overview of life and cultural inspirations come from their belief in a supreme being who presides over a pantheon of ancestral spirits and lesser deities.[15] Africans also believe in a host of existing malevolent spirits, which is where their aversion to and fear of sorcerers and witches comes from, some of whom they believe to be channels for expressing these spirits. Njie's memoir captures this aspect of the African consciousness thus:

> The Banjul of my childhood was a city said to be ruled at night by genies, wizards, gnomes, witches, and sorcerers. They were mythical, of course, and as a child it was all a lot of fun to be scared out of your wits—except later I realized that adults actually believed these things existed: a mysterious illness was to befall the land, but luckily it had been foreseen by a renowned marabout from a land faraway.[16]

Consequently, the African life is one lived with a consciousness of the supernatural, where life decisions and actions are often guided by, among others, indigenous belief systems and the imperial acculturation of Islam and Christianity. Therefore, it will not be out of place to state that African society is aggressively religious. In fact, Paris puts it succinctly when he states that "Africans are unexcelled in their reverence for and devotion to all spiritual phenomena which they readily incorporate in their thought and practice."[17]

Prior to the incursion of colonial and western religious systems, Africans had traditional religious systems, as well as indigenous practices and means through which they connected with the realm of spiritual and divine existence. There are symbols, rituals, objects, festivals, and other activities that characterize African traditional religion. The manifestations of precolonial religious systems are often found in the use of charms, amulets, the consultation of sorcerers (otherwise known as marabouts), and other forms of spiritual fortification, as reflected in the text. These symbols, artifacts, and practices are bridges between indigenous African religious systems and contemporary African society. In Njie's text, there is clear evidence of Africa's conception of the supernatural, which can be identified through daily interactions between the ordinary and the mystical.

> In the eternal throng of people between McCarthy Square and Albert Market, there was sure to be the marabout. I remember, one time, just before a soccer game we were about to play, we ran into one. Historically, marabout is a more precise term, but to us then, and as is the case now, the marabout was a sorcerer, a seller of charms and amulets [...] The Banjul of my childhood was a city said to be ruled at night by genies, wizards, gnomes, witches, and sorcerers. They were mythical, of course, and as a child it was all a lot of fun to be scared out of your wits—except later I realized that adults actually believed these things existed: a mysterious illness was to befall the land, but luckily it had been foreseen by a renowned marabout from a land faraway. To ward off the impending calamity, all inhabitants must perform a ritual bath at the river.[18]

Therefore, this existing rapport between African belief systems and the world of the supernatural accounts for some of the activities of Jammeh's administration, which were considered laughable by western society. These include the president's self-acclaimed status as a healer without a medical degree, as well as his attempts to exorcise women whom he identified as witches with evil powers. The close borders between the world of the supernatural and the natural in the African community are not depicted exclusively in Njie's text. Falola's *A Mouth Sweeter than Salt* provides textual evidence to substantiate claims of a casual integration of the supernatural in the lives of Africans. While narrating his childhood experiences, Falola intimates the reader with experiences that expose the popularity of charms and potions in traditional Yoruba society. For love potions, he denotes that "[t]he morality was always ambiguous; no one emphatically said that it should not be used."[19] The writer examines the mysticism of love potions and their application in people's lives. Oluleye's life story also examines the African belief in the proximity and expressions of the supernatural amidst the natural:

> I had experienced a number of debatable subjects such as spirits [...] people in Efon Alaye and beyond were made to believe that there was a place at Oke Ibase where people who lost their dear one through strange deaths or circumstances could communicate with the dead to clarify doubts and issues.[20]

However, with the coming of western religious systems, foundational religious systems in Africa for generations were demonized. Often, this demonization is expressed in reference to an association of African religion with words and concepts like barbarous, savage, fetishism, paganism, heathenism, animism, or idolatry.[21] This demonization project created a smooth transition from African religious systems to western and middle eastern religions like Christianity and Islam, which are today considered the most prominent religions in Africa. This has led to complex interactions between religion and identity on the African continent.

Among the continents and nations of the world, this book notes that Africa has experienced a long list of religious-inspired conflicts, usually between the adherents of world religions such as Christians and Muslims. For instance, Nigeria, a country of diverse religious and ethnic groups, has since independence had its fair share of ethno-religious conflicts, now so numerous and routine that they consume a lot of national resources. Already divided by the multiplicity of languages and ethnic groups, the incursion of the two predominant foreign religions in the country has exacerbated the divisive posture of the country. This religious divisiveness has resulted in a competition for power among the Christians and Muslims in the country. However, these conflicts over power do not align with the African principles of humanity and brotherhood. In other words, the African identity woven around the concept of community has somehow been lost along the line of acculturation and the adoption of foreign religions.

According to Njie's work, a relative amount of tolerance seems to exist amongst the Christian minorities and Muslims in The Gambia. The text illustrates the interaction of diverse religions and how they frame a people's identity. To express the diversity of his environment, the writer states, "New Street was a very diverse street, too, home to Wolof Gambians, like ourselves, Mandinka, Jola, who were all typically Muslim, and the Christian Aku."[22] As illustrated by the writer, the Muslim home in The Gambia is a large community of family and friends, with multiple mothers, as a result of the permissibility of polygamy in Islam. As described by the writer, a certain boisterousness is associated with the large households that make up Muslim families. In contrast, the writer observes that the Christian homes, which he referred to generally as the Aku families, were monogamous. Although considered a minority, the writer's family and his upbringing were also marked by several interactions with the Aku families.

Consequently, the writer formed several opinions of these families, some admirable and some not. He notes that:

> Many of the Aku adults I interacted with as a child could sometimes be severe or conservative when it came to such things as these, especially with their own children, and Auntie Okeke was no exception. Their severity not infrequently intimidated a few of my brothers and sisters, and some of our friends, but I was always too curious to be discouraged from being friendly with the Aku adults [...] The Aku compounds were often cleaner and more organized than those of other polygamous families; as I grew older, I found I liked the orderliness of these households more than what very often felt like the regular chaos of my own. Passing by, you could tell which were the compounds of Aku families and which ones were not: the Akus kept their compound doors closed. With us, there was simply too much traffic to bother, except at night of course.[23]

The writer implies that the religious affiliation of the families mentioned might have had a big influence on their disposition toward human interaction and their way of life. Yet irrespective of the differences in religious affiliation, the writer notes that the community understood the very essence and concept of community. The writer further attests to this notion by observing that there was a sense of safety amongst the children because the adults looked after every child as if they were their own. Quite conveniently, the writer evokes the African philosophy of raising children evoked by the saying that "it takes a village to raise a child."[24] This principle, as noted by the writer, frames the disposition and attitude of the adults toward the children from their community, accounting for the use of possessive references like "my son" or "my daughter" by the elders when responding to or referring to younger persons of no blood relation.

Among the many aspects of African oral traditions, proverbs and idiomatic expressions also convey the depth of the continent's philosophical insights and values concerning lifestyle, leadership, and conduct. Therefore, given this fact, this study will often summon proverbial expressions to buttress the neglect of indigenous codes of conduct in political exercises of the African continent.

Postcolonial African Political History

The diversity and size of the African continent make generalization a tedious business. William Tordoff opines that Africa is a vast and diverse continent and, therefore, the idea of describing the play of politics in these states as singular would be a misrepresentation of the continent.[25] To substantiate Tordoff's postulation, Chazan et al. describe the African continent as home to a "rich mosaic of peoples, culture, ecological settings, and historical experiences ... the 500 million people of Africa (roughly ten percent of the globe's population) are as diverse as the terrain they inhabit."[26]

The earliest independence from colonial rule in Africa commenced in the 1950s, freeing Ghana and North Africa from colonial domination. In the 1960s, about thirty new states attained independence from colonial rule, including The Gambia in 1965; this earned the sixties the title of the decade of "African independence."[27] The second part of independence commenced in 1974, which led to the final overthrow of colonial powers in Portuguese-speaking countries like Mozambique, Cape Verde, Guinea Bissau, and Angola. Zimbabwe overthrew white rule in 1980 and Namibia in 1990, leaving South Africa to continue grappling with apartheid well into the 1990s.[28] Thus, colonialism and white domination constitute an area of common historical experience for most African nations. However, this section intends to appraise the politics of postcolonial Africa and, in an attempt not to create misleading generalizations, will use Charzan et al.'s approach to examine the frequency of some political systems in the postindependence history of the new African states.[29]

From the start of independence, Tordoff identifies the ex-colonial status of these new African states as one of their commonalities. They had undergone the domination of one of the following colonial powers: "Britain, France, Germany, Belgium, Italy, Portugal and Spain, and South Africa in respect of Namibia."[30] However, many scholars have acknowledged that these states had a precolonial history and, consequently, a precolonial political system. As they sought new identities as nation-states and strove for global recognition as independent from their former colonizers, they also struggled to integrate the variety of people and languages bunched together to attain nationhood.

At different sociopolitical stages, carrying everyone along became more demanding, especially for highly populous and heterogeneous nation-states like Nigeria, often described as the "linguistic crossroad of Africa."[31]

Aside from the economic struggles of these new states and their continued dependence on the provisions of the world market, they also had unstable political cultures. Indigenous political leaders had little or no experience running a government on a national level, compounded by the weakness and inexperience of the various institutions through which the government was expected to work. This, therefore, meant that they were hardly prepared to deal with the demands of governance, leading to the outcome of leadership that has persevered in recent times. This study posits that aside from the circumstantial ill-preparedness, these leaders have refused to put in the work, and they have not extracted and applied the wealth of knowledge resident in the rich cultural philosophies of their African heritage.

Consequently, postcolonial African political history is marred with incidences and reports of tyranny, corruption, mismanagement, brutal killings, disregard for human life, and an endless list of inhumanities that go against Africa's philosophy of humanity and community. This has inspired terminologies like "personal rule,"[32] "politics of the belly,"[33] or "politics of ethnicity"[34] when referring to politics in Africa.[35] Allen describes the political situation of postindependence Africa using terms and ideologies like "centralized bureaucratic politics" and "spoils politics."[36] From another angle, Kura describes the continent's politics as "illiberal civilian autocracies."[37] These terminologies embody and represent the political situation in most parts of Africa. Osaghae considers the analysis of African politics as one littered with dead ends, including the idea that perceptions of African politics are based on the limited opinion of the West, which labels some recurring political events in Africa as its general political situation.[38]

These recurring situations include ethnic politics in nonhomogenous African states like The Gambia, as well as corruption, military coups, and dominant political party systems. However, to truly investigate and evaluate Osaghae's observation about the western conception of politics on the African continent, it is necessary to examine the postindependence systems of government and their operations within the continent. This study maintains that irrespective of the geographical and linguistic diversities in the continent, these nations share similar cultural philosophies and practices, most of which should have positive impacts on the systems and practicality of government on the continent. Therefore, the next section will evaluate the political realities of the continent measured against the Ubuntu philosophy and some proverbs with reference to Njie's *Sweat is Invisible in the Rain*. It will examine the opinions of these indigenous epistemologies toward sociopolitical issues and the failure of their representation in African politics.

Political Monopoly

Political monopolies and dominance of strong political parties are not unusual in Africa. This calls for concern because amongst the many West African nations with multiparty systems of government, dominant ruling parties continue to control the quality and caliber of leaders produced in the country. One-party dominance is prevalent, as in The Gambia, and is considered by Renske Doorenspleet and Lia Nijzink to be anomalous to democracy.[39] Concerning politics in The Gambia, Nyang argues that since the inception of political parties in 1951, the country has witnessed a progressive proliferation of political parties and the seasonal emergence of dominant parties that monopolize political power, silence opposition, and eliminate accountability. He continues:

> The key features of the Gambian political system from the time of independence in 1965 to the present are the continuing dominance of a ruling political party that now embraces almost all the ethnic groups in the country, and the growing weakness of the major opposition party, whose base of support has been gradually eroded since independence.[40]

As defined by Doorenspleet and Nijzink, one-party dominance plays out when "the same party wins an absolute majority in at least three consecutive elections."[41] In this system, a party dominates for long periods, irrespective of regular elections in which multiple parties participate. The dominant party usually garners the majority of the votes cast during elections and often dominates policymaking in the various tiers of government. This system does not permit healthy and normal competition between political parties in a democracy, which means it is inherently harmful to a nation's democracy. Yahya Jammeh overthrew The Gambia's interim civilian government in 1994 and controlled the nation for four years as a military leader, after which he contested for the presidency as a civilian under the Alliance for Patriotic Reorientation and Construction (APRC), a party created in 1996 specifically for Jammeh's presidential ambitions. Jammeh won the election under the umbrella of the APRC, and until 2017, exempting the four years of his military rule, the country's politics was dominated by the APRC.[42]

Party dominance as a system often occurs periodically, sometimes lasting for many years until a stronger party topples it, as in the case of The Gambia. The dominance of the APRC lasted for twenty years through five consecutive elections. Countries like Nigeria have also experienced one-party dominance, which lasted for about sixteen years. The People's Democratic Party (PDP) government came into power and exerted dominance with the election of President Olusegun Obasanjo as the president of the Federal Republic of Nigeria. To buttress this part of history, Madubuike states that:

> In 1999, the PDP won majority of the seats in the National Assembly, most state houses of Assembly, gubernatorial seats, local government councils and most importantly the presidency. It was thus, able to dominate policy making at all levels of government. And through the instrumentality of the state, the ruling PDP has been able to emasculate the opposition parties. The situation became even graver in 2003, with the PDP having a landslide victory virtually in all the political zones of the country in what could be regarded as a very controversial election.[43]

The party also maintained a majority rule in positions and offices around the country and continued until the 2015 elections, which ushered in the All Progressives Congress (APC)-led government.[44] Not surprisingly, this continues to be the case in many other parts of West Africa. According to Madubuike, "the emergence of dominant political parties in democracies of developing countries is an impediment to the development and sustenance of democracy."[45] This sets the tone to explore the impact of a hegemonic political system on the growth and development of African nations. In order to understand this, Simutanyi and Mate have delineated five indices to identify party dominance in a democracy. They contend first that there has to be evidence of seat dominance in the parliament; second, the opposition has to be excluded in decision-making and policy formulation; third, the party has to exert control over the presidency; fourth, there must be proof of a strong alliance impeding opposition; and finally, the presence of an unstructured and weak opposition constitutes proof of party dominance.[46]

The listed indices of party domination in politics are sure avenues to discourage competition and participation in politics; they also lead to patronage politics, a lack of accountability, and the absence of checks and balances, resulting in self-centered policies, general political instability, corruption, and tyranny, like the Jammeh administration presented in Njie's *Sweat is Invisible in the Rain*. Madubuike goes further to provide elaborate outcomes of this situation by stating that:

> [t]he existence of dominant parties narrows the scope of party competition, stifles opposition, impedes political participation, deepens ideological polarization, (where such parties are formed on ideological grounds) and breeds animosity among the parties, and also among the different social, ethnic-religious, linguistic and political cleavages in society.[47]

This is hardly the case in pluralist party systems with healthy competitive environments that encourage the representation of various interests and political participation. The interaction of various parties promotes vision and strategies that make for political stability and encourage development and political growth. The individualistic domination by select party members of the entire affairs and resources of the nation does not reflect the ideology of community and its attendant aim to represent the interests of diverse persons, groups, and units in a society. At the heart of the Ubuntu philosophy is the call for cohesion, harmony, integration, and representation of all people, which frowns on party dominance that has become a peculiar feature of African politics. Drawing insights from the Ubuntu philosophy, Masolo views a positive integration of humanity as a necessity for the sake of humanity: "A life of cohesion, or positive integration with others, becomes a goal, one that people design modalities for achieving. Let us call this goal communalism, or, as other people have called it, communitarianism. In light of this goal, the virtues … also become desirable."[48]

As a result, when there is a dominant party system, there is usually an operative political elitism and a resultant absence of integration; that is, there is an alienation of the interests of other groups or units, which automatically become minorities in the presence of their dominance. This is detrimental to democracy because political parties are crucial to governance. The presence of competition and active opposition guarantees that political structures and offices are not controlled by selfish bureaucrats. Aside from the eventual underdevelopment and political unrest in societies at the mercy of these political hijackers, traces of tyranny and authoritarianism will be attempted and successful coups will also be commonplace.

Democracy and Tyranny in Africa

The monopoly of power structures in a democracy is usually a cause for alarm. This is understandable because government monopoly is usually associated with alienation and divisive and self-centered policies orchestrated to serve the needs and whims of the dictator at the helm. With dictatorship comes irrational government policies that do not express the needs or interests of the citizens. Also, with this negligence of mass interest comes all manner of inhumanity and brutality and a sense of invincibility that continues to fuel unaccountability and godlike disposition while stifling and subduing human expression amongst the masses. In Njie's *Sweat Is Invisible in the Rain*, Jammeh's administration proffers a perfect depiction of tyranny and dictatorship in a so-called democracy.

About the disregard for the interest of the masses, Njie notes that Jammeh started a resistance against the people's freedom of expression. The press constitutes the pillar of every democracy because it holds the government accountable for its actions, demands transparency in governance and provides an avenue for mass expression. Therefore, by restricting press freedoms, democracy is jeopardized: "Chairman Jammeh became President Jammeh, and the character of his regime remained intact. Contempt of the free press and persecution of journalists continued all the same, though still rather discreetly."[49]

Despite operating in a "democracy," tyrannical administrations perpetrate all kinds of inhumane acts without sanction by assuming ultimate authority and control of all agencies in society, including the military. They often wield agencies like the armed forces as weapons against free expression and human rights, hence the growing rate of mass shootings, assassinations, and brutality against civilians. Njie's memoir explicitly conveys government-inspired disregard for human life:

> [...] in response to two separate incidents of police brutality involving young Gambians (for which the persons responsible were not held accountable), students organized a protest in Banjul to bring attention to the matter and demand accountability. The Police Intervention Unit (PIU), a paramilitary police unit, fired into a mass of marching students, killing some and wounding others [...] The results of the investigation were never made public by Jammeh—a clear indication of contempt for the rule of law. And for accountability.[50]

This flippant attitude toward human life does not align with African bioethical principles. Many oral literary devices, particularly the proverb, are often used to emphasize the sanctity of human life and the evil associated with killing innocent people. The proverb is a repository of ethnic knowledge, value systems, and a channel to African epistemologies. According to Rakotsoane and Niekerk, proverbs serve as reference points for the justification of decisions and paths taken in life.[51] Also, more succinctly, Emmanuel Obiechina defines proverbs as "philosophical and moral expositions shrunk to a few words, and they form mnemonic device in societies in which everything worth knowing and relevant to day-to-day life has to be committed to memory."[52]

For the Igbo people of eastern Nigeria, the belief in the sanctity of life cannot be overemphasized. It is often expressed in the naming of children and extended to the proverbs that guide and justify the actions of people in society. Some of these proverbs include the following, alongside their translation to the English language constructively analyzed by Anuolam in his thesis, "Igbo Value and Care of Life."

> Igbo: *Mmadu agaghi eji maka unwu na amu were rie Nne ya.*[53]
> English: One cannot, because there is a famine, eat his mother.

In his analysis, Anuolam views this proverb as an expression of the value placed on human life. In other words, no matter how difficult the circumstance is, there is no justification to take an innocent life. This proverb buttresses the fact that the murder of an innocent is considered an abomination in the Igbo cultural space.

> Igbo: *Ana ekwu maka nwanyi mmiri riri, gi anakwu maka akwa oma.*[54]
> English: A woman who drowned is being talked about, and you are talking of the cloth she is wearing.

From this proverb, one can deduce the importance placed on human life. Life should be valued above everything else, including material things. It frowns on placing value on material wealth at the expense of human life. As noted by Rakotsoane and Niekerk, proverbs emanating from Lesotho in southern Africa also convey the very essence and sanctity of human life. In their work, "Human Invaluableness: An Emerging African Bioethical Principle,"[55] they examine the application of life-related proverbs in varied scenarios in both ancient times and contemporary society. The following proverb and its utility in expressing the value of human life are explored in their work:

> Sesotho: *Ha le fete khomo le je motho*
> English: Let it not go past a beast to kill a human being.[56]

This proverb references the spear used in killing or hunting, and it makes a statement that human life is of more value than the life of an animal. In ancient times, the proverb was often invoked in precarious situations to plead for one's life. It serves as a quick reminder to the assailant of the value and sacredness of human life. However, in recent times, the proverb is often used as justification for various actions made toward preserving life—for instance, the investment of a huge amount of resources in the treatment of a loved one.

In addition to proverbs, naming in Africa is not considered with levity. Names across the continent often express the values and philosophies of the people. The use of names to convey ethnic epistemologies is prevalent in Africa; we can see this through the naming system of the Igbo people. With reference to the sanctity of life, amongst the Igbo people of eastern Nigeria, certain names convey the strong cultural notions of the people about life. Some of these names, as examined by Anuolam, include the following:

> Igbo: Ndubuisi
> English: Life is primary and first[57]

In other words, to the Igbo people, life is principal and should be preserved, valued, and protected.

Igbo: Ndudinakachi
English: Life is in the hands of God[58]

The above name implies that the power of life and death lies in the hands of God and not man; therefore, man should not play God by taking the lives of innocent people. This stands in contrast to tyranny and unlawful killings of innocent people. But these philosophical provisions notwithstanding, governance and politics on the African continent continue to run contrary to these indigenous principles, and contemporary African politics is a misrepresentation of ancient African epistemologies.

As stated earlier, tyrannical governments are characterized by the enactment of self-serving policies and acts that do not take into consideration the interests and welfare of the masses, much like the Nigerien President Mamadou Tandja, who was democratically elected in 1999 and then dissolved the national assembly and passed a constitutional referendum to extend his position as president for another three years.[59] This is also reflected in Njie's *Sweat Is Invisible in the Rain*. In response to the earlier excerpt depicting the brutality of the armed forces against protesting students, Jammeh enacted a policy giving him authority to absolve the perpetrators of police brutality: "Later in the year, the Jammeh government passed the Indemnity Act. This law essentially gave the executive—that is, Jammeh—unilateral power to grant amnesty to any 'member of the security forces accused of misconduct during a riot or state of emergency'."[60]

Ideally, democracy should be an assurance of fundamental human rights. Therefore, in cases like The Gambia, where people are hassled for the mere expression of these rights, citizens usually agitate, creating civil unrest and a tempestuous atmosphere. Often, a natural alliance emerges for the masses to take back the power hijacked from them. In situations like this, the hint of opposition puts the dictator on edge, leading to irrational and vengeful actions to silence attempts at revolution. This fosters a dense feeling of insecurity, powerlessness, hopelessness, and fear amongst the masses. By creating an atmosphere of fear and helplessness, crime goes unaccounted for, human rights are infringed upon, bizarre activities go unquestioned, societal conditions continue to deteriorate, and development is put on hold.

To lend credence to this opinion, Njie observes that: "Something new was happening: the Jammeh regime felt it no longer had to behave as carefully as before. The regime discovered in 2000 that it could openly practice its authoritarian modus operandi without popular resistance."[61] In several instances in the text, Jammeh is associated with assassinations, unlawful imprisonment, public executions, and the creation and use of paramilitary forces to intimidate the masses. Njie also notices a devastating deterioration of society and a thick silence and fear that hung in The Gambia's air at the time. Irrespective of the attempts of a dictator to silence and incapacitate society, there are usually agitations, uprisings, and plots to topple the dominant authority. Therefore, concerning party dominance, stronger opposition parties, as in the case of the 2015 Nigerian elections, are formed to overthrow the dominant party. But in the occasion of a single dictator, as typified by Jammeh in Njie's account, violent coups are a typical result.

Righting the Wrong

The continued presence of a dictator at the helm of a country's leadership fosters restiveness in society, hence the history of attempted and successful coups in Africa. Tyranny and dictatorship in a democracy predispose a regime to unconstitutional efforts geared toward unseating it. A tyrannical administration also runs the risk of being toppled when it fails to meet the democratic expectations of the masses. Njie's text is introduced with a Wolof proverb: "Bu bey dahehsacha see kerr, haj war naarus," translated as "When the goat chases away a thief from the compound, the dog should be ashamed."[62] In literal terms, one can infer that the proverb juxtaposes the play of strength and power between the goat and the dog. Ostensibly, the dog is stronger, faster, and more aggressive and, therefore, in the best position to chase the thief away from the compound. This dog represents authority in the right position to provide economic, political, and social security to the masses. However, when it leaves its assigned duties to others, like the goat in this proverbial analogy, the administration should be ashamed, as prescribed by the distilled wisdom and African value in the proverb.

As reflected in the text, Jammeh's administration abandoned its appropriate responsibility to the lives and properties of the Gambian people and instead became an oppressor. The text presents several coup attempts by silent elite opposition groups to reestablish democracy in the country. Also, just like The Gambia, in a bid to restore or reinvent democracy in society, several countries have resorted to the use of force, often expressed in a coup d'état. According to Derpanopoulos et al., "[c]oups are successful efforts by the military or other elites within the state apparatus to unseat the sitting executive using unconstitutional means."[63] Jammeh spearheaded a coup that installed him into the Gambian government in 1994, ousting the Jawara government. Comparatively, the coup was rather bloodless, given that Jawara fled the country without engaging in reprisal attacks on the military lieutenants who fought to unseat him.[64]

Jammeh's tyrannical administration itself attracted several unsuccessful coup attempts, one of which Cherno Njie, a representation of the agitated elite, spearheaded. Furthermore, The Gambian experience with coups is not an isolated one. As noted by Derpanopoulos et al., in 2010, the incumbent president of the Nigerien republic, President Mamadou Tanja, was arrested and ousted from the presidential palace by military troops. This was in response to the maladministration and distortion of democracy in the country by his incumbent government. Derpanopoulos et al. also attest that the 2010 coup was not the first of its kind in the country. Prior to the elections that ushered Tanja into government, there had been a previous coup resulting in the death of Ibrahim Bare Mainassara, an aggressive ruler who had ruled the country since 1996.[65]

Also, the Nigerien and Gambian experiences are hardly isolated. Africa has experienced over 200 coups since the 1950s,[66] including the extreme case of Guinea Bissau, which has never had a president complete his term. Nigeria, which is considered a strong force in Africa's politics, has gone through a series of failed and successful coups too, with four coups in a particular ten-year period (1966–1975). The same can be said for Mali, Guinea Bissau, Burkina Faso, Burundi, Chad, Ghana, and Uganda. In Nigerien political history, there is a long list of overthrows and replacements, starting from the first attempted coup that left in its wake a list of casualties and led to the country's brutal civil war. The countercoup in 1966 ushered in the government of Major General Yakubu Gowon and ousted Major General Aguiyi Ironsi.

In Chinua Achebe's account in his memoir, *There was a Country*, the writer attests to having predicted a coup, given the extent of the country's deterioration in the early years of independence.[67] Achebe explores the ensuing disintegration and blames it on the endemic tribalism and corruption in the country. However, making political decisions with tribal bias goes against the concept of oneness, community, and kinship embedded in African cultural philosophies. Although some coups are carried out with good intentions, such as to eliminate corruption and reinstate good governance or democracy, Derpanopoulos et al. opine that the new government is sometimes no different or even worse than the one that was toppled. They also agree that most coups are ostensibly carried out with the sole intention of transforming society. In their opinion:

> [T]he basic goal of a coup is to bring about change in leadership, but often coup plotters also seek more substantial political transformation. They may announce their intention to hold democratic elections in the near future and even offer a timeline for the transition. However, they do not fulfill such promises.[68]

This excerpt, in some ways, mirrors the intentions and approach of the Jammeh-led coup in the text. According to Powell and Thyne, the shock of a coup is rather necessary to create a form of political liberalization.[69] The writer admits that the previous Jawara government had run out of ideas on how to run the country, and the country was wallowing in stagnancy and growing deterioration. With this reality, the idea of a coup appealed to the masses, while the Jammeh-led military administration provided a timeline for a smooth transition to a democratic government. Yet as Derpanopoulos et al. observe, often, a coup brings nothing more than a replacement of the old tyrants with new ones, as seen in how the Jammeh-led administration under the military and civilian government did nothing but worsen the country's situation.

Among the many motivations of a coup is patriotism: a devotion to one's homeland, an ache or desire to right the wrongs of incompetent rulers and restore a nation to its deserved glory. In the most simplistic definitions, patriotism can be viewed as love for one's country, but the concept of patriotism runs deeper than the simplistic connotations of love. As noted by Mitja Sardoc: "Both historically and conceptually, patriotism has been one of the foundational characteristics that defines the very essence of one's attachment, identification, and loyalty to a political community and a basic virtue associated with citizenship as a political conception of the person."[70]

Therefore, one's attachment and loyalty to a country or hometown is a clear expression of the concept of patriotism. Sardoc also states that the willingness to kill or die for one's country is considered a profound and genuine expression of patriotism.[71] This calls for an exploration of Njie's actions as represented in his text using the parameters provided by the concept of patriotism. Among the parameters provided are devotion and loyalty to one's country. As depicted in his text, Njie's actions can be interpreted as acts of patriotism. Although the writer had been away from his home country for many years, he admits to having been burdened by the turn of events in The Gambia, and his disposition toward Jammeh's tyranny and the situation at home is expressed thus:

> In the last decade, however, I felt increasingly a tugging from somewhere over the Atlantic, in the direction of The Gambia. In 2011, Yahya Jammeh, a president who was becoming more and more a dictator, won a fourth term. I was at this point quite invested in his defeat; the outcome of the elections threw me into a cycle of detached apathy and despairing hopelessness. An acute sense of the uselessness of expending my time and resources on legal actions to resist Jammeh plagued me; from the United States, even with the help of Gambians of the diaspora and international advocacy groups, we accomplished very little. I was caught in a bind: I felt required to act concretely upon what I felt was a responsibility to The Gambia, upon a sense of civic duty as a successful Gambian of the diaspora. The noisy crashing of calamity across the Atlantic held, however, a deadening power over me. I experienced in the months after Jammeh's victory in 2011 an odd sort of paralysis.[72]

The above captures the intensity of Njie's devotion and commitment to the reestablishment of democracy and eradication of tyranny in his home country. In subsequent pages of the text, the reader is privy to his various financial and material commitments to the cause of toppling the tyrant plaguing his home country.

Another parameter is people's readiness to die or kill for their country. As depicted in the text, supporting and adopting a series of constitutional approaches to expel Jammeh from power and the repeated failures of these approaches led Njie and a group of other expatriates, most of whom were in exile from Jammeh's government, to consider the use of force to expel Jammeh from power. This resolution led to the creation of the D30 group, an acronym for the plotters of the failed December 30th coup attempt on the Jammeh administration. This group varied from real estate developers to ex-military officials, and they understood the implications of their actions. They understood that carrying out a coup to overthrow a government in full control of a nation's military could mean death by crossfire or being charged with treason if caught.

But given their devotion, planning, and commitment to the cause, their love and loyalty to their home country became apparent. Most of the members of the D30 group, aside from Papa Faal, who betrayed the rest of the group to seek absolution for his involvement in the coup, embodied a true sense of patriotism. As the ultimate demonstration of that patriotism, Col. Lamin Sanneh, Capt. Njaga Jagne, and Alagi Jaja Nyass died in action while trying to rid The Gambia of a dictator who had systematically robbed the people of their lives and free expression.

However, irrespective of the sentimentality attached to patriotism, some scholars consider parts of its expressions and approaches controversial, which is why Sardoc believes that there is no concept in political philosophy, citizenship, and contemporary studies more prone to abuse.[73] Therefore, at what stage can an aggressive show of solidarity and loyalty be considered a mere display of violence, treason, or even terrorism? Mark Twain, Leo Tolstoy, and Oscar Wilde, all cited in Sardoc, view patriotism as "immoral and questionable," as the "virtue of the vicious," and "the last refuge of the scoundrel," respectively.[74]

These reservations toward patriotism show that love for one's country often emanates from the aggressiveness of its expression and are worsened by Horace's opinion that it is sweet and fitting to die for one's country. These opinions that romanticize dying for one's country arguably stem from a place of extremism in dealing with issues that pertain to society. This opinion must have also influenced the members of the D30 group who were residents in the United States before their coup. Njie was tried and convicted for violating an obscure section of US federal law originally established by the Neutrality Act of 1794. Yet as part of his expression of patriotism, Njie categorically states:

> Having been afforded little opportunity to speak for myself and much time for reflection, I guess the first thing to say is that I have never regretted the collective action we took. That the use of force was necessary to unseat Jammeh has been borne out by history [...] At any rate, regret has no place in a moral decision such as this. Our actions, sacrifices, successes and failures were expressions of the real, material pursuit of liberty. Escaping Gambia, I did not consider the attempt as an absolute failure, but rather an initial foray, a malfunction that meant only regrouping and reorganization.[75]

Also, the continued commitment of the surviving D30 group members to the country's welfare, even after the eventual exit of Jammeh from office, provides another layer of proof of the writer's patriotism and his commitment to the growth and development of The Gambia. This commitment and investment in the welfare and development of one's country fit the description and expression of the Ubuntu philosophy that preaches humanity, interdependence, and altruism. In addition, given the controversial nature of some expressions of patriotism, such as a coup, Njie uses *Sweat is Invisible in the Rain* to explain his actions and motivations to clarify any possible misconceptions about his intentions.

Conclusion

Given the self-serving political situation in the continent, one may hastily infer that it is characteristic of indigenous African leadership ideologies to promote individualism, greed, tyranny, and brutality. On the contrary, however, this chapter has argued that these attributes and dispositions of some modern-day African leaders like Jammeh are alien to African ideals and values that are usually centered on humanity and community. By exploring the cultures, philosophies, and practicality of African politics with reference to the selected primary text, this study postulates that the modern-day political situation in Africa, among other things, clearly misrepresents the continent's sociopolitical ideologies and philosophies.

Notes

1   Diana Raab, "Creative Transcendence: Memoir Writing for Transformation and Empowerment," *The Journal of Transpersonal Psychology* 46, no. 2 (2014): 1–21.
2   Desmond Tutu, *God Has a Dream: A Vision of Hope for Our Time* (New York: Doubleday, 2004).
3   Tutu, *God Has a Dream*, 25.

4 Tutu, *God Has a Dream*.
5 Cherno M. Njie, *Sweat Is Invisible in the Rain* (Austin: Pan-African University Press, 2020), 4.
6 Toyin Falola, *A Mouth Sweeter than Salt: An African Memoir* (Ann Arbor: University of Michigan Press, 2004), 19.
7 S. Gbadegesin, *African Philosophy: Traditional Yoruba Philosophy and Contemporary African Realities* (New York: Peter Lang, 1991).
8 Njie, *Sweat Is Invisible*, 14–15.
9 Ezekiel Mphahlele, *The African Image* (Uppsala: Faber and Faber, 1962), 12.
10 Roger Abraham, *African Folktales* (New York: Pantheon Books, 1995).
11 Ayo Kehinde, "Story-Telling in the Service of Society: Exploring the Utilitarian Values of Nigerian Folktales," *Lumina* 21, no. 2 (2010): 1–17.
12 Njie, *Sweat Is Invisible*, 14–15.
13 Peter J. Paris, "The Spirituality of the African People," *Journal of Black Theology in South Africa* 7, no. 2 (1993): 114.
14 Njie, *Sweat Is Invisible*, 175.
15 Njie, *Sweat Is Invisible*.
16 Njie, *Sweat Is Invisible*, 19.
17 Paris, "The Spirituality of the African People," 115.
18 Njie, *Sweat Is Invisible*, 19.
19 Falola, *A Mouth Sweeter Than Salt*, 181.
20 James Oluleye, *Architecturing a Destiny: An Autobiography* (Ibadan: Spectrum Books Limited, 2001), 19.
21 Joseph O. Awolalu, "What Is African Traditional Religion," *Studies in Comparative Religion* 10, no. 2 (1976): 1–10.
22 Njie, *Sweat Is Invisible*, 175.
23 Njie, *Sweat Is Invisible*, 7.
24 Njie, *Sweat Is Invisible*.
25 William Tordoff, *Government and Politics in Africa*, 2nd ed. (Basingstoke: Macmillan International Higher Education, 1993).
26 Naomi Chazan et al., *Politics and Society in Contemporary Africa* (Boulder: Lynne Rienner Publishers, Inc., 1992), 5.
27 Chazan et al., *Politics and Society*.
28 Chazan et al., *Politics and Society*.
29 Chazan et al., *Politics and Society*.
30 Tordoff, *Government and Politics in Africa*.
31 Tordoff, *Government and Politics in Africa*, 5.
32 Chris Allen, "Understanding African Politics," *Review of African Political Economy* 22, no. 65 (1995): 301–320.
33 Jean Francois Bayart, *The State in Africa: The Politics of the Belly* (London and New York: Longman, 1993).
34 Kenneth Ingham, *Politics in Modern Africa: The Uneven Tribal Dimension* (London: Taylor & Francis, 1990).
35 Kenneth Kalu, Olajumoke Yacob-Haliso and Toyin Falola, eds., *Africa's Big Men: Predatory State-Society Relations in Africa* (London: Routledge, 2018).
36 Allen, "Understanding African Politics."
37 Sulaiman B. Kura, "African Ruling Political Parties and the Making of 'Authoritarian' Democracies: Extending the Frontiers of Social Justice in Nigeria," *African Journal on Conflict Resolution* 8, no. 2 (2008): 63–101.
38 Eghosa E. Osaghae, "The Study of Political Transitions in Africa," *Review of African Political Economy* 22, no. 64 (1995): 183–197.
39 Renske Doorenspleet and Lia Nijzink, eds., *One Party Dominance in African Democracies* (Boulder: Lynne Rienner Publishers, 2013).

40 Sulayman S. Nyang, "Politics in Post-Independence Gambia," *A Current Bibliography on African Affairs* 8, no. 2 (1975): 113.

41 Doorenspleet and Nijzink, *One Party Dominance.*

42 Njie, Sweat Is Invisible.

43 Okechukwu Madubuike, "Party Dominance and Democracy in Nigeria: A Study of the People's Democratic Party (1999–2007)" (Thesis, University of Nigeria, Nsukka, 2007), 2.

44 Ademola Azeez, "Ethnicity, Party Politics and Democracy in Nigeria: People's Democratic Party (PDP) as Agent of Consolidation?" *Studies of Tribes and Tribals* 7, no. 1 (2009): 1–9.

45 Madubuike, "Party Dominance and Democracy."

46 Neo Simutanyi and Njekwa Mate, "One-Party Dominance and Democracy in Zambia" (Paper, Framework of the Fredriech Ebert Stiftung Mozambique Regional Study on Dominant Parties and Southern Africa, 2006).

47 Madubuike, "Party Dominance and Democracy in Nigeria," 3.

48 Dismas A. Masolo, *Self and Community in a Changing World* (Bloomington: Indiana University Press, 2010).

49 Njie, *Sweat Is Invisible*, 75.

50 Njie, *Sweat Is Invisible.*

51 Francis C. L. Rakotsoane and Antone A. Van Niekerk, "Human Life Invaluableness: An Emerging African Bioethical Principle," *Southern African Journal of Philosophy* 36, no. 2 (2017): 252–262.

52 Emmanuel Obiechina, *Culture, Tradition and Society in the West African Novel* (Cambridge: Cambridge University Press, 1975).

53 Charles Anuolam, "Igbo Culture and Care for Life" (PhD dissertation, Universidad de Navarra, 1993).

54 Anuolam, "Igbo Culture."

55 Rakotsoane and Niekerk, "Human Life Invaluableness."

56 Rakotsoane and Niekerk, "Human Life Invaluableness."

57 Anuolam, "Igbo Culture."

58 Anuolam, "Igbo Culture."

59 George Derpanopoulos et al., "Are Coups Good for Democracy?" *Research & Politics* (2016): 1–7.

60 Njie, *Sweat Is Invisible.*

61   Njie, *Sweat Is Invisible.*

62 Njie, *Sweat Is Invisible.*

63 Derpanopoulos et al., "Are Coups Good for Democracy?"

64 Njie, *Sweat Is Invisible.*

65 Derpanopoulos et al., "Are Coups Good for Democracy?"

66 *Al Jazeera*, "Why Are Coups Common in Africa?" *Al Jazeera*, September 18, 2015, https://www.aljazeera.com/programmes/insidestory/2015/09/coups-common-africa-150917161949909.html.

67 Chinua Achebe, *There Was a Country: A Personal History of Biafra* (New York: The Penguin Press, 2012).

68 Derpanopoulos et al., "Are Coups Good for Democracy?"

69 Clayton L. Thyne and Jonathan M. Powell, "Coup d'etat or Coup d'Autocracy? How Coups Impact Democratization, 1950–2008," *Foreign Policy Analysis* 12, no. 2 (2016): 192–213.

70 Mitja Sardoc, "The Anatomy of Patriotism," *Anthropological Notebook* 23, no. 1 (2017): 43–55.

71 Sardoc, "The Anatomy of Patriotism."

72 Njie, *Sweat Is Invisible.*

73 Sardoc, "The Anatomy of Patriotism."

74 Sardoc, "The Anatomy of Patriotism."

75 Njie, *Sweat Is Invisible*, xv.

Chapter Five

THE YORUBA WORLDVIEW, MEANINGS, AND IDEALS OF LIFE IN MICHAEL AFOLAYAN'S *FATE OF OUR MOTHERS*

Introduction

The Yoruba world is a distinct pool of cultural wealth shared by a group of people united by their rich tradition, deep moral values, unique knowledge system, common beliefs, and shared space and narratives. It is described and interpreted through its language, the words, and the unique and meaningful linguistic and semantic shifts and tones. It is sustained by a universal education in oral literature and "orature" that constitutes the auditory and sensory ambiance for the narratives emerging from the children of Oduduwa. The contours of the Yoruba world and its people—the craft of the Yoruba beliefs, ideologies, and histories, the pantheons of deities and ancestral bodies, and the shared experiences of its members and their connection to a physical space—are uniquely carved into the peoples' constellations and give them substantiation as a distinct people.

The Yoruba people trace their origin to Oduduwa and the city of Ile-Ife, in the southwest of Nigeria, which is also fabled as the spot where God created all humans, white or Black.[1] This faith and mythology of Oduduwa, spread through his descendants, intrinsically ties the Yoruba world to the physical world, each shaping the other into mirror images. The physical world is assembled out of different domains: the atmosphere, the depths of space, and the astral bodies; land and the vegetation that grows from it; freshwater flowing inevitably towards the depths of the ocean; so is the organization of the Yoruba world. It encompasses its spatial symbolism, temporal narrative spaces, the meaning ascribed to cosmic bodies, and the effects on the people within it caused by interactions between the different divisions of the world.

The word "Yoruba" is rooted at the center of the intersection of language, people, and land. The word is the name of the language, which is the base material of how the people give and communicate meaning. Beyond language and ethnicity, Yoruba represents the choice of words, actions, demeanors, and the biological presentations and meanings of appearance that combine to describe a culture and make it easy to identify someone as a Yoruba based on their ingrained belief system and origin. Yoruba is the physical and symbolic spatial figuration and how they describe and inform the people and the language. Yoruba receives into its soil the bodies of its people both literally and figuratively, and the land continues to speak for these bodies long after they have perished. In this way, the land serves as the index of lives that have spent their span on or beneath it, or both, and the prism through which they are understood.

This chapter is divided into four broad categories, and each section will explore the sociocultural, political, religious, and economic configurations of the people, language, and the Yoruba world and its depiction in *Fate of our Mothers*. The Yoruba memoir gives details of the cultural products, narrative texts, medical practices, knowledge systems, traditions and customs, religions, and economy of the Yoruba people, allowing for the appraisal of the Yoruba cosmology and the narrative space of its sociocultural organization. The four categories are Religion, Society, Literature, the Arts and Recreation, and the Natural World.

Religion

This part of the chapter will appraise the religious and ritualistic aspects of the Yoruba world in Michael Afolayan's *Fate of Our Mothers*. In this section, the traditional belief systems and framings that indicate the Yoruba's distinct pool of cultural resources will be addressed.

The oracular belief in Orí and àdáyébá

After Olodumare, the Divine God within the metaphysical structure of the Yoruba world, creates someone and they have knelt before him to receive their àdáyébá (destiny), Orí personally witnesses their fate.[2] In order words, Orí is present when a human is created and serves as a personal signifier to their fate. It is why Segun Ogungbemi claims that in the structural belief system, Orí (the personality soul or the guardian spirit) is constantly appeased with appropriate sacrifices and veneration. The impression given by the Yoruba in their theology is that Olodumare and his ministerial agents made humans dependent on him.[3] In Yoruba cosmology, fate and destiny are synonymous. Àdáyébá is known as destiny, which means "what awaits one on earth after birth." This is why the Yoruba believe that "àyànmọ́ ò gbóògùn" (destiny cannot be altered using charms). Àdáyébá, to a large degree, is fixed and determined by the Yoruba high god, while Orí becomes instrumental to the progress of a predestined life.

Afolayan argues that the Yoruba world operates on the totemic system of Orí and Àdáyébá, as destiny is fixed before the individual makes entry into the world. Orí gives direction to the course of man's destiny, and it is reliant on the oracular power of the Orí to determine the choices a Yoruba makes in the physical world and beyond. Fate and destiny refer to Àdáyébá in the Yoruba world, and it is installed in their philosophy, traditions, and religion as the preordained signature of Olodumare on every individual. The Orí may dominate the choice of a career or making the right decision. For instance, as a child, the author wants to choose farming as a career, but his stepmother cuts in to implore his Orí to intervene so that he will choose a better occupation. This is why in Afolayan's memoir, Mama Kekere, the author's stepmother, who deeply cares for him, invokes his Orí to save him from choosing the life of a farmer as a career. A person may decide to travel to a place filled with danger unknown to the individual, and

Orí may decide to save him/her by either changing the route or delaying the journey through different events till the danger passes or expires. In this, the Orí is instrumental to fate/destiny in Yoruba cosmology.

In the cosmic world of the Yoruba, Orí represents the essence of a human within metaphysical space. The fate of a person is determined by the choices made by their ori, to the extent that the Orí may be influenced by malevolent forces to work against its human and force them to follow the enemy's path. Orí is the lever to the shape of the life of a human, and so the Yoruba call upon and venerate it when they say, "Orí là bá bo, à bá f'orìsà sí lè" (One should serve and venerate Orí and leave the worship of the Yoruba orìsà (deities).) This is commonly used when the Orí plays a significant part in the life of a person who is lucky or avoids misfortune due to his Orí's intervention. In the Yoruba knowledge system, Orí is invoked, placated, sacrificed, and prayed to as it is the life force of human destiny, though they also believe that whatever happens to anyone in life has been preordained.[4] Àyànmó and kádàrá (known as fate) are predetermined, while the ori, the personal witness to fate, is powerful enough to influence one's choice.

Afolayan reiterates that apart from the Creator, only the person's Orí or personal god would be in attendance to witness the entire decision-making process. Having been given the opportunity to decide and choose what they wanted to become upon arriving into the world, each person would kneel before Olodumare and give a long, well-itemized list of what they would like to become, whether they would like to achieve everything on the list, and even when to finish all of the world's activities and join the ancestors. As soon as a person voluntarily made their choice, the Creator God would ring a bell in heaven and yell out to the person's ori, asking, "Have you or have you not witnessed?" The Orí would respond that he had witnessed. Then the Creator God would ring the same bell seven times, saying, "Àse! Àse! Àse!" each time. On the seventh ring, all the spirits would chorus together with the Creator God, "Àse!" Immediately after this ceremony, the person who just made a choice would then jump into Okun Ìgbàgbé (the Sea of Forgetfulness) and swim into the world.[5] This means that the seal of authority has been placed on the decision made in heaven, as witnessed by the Orí and presided over by the Olodumare. This stamp signifies the finality of the destiny of the person and puts the Yoruba at the mercy of the Yoruba high god for intervention.

The totemic function of oríkì

According to Sola Adeyemi, oríkì, a Yoruba folklore form of literature in which a praise poem or poetry venerates and immortalizes the existence of a person or family, is linked directly in the Yoruba to the historical narratives of individuals, collective groups, or the entire community. It reveals the characteristics of the people, their taboos and exploits, the nature of their relationships with other groups, their totems, and a myriad of other types of information, all of which define the social identity of the person or people whose oríkì is recited. And because of the crucial significance of oríkì in defining relationships, it exposes connections and hidden aspects of society that would otherwise be inaccessible to many people.[6] The hidden aspect includes the essential ingredients or makeup of a society of an individual, which, when invoked by malevolent forces, has serious implications for the community or person involved. This means an individual's spiritual frame/structure and totems are embedded in the *oríkì*. These hidden aspects are inaccessible to others because they are esoteric, and only a few people possess the historical and spiritual details of the individual or community.

Oríkì is the totemic poem or panegyric of a family, connected to individual members through their identities and nomenclature, a form of oral literature that confirms the existence of literature in Africa before the advent of Western education. It is a long epic that tells the story of the beginning of each lineage and the first progenitor, a man from a remote land.[7] The family's *oríkì* (*oriki orile*) offers the origins and essence of each family as well as their totems. The Yoruba believe in the metaphysical significance and totemic functions of oriki to nurture, calm, arouse, and incite an individual when their personal oriki or their family's is being chanted. In the Yoruba world, the oriki is usually sung or chanted to every child born into that particular family every morning.

Oriki can be chanted or performed like a song and is usually done as a daily rendition for the length of their childhood. The poem is meant to bring the child closer to their ancestors and progenitors and to familiarize them with the heroism of their lineage. In chronicling their successes, trials, bravery, prowess, and failures, it celebrates the wisdom of their sages and ancestors. Women, especially mothers, are the custodian of this family panegyric poetry, preserved as poems, songs and stories, folklore, etc., until it is drawn upon when a situation calls for its performance. The women are taught through performances and training before marriage. The women's education captures these aspects of reciting, learning, and acquiring oratorical skills in folklore and poetry. Notably, their education runs from childhood to adulthood when education in oral literature, among others, comes into the limelight.

There is also praise poetry for different aspects of life in the Yoruba world, such as verses honoring foods like palm wine or iyán (pounded yam), spiritual beliefs about deities, or other plants significant to the Yoruba. This type of poetry is used to exult the crop, the food-making process, the finished product, and its benefits to the body. The Yoruba people use these poems to acknowledge the efforts of farmers, the climate and other elements necessary for crops to grow, the cultivation of these crops, and the women who complete the process by transforming them into something edible. The Yoruba people love to appreciate efforts, things, people, and ideas, and they do this by writing poetry. To the Yoruba people, appreciation and acknowledgment are important ingredients of sociocultural cohesion. It cements the people's ability and will to seek immortality and productivity and honor people who have done their best to provide these food items. These values are transferred to posterity through the composition, performance, and appreciation of these praise poems. Women's social roles as custodians of oríkì also appear in the rendition of these poems as they sometimes double as performers of the poetry and subjects of the same. Women as custodians of oríkì aid the appreciation, vitality, and reproduction of the subjects of these nonfamilial poems.

Taboos and superstitions

The breaking of a traditional taboo is expected to be followed by a supernatural penalty because it is supernaturally forbidden or regarded as culturally immoral and improper.[8] The penalties of breaking a taboo may require sacrifice to appease the gods to avert consequences like famine, drought, death, infertility, or barrenness. Though the penalties for breaking these taboos are usually instant, they can last for a long time. In the Yoruba world, traditional principles regulating people's actions and behaviors are embedded into taboos from which people take cues, thereby acting as social control. The socially institutionalized taboos are a method by which the structure of the Yoruba world works to control society's stability and cohesion.

Olatubosun observes that "taboo is a major component of the Yoruba culture, a way in which Yoruba society expresses its disapproval of certain kinds of behaviors believed to be harmful to its members, either for supernatural reasons or because such behavior violates a moral code."[9] These taboos are many and sectioned into categories such as cleanliness, family relations, sexual intercourse, morality, or religion and deities, and every Yoruba community or society has taboos peculiar to them. Taboos are structured for the sociocultural, psychological, political, and spiritual tranquility of the social institutions of the Yoruba communities by instilling values such as proper behavior, sexual purity, and cleanliness.

Taboos are part of the structures in the Yoruba world to uphold responsibility and mores at a variety of levels of the community. Every Yoruba family, community, or society has a taboo or string of taboos to keep its members in check and ensure they are kept whole and safe. Taboos and superstitions were the safety valves that engendered Yoruba survival, Afolayan claims.[10] They serve as the Yoruba's belief systems, guiding and protecting their heritage and posterity. To ensure that rules and warnings are respected, they are couched in lessons of cause and effect and made to either teach morals or instill fear in children and adults. These taboos impart lessons on cleanliness, morality, accountability, fidelity, and other Yoruba values.

Afolayan recounts lessons such as the fear and reverence for deities, obedience to the rules of the community, and service to humanity. His father, Baba Agba, states that when a star fell, symbolic of death, it dropped into the abyss and indicated that someone who offended their ancestors must have died an awful death from which his soul would never reincarnate. The size of the star would determine how important the person who just died was on the social scale of life.[11] Other omens served as ominous signs for the Yoruba people to herald the occurrence of an event, as when Afolayan notes that people in the village believed that the wailing of dogs before dawn was always a signal that someone was about to die.[12] The purpose of taboos in the Yoruba world is to stabilize the sociopolitical/sociocultural structure of society. They act as control or bridle to youthful exuberances and adult excesses, as the fear of the consequences of breaking the taboos leads to prudence and a reduction in crimes. Taboos are like ethical guides of the community for proper social, cultural, and political governance.

The twins and their metaphorical significance

The Yoruba people value and recognize that twins are a special kind of people from the Supreme Being. One of the customs of the Yoruba is the veneration of the mythological twin children Taiwo and Kehinde through singing the "Twins Songs." This veneration is done for all twins born in the Yoruba world as a way of immortalizing their existence. Unusually, Taiwo (meaning "taste life first") was the first to be born but is regarded as the younger twin, while Kehinde (later arrival) was considered the elder. This is tied to the belief that older people often protect the younger ones by coming behind them to ensure their safety.[13] According to Yoruba traditions, when one of the twins dies, the mother enquires from the gods about what should be used to appease the spirit of the deceased twin, sometimes making a bust or carved image of the dead child and going about with it as she sings the special song:

Tayelolu said I should greet you all,
And I will greet you all, one by one.
Two jolly friends said I should greet you all,
And I will greet you all, one by one.

Omokehinde said I should greet you all,
And I will greet you all, one by one.
Two jolly friends said I should greet you all,
And I will greet you all, one by one.[14]

This is followed by the praise poetry for the twin, using the Yoruba general poetry for twins. Twins are believed to be special children and likened to a deity which is one of the reasons the ìbejì figurines are carved in the Yoruba world. The death of one of the twins is perceived as a threat to the other twin, as it is believed that they possess a kindred spirit and soul. This is chanted while she goes around the community, receiving offers for some token meant to pacify the spirit of the dead twin child. The twins are sometimes referred to as orìsà—to be venerated and worshipped as special kinds of humans. The mother of the twin is also required to cook a special meal of beans called ẹ̀wà ìbejì for people to eat and bless these supernatural beings on earth.

The belief in àbíkú and reincarnation

In the Yoruba world, àbíkú is a phenomenon whereby the spirit of a child who dies at birth or at a young age returns to the same mother to be born and die again and again. As a result, parents who have already suffered the loss of a child take preventive measures to prevent the return of the àbíkú through sacrifices, divination, and other rituals. The Yoruba belief in reincarnation goes far beyond the rebirthing cycle of the àbíkú and is expressed in the naming of children. Names like Iyabo (mother has come), Yewande (mother has sought me out), and Babatunde (father has come again), given to both female and male children immediately after the death of their parents' father or mother, symbolize the reincarnation of ancestors in the present generations, connecting members of a family to its history. The time and circumstances surrounding the birth of a child, as well as the child sharing some perceived characteristics with a deceased relative, connect these names to the belief in reincarnation. The child born around or after the death of the parents' relative is believed to be the incarnation of the deceased relative.

The belief in àbíkú and reincarnation are important aspects of the Yoruba philosophy and worldview. Afolayan makes allusions to them, recycling and rebinding them in his memoir, *Fate of Our Mothers*. In oral tradition, the presentation of àbíkú and reincarnation has sociocultural significance to the parents and society. Reincarnation connects the ancestor to their posterity while securing these offspring to their roots and progenitors. The belief in àbíkú and reincarnation are replicated in popular fiction, such as represented by *Fate of Our Mothers*. In fiction, the presentation is mystical, with magical realism as a frame for capturing metaphysical traits and powers. The birth of the àbíkú is usually extraordinary, with exaggerated demonstrations of power in the terrestrial and extraterrestrial spaces. Reincarnation is, however, imbued with spiritual and moral significance as a display of the cultural importance of this quasi-religious aspect of oral tradition.

Death as debt

"Gbèsè ni'kú" is a popular metaphorical saying of the Yoruba people that refers to the necessity of death as a debt that everyone owes and must be paid at the appointed time because after the physical termination of life, there is another world that dead people go to live. To the Yoruba people, death does not indicate the end but a continuation of existence in another world different from the present. While reincarnation is the duplication of ancestral life in the present generation, individuals who die continue to exist as ancestors in the afterlife. According to Ajibade, this Yoruba concept reminds individuals to do good things while on earth in order to qualify to live with their ancestors.[15] This is encapsulated in the saying, "Awáyé má kú kò sí, òrun nìkan làrè ma bò," meaning "There is no one that will not die (physically) on earth; it is only heaven that one cannot (physically) return to."

Yoruba gods and deities

A pantheon of deities and ancestors are worshipped in the Yoruba world. African traditional religions are myriad and sectionalized, and within the Yoruba world, some worship Ifá, Ògún, Ṣàngó, Èṣù, Oya, Obàtálá, Égúngún, Òṣun, and others, each with its own system of worship and veneration. For example, hunters and blacksmiths are known to be followers of Ògun and sacrifice dogs as ritual material, while others use chicks, ducks, and goats placed or slaughtered by the junctions/pathway for the deities to devour as their meal. Other professions like the traditional healers and Babaláwo worship Ifa, also known as Òrúnmìlà, Àyàn (drummers) also worship their deity Àyàn Àgalú, as stated by Oladosu.[16]

Egúngún is a Yoruba deity venerated by followers who believe that this ancestor-cum-deity is a celestial body from heaven. He is always impersonated by a male member of the Egúngún family who has been initiated into the cult. The Egúngún festival is held for the people to appreciate their ancestors through impersonation—sometimes as a serious ritual and other times just for entertainment—by masquerades representing the spirits of the ancestors or departed relatives. All the family members or descendants (ọlọ́jẹ́) of this deity adhere to the worship; however, men are the only ones allowed to wear the costume (èkú). The worship is open to all adherents and the direct descendants of the Egúngún families. The impersonator represents the spirits of the ancestors, and he is covered up so that people cannot see his face.

Another of the major activities during the Egúngún festival is the street flogging and whipping of youth and children by the followers of the Egúngún to shield the deity from being crowded while they move about the community, street, and marketplace. These beatings are more of a spectacle than a serious infliction of injury on the children and are sometimes done to create a safe distance between them and the performing Egúngún. During the festival, many Yoruba children are immersed in certain herbal concoctions in a well-known ceremony called "wíwẹ àgbo" (bathing in the concoction). Having bathed in the àgbo or oògùn, the belief is that the body is no longer susceptible to the pain of beating, laceration, or mutilation caused by heavy whips.

Olawole Famule opines that Egúngún originated from Ọlọ́gbin Ológbojò, who is also known as Baba Egúngún (the overall father/coordinator of the Oyo-Yoruba Egungun; Alápinni (the chief of Egungun cult), and Ọlọ́jọwọ̀n (the carver of the headpieces for Egúngún).[17] There is a leader known as the Alagbaa who directs the activities of the Egúngún cult. Members of the Egúngún cult are obligated to keep and conceal the cult's secret. The veneration of this deity is rooted in the Yoruba belief that their deceased ancestors are not truly dead but have merely been transposed to another space known as orun (heaven). This transition is substantiated by saying that their ancestor has been transformed (wọ́n ti pa'pò dà).

Famule goes further to say that as the ancestor reincarnation pertains to Egúngún, upon the invocation of the spirits of the dead, especially through the Ọdún Egúngún (the ritual festival for Egúngún), the ancestor(s) of the Egúngún's family lineage manifest physically in the appearance of Egungun (masked figures or masked performers.) thus, not only is Ọdún Egúngún an important form of ancestor veneration, but it is also one of the many ritual devices that the Yoruba explore in order to provide a form (or tangibility) to their abstract, metaphysical, or ontological concepts and ideas.[18] Offerings and sacrifices are made to this deity at the Ojúbọ Egúngún (the Egúngún's shrine), with propitiation items like goat, ram, bitter kola, alligator pepper cock, palm oil, kolanuts, snail, wine, smoked rats, pigeon, and other edible items. The Egúngún prays for the adherents, and they respond with Ase (Amen).

There are also taboos and rules associated with the worship of each deity, as well as special dresses, costumes, and decorations for each that are recognized by anyone in the community. For instance, the Egúngún has its costume known as the "èkú," which the representative of the deity wears for the performance at the marketplace or as it moves about the community and visits houses of chieftains and eminent people offering prayers. All of these gods have specific custodians and days of celebration or festivals where all adherents come out to venerate and show appreciation for the year and blessings they have received from the deity they worship.

Different food items, raw and cooked, are provided to be offered to the deity and also to be eaten. These food items are either accepted as offerings to these deities or material for them to consume. Ogungbemi agrees with this, noting that each deity has its own appetite and taste, which devotees recognize and adhere to when occasions call for worship.[19] People in Yoruba societies can venerate multiple deities, such as communal and family deities. For instance, a community may worship the Ọ̀ṣun river (as in the Osun-Osogbo festival) as the general communal deity, while some families have deities such as Ọbàtálá, Egúngún, and Ifá. There is a plurality or multiple veneration of Yoruba deities because there are a plethora of them.

According to Afolayan, the bàtá drum assembly featuring performers, priests, and priestesses drumming, is traditionally used to represent the macho-militant nature of Ṣàngó, the Yoruba orìsà or deity of thunder and lightning. Olodumare has assigned the orìsà duties and responsibilities as intermediaries between the Yoruba high god and humans. The deities are male and female divinities and are categorized into those who are ancestors-turned-deities and the ones created by Olodumare. The orìsà created by Olodumare are primordial divinities, while the deified orìsà are humans who have been transformed into ancestors because of their impact and contribution to society and people. Ṣàngó is believed to be acrimonious, vindictive, and hot-tempered. He was the only one

Figure 5.1 Michael Olajide Afolayan

in the pantheon of orìsà known to have actually been a Yoruba king, and he was said to be the fifth Aláàfin (ruler) of the ancient Yoruba city of Oyo, considered the political capital of the Yoruba people.

Ṣàngó worshippers and dancers have a peculiar ensemble they wear for their performance as they celebrate,[20] skirts and heavily ornamented blouses or vests that look like the ancient regalia of the distant knights of Europe. The blouses are decorated with assorted cowries, emerald stones, beads, amulets, and miniature gourds, and all of the participants look and dress like women, regardless of sex. Ṣàngó dancers are the only men who traditionally plait or weave their hair among the Yoruba, and they only do this whenever they are going to perform. Some even have their ears pierced and wear makeup like women.[21]

Oya is another deity in the Yoruba pantheon, who Afolayan claims was a Yoruba river goddess and is believed to control the forces of violent winds, flooding, and earthquakes, and that she was the first wife of Ṣàngó, the acrimonious god of thunder and lightning.[22] This deity is female and has the power to control the aquatic world and is known for her support of women and female leadership. Oya's connection to Ṣàngó is legendary because of her impact on manipulating the weather, which is also a feature that connects her to her husband-deity (Ṣàngó). This deity is known to possess a warrior's ability and strength. To seek Oya's help, it is required that one offers her favorite food items, such as shea butter, kola nuts, and hen.

The list of the Yoruba religious pantheons is long, and each has a cult that celebrates the deities with festivals known as Odun. These cults are organized by the adherents of these deities for veneration, prayers, and propitiation. Each of these orìsà has his or her priests/priestesses and devotees. In Yoruba traditional religion, the orìsà have their sacred days of worship, and the big events are the festivals, as Ogungbemi opines.[23] These festivals are special events/occasions where adherents come together with colorful attires to venerate the existence and importance of these deities. The festivals have the sociocultural significance of bringing the adherents and their descendants together and continuing the tradition of passing the religious belief to posterity. Ogungbemi further claims that these festivals synergize religious plurality among the Yoruba, explaining the elasticity of tolerance and accommodation in their society.[24] It validates the coexistence and relationships amongst these varied cults of the Yoruba deities as there exists fluidity of veneration amongst devotees in the Yoruba societies.

The Orò male cult

Using Ajibade's definition, a cult is a religious group that promotes the worship of a human leader or devotion of one's life to a specific purpose with a "specific system of religious worship, especially with reference to its rites and deity."[25] There are several cults of different kinds in the Yoruba world, as well as fraternities with gender specifications. With the large pantheon of Yoruba deities, these cults have their own organized systems of worship, ritual, shrine, leaders, poetry, divination system, and mementos. Potential members must fulfill the necessary processes and eligibility requirements according to the deity's rules and principles.

The Orò all-male cult in the Yoruba land is shrouded under secrecy and mystery. As captured by Akanji and Dada in their examination of this institution, this cult is reputed for performing political, judiciary, and religious functions in the community.[26] This cult is important in the Yoruba world because the members were responsible for the administration of the community in the precolonial period. Members of this cult are kings, traditional rulers and chieftains, and important social figures in the community. They are initiated into this cult based on a pact of secrecy and sensitivity. The word "Orò" refers to fierceness famed for its terrifying demeanor and structure in the Yoruba societies. This cult is an important aspect of the sociocultural and political structure of the Yoruba community because of its ancestral origin.

Akanji and Dada note that Orò is a symbolic deity fashioned in the image of bamboo wrapped with strips of cloth and which produces a whirling sound.[27] Women are forbidden from taking part in, or even spying on, the ritual activities of Orò,[28] reflected by the poetry used to venerate the cult and sing about its sacredness:

Awo egungun l'obirin le se;
Awo gelede l'obinrin le mo;
B'obinrin ba f'oju kan oro,
Oro a gbe e.

[The cult of the masquerade is open to women;
The cult of gelede is available to women;
If a woman dares to catch a glimpse of the cult of Oro,
Oro will abduct her].[29]

This all-male cult is a powerful one where members pride themselves on their ability to stay sacred and exclusive to the male gender. The cult, a subdivision of the Ogboni cult, exercised a check on the "excessiveness of any traditional king in Yorubaland."[30] This means the cult influences the sociopolitical administration of the Yoruba societies. Members of the Orò cult have the power to execute criminals; in such cases, Orò is said to have devoured the bodies.[31] This translates to the ability to carry out judicial functions in the community, such as exiling offenders/criminals, excommunicating malicious people, and sometimes exposing evil people like witches. Also, this cult performs religious roles such as purification rites and exorcism of evil spirits from possessed individuals in the community.

Unlike the Egúngún and Gèlèdè cults that are open to women, the Orò cult is feared and said to abduct any woman that is unfortunate to be found outside of her house when they are on patrol or going about. There appears to be no sanction for this act of abduction, which is believed to be the consequence of violating the sacredness of this cult.

Traditional magic and power

The traditional Yoruba magical powers are based on bodies of natural and supernatural codes used by herbalists, hunters, or priests versed in esoteric knowledge. This form of knowledge is known as oògùn, a traditional science of the Yoruba that requires ingenuity and knowledge of the cosmos command and brings about the desired changes sought by the magic user. The Yoruba believe that oògùn can either be used for a good cause or be manipulated for malicious intent. Incantations of magical words and phrases are used by people who have magical powers, such as herbalists, priests, and traditional leaders who are believed to possess the power to issue them as commands. They can be as short as a line or two or very lengthy, depending on their purpose, the situation the magic user is attempting to address, the context, and the performer's objective.

In addition, they can be used to complete a vanishing act to flee danger, demand specific changes such as taking the form of an animal or transitioning from one to human form or subvert a natural course of action. Belief in these magical powers and incantations is a significant aspect of the Yoruba supernatural world, regardless of whether they can be explained empirically. Charms and amulets are another part of Yoruba traditional magic and supernatural power that use an understanding of the mystical world and the manipulation and permutation of the required cosmic elements to perform a certain function. The knowledge of the cosmos and symbolic codes are mechanisms in charms and amulets of the Yoruba traditional magic. These are combined in the manipulation of supernatural and terrestrial forces in the Yoruba world. They are worn as magical insignia and symbols to protect against malevolent forces and bring good fortune or as channels for making magical weapons.

Soetan notes that, among the Yoruba people, "the use of charms is as ancient as the creation of the earth even if it is a practice that has evolved, changing forms through the ages and the colonial experience."[32] The belief system, he continues, "serves as a natural science developed by initiates schooled in the codes that unlock the powers that emerge from a synergic exchange between the transcendental heavens and the immanent earth."[33] This science is rooted in religion and a product of mythology but is also an attempt by the Yoruba to study and understand the physical world.[34] By introducing colonialism and its attendant institutions, such as Western education and religion, Islam and Christianity have shaped the way people view Yoruba spiritual beliefs. Yoruba spiritual beliefs are now being seen as "the practice of evil and he or she is either an unbeliever or a soul condemned to burn in hell—this is the general assumption in modern-day Nigeria that has become a religious enclave for Christians and Muslims as averred by Soetan."[35]

In the Yoruba world, herbs can also be used as magical substances, along with incantations, magical powers, chants, and amulets. The Yoruba believe in using herbs and plants for liberation from health maladies or unwanted situations. When these herbs or plants are chewed, they are believed to release special powers that the eater can draw from. Àféèrí, a form of invincibility; ayeta, the ability to become bulletproof when shot at; and òkígbé, protection from getting attacked with a machete or being cut open, are few magical abilities and powers that reside in the manipulation of traditional Yoruba metaphysics.

This list of powers is not specifically gained from the herbs or plants mentioned above but are examples of powers and demonstrations of traditional magical power. There are other herbs that require incantations to be effective. Afolayan underlines the importance of incantations thus: "Without the incantations, the herbs are vegetables and for them to be effective for whatever purpose, herbs must be gathered in broad daylight."[36] This means that the herb/plants do not possess extraordinary properties to perform these metaphysical demonstrations on their own, except they are accompanied by these incantations. However, this relates to incantatory compound charms, the potency of which is dependent on the added element(s). In the Yoruba culture, this translates to the existence of many forms of charms, amulets, and incantations.

Traditional medicine and healing

In the Yoruba world, there are several traditional medicine practices and ways of healing ailments and diseases through herbs and traditional knowledge that stretch back far before the introduction of Western medicine. These healing systems and knowledge are part of the belief system of the Yoruba. The medicinal properties and functions of plants and herbs are directly linked with their belief in the efficacy of the ingredients and methods of healing, requiring learned traditional healers who have studied medicinal herbs and how to apply them to different health issues. The Yoruba beliefs/worldviews are the manuals for the healing and application of healing properties to any medical issue.

For instance, in the selection of herbs, the Yoruba people believe that herbs for healing are to be picked/plucked in daylight to be effective. When the herbs are plucked at night, they affect their effectiveness or render them ineffective. Oníṣègùn is the name for this traditional healer, who may also be Babaláwo, a priest who doubles as a healer. The Babaláwo performs traditional medicine and other sociopolitical and cultural functions, while the Oníṣègùn deals primarily with traditional medicine. The Babaláwo enjoys a place of esteem because of his office and function in society.

Society and Its Core Institutions

In this section of the chapter, the sociocultural organization of the Yoruba world, as captured in the text, will be explored. This will reveal how society is organized, the arrangement of the marriage and the family system of the Yoruba, the customs binding the community, and the various aspects of the social and cultural behavior/ attitude that characterized this division.

Traditions

Traditions serve as external pressure plugs and internal stabilizing forces in the Yoruba society, allowing them to maintain their culture, values, mores, and knowledge system. These traditions used to be an unquestionable guardian of the rituals and practices of the Yoruba society, which, more often than not, were replicated in the social institutions. Ṣíṣú lópó is a Yoruba tradition where a widow is passed on to a member of her husband's family after his untimely death, leaving her re-possessed or inherited by her husband's brother or another male relative. Ṣíṣú lópó stabilizes the family and marriage as social institutions. The woman stays connected to her husband's heritage and family by remarrying her late husband's relative. It also keeps the child(ren) of the man under the same protection and household.

Ṣ̣iṣú lópó is an important aspect of the Yoruba social institution with its own ways of operation. Another tradition observed when a person dies is that, following the customs of the land, a live chicken of propitiation, called adiẹ ̀irànà (literally meaning "the buyer of the road"), is held a few yards ahead of the pallbearers as a sign to others that a corpse is being carried along that way and to clear them from the route. This is based on the belief that when a corpse is transported over a river or water, it becomes heavy and resistant to cross or move until the chicken's feathers are plucked while the praise songs of the deceased person's family are sung or chanted.

There are traditional gender roles for men and women in the Yoruba world in the home and in public. By nature and tradition, women are caretakers of their households through various means, including nurturing, caring, and providing. At the same time, men are the sole providers and breadwinners of the family, and they represent the family at different public functions or provide guidance and direction. Traditionally, men inherit their family's property and wealth, while their female siblings may receive some smaller portions of the property or more in certain circumstances. Afolayan describes a woman inheriting her father's farmlands in the absence of any male family member. Regardless of inheritance, when the head of the family dies, it is the duty of the eldest daughter to create an effigy in honor of her father and take care of his resting place. Afolayan presents these traditions to explore the varied positioning of women in Yoruba society while also criticizing some of the negative aspects that impact the fate of women as a gender constantly under the grip of patriarchy.

Courtesy and social organization

It is customary to break kola nuts before one addresses an elder and seek the gods before an important meeting or deliberation. To the Yoruba, kola is known to wave away death and disease, "obì ní b'ikú, obì ní b'àrùn" (the kola chases death and diseases) because of the medicinal attachment and properties it carries and as propitiation items for the deities' consumption. Palm wine is served before the commencement of any meeting or talk by a young male child, who is required to be the first person to taste it before offering it to the elders as a sign of respect and courtesy. Also, the oldest male member in a family is consulted when a man decides to take a wife to discuss the matter and prepare him on how to go about it. Usually, these elders are the spokesperson when the groom's family visits the girl's family, and they converse with the elders in her family on what is required of the groom-to-be. As a sign of respect and responsibility, it is also expected of a Yoruba child to assist an elder carrying some loads.

Social rules like these are observed in the Yoruba world to stabilize the hierarchy in social institutions and maintain the force of traditions. Afolayan explores how these rules reflect and maintain the values of the Yoruba society, such as the expectation that women, especially wives, will follow the unwritten rule of cooking excess food so that in the event they have visitors who come greeting during mealtime, the guests will also be served the meal. Another rule in the Yoruba world during important social gatherings or meetings is to pour a libation—palm wine or another indigenous drink—on the ground before the commencement of the meeting. This action is meant to pay homage to the Yoruba deities and to offer them dues so the deities can preserve and protect their followers. The libation plays the role of an offering to the deities, who, in turn, stabilize the social gatherings/meetings.

It should be noted that tradition excludes children and women from these gatherings. The rules guiding behavior and comportment in the Yoruba society order both the old and young, men and women, through regulating systems of social institutions that control every aspect of human activity.

Greetings and respect

In Yoruba society, greetings and respect are essential elements of social institutions. It is compulsory for younger people to pay their respects to the elders in the community by greeting them in a prescribed manner. Tradition stipulates that the men prostrate in greeting while the women or young girls kneel. Furthermore, if any child was born in a family before a woman was married into it, the woman was treated as junior and subservient to that child within the family.[37] As a sign of respect in the Yoruba world, one must remain prostrated or kneeling until the elder asks you to rise. This manner of greeting symbolizes the social relationship between an elder and a youth, placing the elder at the top of the social rungs and the youth at the bottom of it.

Respect is highly essential in the Yoruba culture, and it is valued differently than it is in the Western world, where there is a more leveled field between two parties. Among the Yoruba people, tradition places a premium on birth order and position in the family. When a man or woman is older than another person by a few years or more, one is required to call the person "little father/little mama" (Bàbá Kékeré/Màmá Kékeré). This respect is nonnegotiable and violations, such as a youth looking an adult in the eye when being spoken to or addressing them, are considered a social crime for daring to disrespect an elder. Such behavior is strongly condemned, and the person may be publicly chastised as a social deterrent to others.

The Yoruba view and use greetings as necessary expressions of fellowship between individuals and the community; indeed, greetings function as the lubricant in the Yoruba "machinery of social harmony."[38] There are greetings for every occasion, time of the day, month, season, year, festival, and ceremony in the Yoruba community. They are not mere salutations or meaningless expressions about the time of the day but rather the symbol of the Yoruba mutual fellowship and their understanding of the psychotherapeutic communication of emotions and good wishes that have been couched in these greeting forms.

Smith notes that the Yoruba people value greetings as part of the core of their culture. Not only are they a vital mode of communication, but they are also a vast storehouse of cultural information that serves as effective agents of socialization. Embedded within them are glints of the culture's philosophy, worldviews, religious beliefs, views of time, space and natural phenomena, means of conflict resolution, core moral values and taboos, codes of conduct, and social ethics.[39] These greetings are significant to the Yoruba people as they reflect the intertextuality of the Yoruba space, time, situation, festivals, emotions, and philosophy.

These varied greetings are texts that take stock of society's diverse social-cultural, sociopolitical, physical, and psychological frames. The time, as a subtext in greetings like ẹ káàárọ̀/ẹ kú ojúm (good morning), ẹ kú ọ̀sán (good afternoon), ẹ kú ìrọ̀lẹ́ (good evening), indicates a time-bound greeting appropriate for that time of the day. The greetings are also situational-bound in that there are varied greetings to capture/ frame situations like death, birth, and different celebrations, such as "ẹ kú àsìkò ọyẹ́" (ọyẹ́ is the harmattan) and "ẹ kú ọwọ̀ l'ómi" (to greet a woman who just gave birth to a baby). There are festivals with peculiar greetings, as well as occupations: For example, "À bọ'rú bọyè, àbọyè bọ ṣíṣẹ o" is to greet a herbalist or priest, and "Oòyà ó yà o!" meaning the comb will perform its work, is used to hail or greet traditional hair-makers.

In terms of emotions and philosophy, greetings communicate belief systems and feelings, especially at crucial or sensitive moments. "Ẹ kú ìpalẹ̀mọ́," "Éyìn wọn á dára" (this is used to cheer the children or family of the deceased), "ẹ kú ilédè," and "ẹ kú ìdèlé" (are employed during the departure of a relative). These greetings capture every nuance of life in the Yoruba world—the combination of different texts of sociopolitical, cultural, physical, and psychological milieu.

Diplomacy and secrecy

In the Yoruba world order, secrecy stands as the stamp of security. Afolayan notes that even the gods that villagers worshiped were shrouded in secrecy.[40] Secrecy and diplomacy are linked as two seeds in a pod, and keeping one's secrets and mouth closed is seen as an essential diplomatic tool of the Yoruba people. There are many proverbs and idioms of the Yoruba that warn against talkativeness and encourage people to keep their secrets to themselves. As Afolayan recounts in the memoir, he was admonished and taught to be diplomatic in handling issues with friends and family members, even as a child: "Secrecy. Secrecy guarded our lives. Every aspect of our life was enveloped in the shroud of secrecy." Villagers would always say, "Ẹnu aráyé lẹbọ," which describes the power of the mouth and the creative and destructive capacities it carries. It means that the gods were gods because we called them so, and since we anointed them with power, they would cease to be gods if we decided to kill them with our mouths.[41]

In the Yoruba world, this close-mouthed secrecy and delicate diplomacy are highly advised in several areas of domestic and public life. In the structure of the overlapping fields of family, community, and settlement, the Yoruba people are accomplished diplomats who hone this skill as a protective and security measure against malevolent forces who work with tact and wisdom in their public and private matters. Premium is placed on secrecy and diplomacy as one of the methods of avoiding unnecessary publicity and loophole for evil to thrive. It is highly valued as a sociocultural treasure within the Yoruba world. The elders are praised for their diplomacy in handling tricky issues, especially when settling disputes between friends, husbands and wives, co-wives, and others. Sometimes the elders are invited when issues such as infidelity, land dispute, and loan/financial quarrel cannot be settled quietly. They are invited based on their wisdom and experience on such matters and may be related to the people involved or respected elders of the community.

In Yoruba society, the ability to keep one's secrets is ingrained and reinforced through philosophies, proverbs, idioms, and education. These are ingredients and skills that the Yoruba people teach their children through stories, folktales, proverbs, and real-life experiences, as explored in Afolayan's work. The author gives an instance of how his father used a folktale and sometimes firsthand experience to impact a lesson about life to him. Both adults and children are taught the art of diplomacy—through real-life experiences and explanations of the Yoruba philosophies about life, coexistence, hard work, and resiliency, which are codified in various Yoruba proverbs and idioms—rather than being a tale bearer who creates discord in the family. A child goes through varied lessons about life in every phase of life, which are transposed as physical and spiritual nuggets. Idioms are lessons about the Yoruba people's ways, values, and culture, and idiomatic expressions are used to reinforce these skills.

Polygamy and polygyny: The marriage system

One institution of the Yoruba world that shapes the structure and organization of a home and household is the polygamous marriage system. The Yoruba man marries more than one wife, operating on a preliterate modus operandi to gain a multiplication of their posterity effort to continue their community and the life of their lineage. It is important that the man marries enough wives to let his family name resound forward through history. This marriage system is one of the grandest and oldest social institutions, with its tenets and values encapsulated and supported in their proverbs about procreation. Gbadegesin opines that marriage is one of the most important traditional rites of passage because it is the only rite that the individual witnesses and actively engage in, and which still retains its meaningfulness to almost all of its members.[42] Other rites of passage in the Yoruba society, such as birth, death, or burial, are done without the person's knowledge and participation.

Marriage rites and customs

A marriage contracted between a man and a woman is another field where Yoruba customs and traditions must be observed. First, there is a step known as ifojú s'ódè, meaning searching for a suitable bride by either the man or his family members. Then representatives from the intended groom's family will visit the girl's family to announce their son's intention and reach an agreement on the time and material requirements for the engagement and marriage, a process called itoro (literally, "asking for").[43] Usually, these delegates from the intending groom's family are elders who meet with the elders of the potential bride's family. After the discussion and deliberation about the proposal, the delegates from the man's family are entertained as custom stipulates. They then return to their family to relate the negotiation.

Before and during these negotiations, there is an additional series of actions going on in the background. After the elders in the groom's family begin to talk with the elders in the potential bride's family, the man's family will proceed to make inquiries to investigate the woman and her family to ascertain whether she is from a good home or family with no questionable behavior or criminal record, or a disease or ailment. While traditional, this is carried out covertly to ensure that the woman would not bring shame and disgrace to the man's family.

Afolayan notes that this investigation may take up to a year or even longer before determining that the woman's family is decent and giving their son positive feedback and formal permission to speak with the woman and propose to her. In the memoir, the author gives a personal illustration of his sister's experience on the issue of proper investigation and inquiry into the family. Tradition stipulates that the woman's family must wait until seven market days before responding, after which they will also send their own emissaries to investigate the man's family.[44] The investigation continues for both families until all parties are satisfied with the outcome of the inquiries.

After these investigations, both families will meet and proceed to the next stage, where the man can talk to his intended bride, make his intentions known to her, and openly court her. After the wedding has been agreed to, it is customary that every new bride brings with her a young companion called *emini*. The *emini* goes on errands for the new bride, as it is considered rude for the bride to send a child on errands in the new compound she was just being married into.[45] Most times, the *emini* stays with the bride for years as a handmaiden to help her settle in her new home.

Ẹkún ìyàwó is a traditional bridal chant performed by the bride in this transitional period as she prepares to leave her family and friends to be joined in marriage to another man and his family. The bridal chant or poetry is taught to the prospective bride by the women in her family among the skills and knowledge she will need in her new home. The bridal chant is performed to the bride's family, friends, and relatives, and it eulogizes her parents' efforts, affection, and training. It gives the bride an outlet to release her emotions to the audience, who are witnesses to the symbolic and metaphorical expression of values and mores absorbed as a girl in her formative years. Going to different houses in the village, the bride chants about how she was raised, thanks her parents, expresses gratitude to her friends and family, and describes her trials and successes.

Afolayan gives a translated example of ẹkún ìyàwó:

I passed by my husband's house
My husband applauded me.
I passed by the oba's palace,
The oba offered me the velvet garment.
I passed by a secret admirer's house
The secret admirer ushered me with a myriad of gifts.
Please, give my message to the husband that I embrace his love.
Please, give my message to the oba that I admire his generosity.
And please, give my message to the secret admirer that I welcome his wasteful spending.
Because wastefulness is the name of a concubine's spending on someone else's bride.
Fortune for my head, today,
I know, it is fortune.[46]

This special kind of poetry requires long years of practice and dedication and a good memory as the bride chants about traditional love, knowledge, admirers, the courting system, and other important aspects of her life. This poem is an important example of the oral literature tradition in the Yoruba world, established as a unique form of verse performed during a marriage ceremony. While the bride goes to every house to chant the ẹkún ìyàwó, her neighbors pray for her and receive wishes for good fortune in her new home. Sometimes, the bride is given some advice or admonished in a lengthy manner to be patient and learn in the unfamiliar home of her husband because "ilé ọkọ, ilé èkọ́" (the husband's house is a ground for re-education).

When a woman marries a man, she begins to learn and study the personality and frame of her husband and home, absorbing new information about the new household and navigating the ideas to sustain it. As with the instruction of children about the Yoruba world, proverbs and idioms are employed in these pieces of advice, including cooking tips, the proper attitude and disposition she needs, and the importance of temperance and good behavior to give the new bride a guide for her to have a peaceful home.

One other custom performed during the marriage ceremony is that water is poured on the roof of the bride's house, and she steps out to walk through the dripping water. As she does this, she is welcomed with the chorus, "Éyìn ìyàwó ò ní m'ẹní o," which means, "May the back of the wife not get used to lying on the mat." This was a prayer for procreation always offered to the newlywed, marking the end of the chanting ritual.[47]

Another of the Yoruba world's ancient marriage rites happens when the girl is resistive to the marriage. In the ironic ìgbéyàwó ceremony, the girl is usually tricked into going to her suitor's house. This may involve sending the girl to purchase an item in the particular house or to run an errand within the vicinity that has already been prepared for the occasion. The girl is then captured and detained in the suitor's house while a message is sent to her family about the successful apprehension of the resisting girl. Her family is not only aware of this plan, but they also are involved in the ceremonial "kidnapping." Afolayan claims that this process is the oldest form of marriage among the Yoruba, and it is why when a man and woman become husband and wife, it is called ìgbéyàwó,[48] translated as the act of kidnapping a woman to make her a wife.

Mother and motherhood

Mothers in the Yoruba world are venerated like goddesses. They are the pillars of their houses and community, determining the tone and hue of events. They are more like a constellation fixed in the stars of the Yoruba people. Afolayan attests that "mothers, literally and figuratively, took the fall for us so we could stand upright and walk."[49] They were the "custodians of the wisdom of the fathers," as they often doubled as their husbands' confidantes and advisers. Mothers were teachers, storytellers, poets, and performers, and they were the source of domestic knowledge and home education.

Motherhood is a phase in the life of a Yoruba woman that represents the rite of passage from being a girl to an adult. In Yoruba society, mothers are referred to as gold, and songs are composed to honor them as mothers or mothers-to-be. Motherhood is more than just the physical reality of birthing a child. It is a societal role with deep meaning and spiritual functions. Mothers are priceless because they are indispensable to their husbands and their children. They represent the voices in the background that have enough force to propel fathers to perform and push the youth and children to succeed.

Motherhood also has cultural significance for the fathers, attesting to the men's virility of the men and their ability to reproduce and replicate themselves through their children. Motherhood carries the emblem of men's fertility for growth and expansion of wealth, establishing them as the provider of shelter and the progenitor of a family line and generation. As it bestows such a position on the male gender, motherhood aids fathers' sociocultural status. The link created and enhanced by the union of the mother and father guarantees the transition to another phase in the social institution. Motherhood is one of the crucial ingredients in the organization and socialization process of society. It is a threshold of support for fathers in that mothers assume leadership and control in the men's absence. In some cases, such as when their husbands die, mothers take on the fathers' responsibilities alongside theirs.

From the earthly phase of nurturing children to the celestial epitome of grace, affection, and even immortality, motherhood in the Yoruba culture is a point of transcendence for women. Mothers and motherhood are celebrated to mark the importance of a gender and a phase that keeps the Yoruba lineage and posterity flourishing. However, this phase has a drawback because it casts the female gender into a mold enabled and controlled by patriarchy. It continually keeps the female gender subordinate to the male gender, as the "other" in the system, placing the male gender at the top with a large share of power in society.

Names and their symbolic meanings

Naming is an integral part of Yoruba culture, and it is compulsory that a formal naming ceremony is held for a newborn. Before the naming ceremony day where their permanent name is bestowed, a baby is given a tentative pseudo-name, such as Ìkókó, Túnfúlù, Àlejò, or Aròbó. A myriad of sociopsychological, environmental, and cultural factors are considered when a name is given to a child, and Yoruba names (an individual's personal name in particular) are a bundle of information about the bearer and their family. Events before, during, and after birth play significant roles in the name to be given to the child.[50] Harrison Adeniyi identifies a classification of Yoruba names, alluded to in the saying "ilé làá wò ká tó s'ọmọ l'órúko" (the condition of the home determines the name of the child).[51] Some names are called àmútòrunwa (divine names), which refer to the condition of the child during birth or certain features about what is observed on the days that such children are born.

As listed by Adeniyi, some examples of these orúkọ àmútòrunwa (divine names) are Taiwo (the first to arrive of a set of twins); Kehinde (the second to arrive of a set of twins); Idowu (a child born after a set of twins); Alaba (a child born after Idowu); Oke (a child born with an unbroken amniotic sac); and Ige (a child that came out of the womb with feet first).[52] Adeniyi also identifies other types of names in the Yoruba world according to the profession or occupation of the family, such as Ayanwale (the drummer sire has come back home); Ayanbola (this child, a drummer-to-be, has found honor); Olonade (here comes a craftsman); and Onadeji (the craftsmen-to-be are now two in the family.[53]

Orúkọ̀ àbísọ (birth names) are names given after birth (during the naming ceremony) by parents and other family members, according to the deities worshipped in the family. Oríkì àbísọ ("personal praise names") like Asake (one selected to be pampered); Ayinla (one selected to be praised); Aduke (one whom everybody scrambles to care for); Ajoke (one whom everyone pampers); Alamu (the chosen one); Akanni (the elected one); and Atoke (raised to be cherished) are personal oríkì or praise names given to male and female children.

In the Yoruba world, the importance placed on names and naming children is done deliberately and with purpose. Names are tied to an individual's fate and the symbolic depiction of the child's future or as markers of position and status in the family and the world. Like Afolayan notes in the memoir, as he was the eighth child in his family, his name "Oladejo" means "My honor and riches have increased to eight."[54] These names reflect the wishes and prayers of the parents for their children, which are carried with these children as the emblem of their being. Names like Oladele (wealth has come home), Oladipo (wealth is glued together), Ogundele (Ogun has come home), and Olaosebikan (fortune has no fixed space) are significant to the child and the parents of the child, as they reflect and represent not only the parents' wishes for their children but also what each child adds to their household. The child is also connected to the broader set of relations within his family and community by receiving an oriki as part of their name.

As a final note, Afolayan observes that only the elders of the house call people by their praise name and then usually only when greeting or praising someone or when they are appealing for a favor.[55] As a child in a household, there is a general oriki for the family, and his personal oriki reveals the broad connection to the lineage's oriki as the tradition of the family and the community.

Naming ceremony

The naming ceremony is another essential aspect of the Yoruba people's customs and way of life. Day seven or eight after the child is born—depending on the gender of the baby—serves as the naming ceremony day. Usually, the oldest woman in the family carries the newborn child while someone pours a bowl of water on the roof of the house on the designated naming ceremony day. The woman runs to catch the droplets of water on the baby seven times if the baby is a girl and eight if it is a boy. While this is being done, prayers are offered concerning the child. Water holds a strong place for the Yoruba as an instrument of prayer, along with other designated items such as dry fish, honey, kola nuts, bitter kola, palm oil, and salt. Afolayan explores the significance of these items in prayer. An older woman picks up a tiny piece of each of these condiments, touches the head and the lips of the baby, as if the infant had eaten it, and then gives it to the baby's mother to eat.[56]

The significance and meaning of these food items placed on the lips of the child and mother is to bless the child, and since the baby is too young to eat or chew the offered food items, the mother eats them on the child's behalf. Each of these items has a reason for being selected as an item of prayer for the newborn child: orógbó, the bitter kola, is believed to give longevity of life, while obi, the kola nut, is believed to clear away death among the Yoruba people.[57] Other significant items for the life of the baby are each tasted by the baálé (the oldest male adult in the family): water, which stands for life; ataare (alligator pepper), in order for the baby to have as many children as there are seeds in the pepper; oti (dry gin) to prevent the life of the baby from going sour; orógbó for long-life; iyọ (salt) so that the baby will be indispensable and important; àádùn (honey, sugarcane, grinded corn mixed with palm oil) for the baby to enjoy the sweetness of life; dried rat or fish so that the child will have more than enough to eat in his or her lifetime; palm oil for an easy and comfortable life; and money, so that the child will have more than enough to spend in life.

It is expected that the baby's mother will keep the money in her custody or buy one or two domestic animals on behalf of the baby.[58]

The father of the child is also present at this ceremony, and at one point, he is handed the child, and he places their feet on the ground to symbolize the child's ability to walk, work, and stay above the ground until a natural death at an old age. Every member of the parents' families is present, and during the ceremony, all adults are called upon to give the baby a name, with the grandparents going first. Each person takes out a few coins from their pockets, puts them into the water, and then proclaims the name they want the child to be called.[59]

Circumcision and facial marks

Circumcision is a Yoruba ritual that dates back to the preliterate period and is still practiced by some today. In the Yoruba community, both male and female children are circumcised by a native surgeon, the olóòlà, who is a professional in the field. While the male child's circumcision is done very early in childhood, the female child might wait a little longer as their genital organs are different. Female children are circumcised based on the belief that they would be sexually loose and be rejected for marriage if they were not. Part of the circumcision procedure for the female child requires a male member who loves her to be present and also be given about twenty-one incisions on the arm. This olóòlà may be male or female, depending on the sex of the child being circumcised. The olóòlà cuts the female child between her legs and in the genital area, causing a lot of pain to the girl and requiring her to lie on her back for some days after the circumcision in order to recover.

Afolayan describes that the ritual requires the olóòlà, in this case, a woman, to be dressed in all-white apparel, as are her apprentices who carry the instruments to be used in calabashes or bowls containing knives of different sizes, napkins, chopping wood, and other tools. The profession of the olóòlà is still highly revered and reviled strongly by children. The olóòlàs were immensely proud of their primordial vocation, and the skill was passed from generation to generation within the same family.[60] They are called dákódákó, which means "people who pierce the penis," but they also do facial marking, another tradition that has been among the Yoruba since time immemorial.[61]

Facial marks hold a more complex meaning than just ornamentation as beauty marks, as they were primarily identification marks for many families in the Yoruba society to identify their kin and members of their community. The transition of facial marks for identification to ethnic/family symbols or insignia moves through a naturalization process due to the function of distinguishing children from different families or communities. These marks or body adornments emphasize sociocultural, political, and religious positions in Yoruba society. They may represent the transition from childhood to adulthood or the attainment of sexual maturity. In some cases, they symbolize spiritual experience (in the case of an àbíkú) and differentiate between indigenes and slaves in the community. These are encoded within the Yoruba culture and tradition to indicate communal/ethnic or kinship affiliations and installed as traditions and rites of passage. But there are also marks made on the body for special or spiritual purposes, such as protection from malicious people or to stop àbíkú children from dying and coming back to torment their parents.

Facial marks and body marks are sometimes done to treat an ailment or affliction such as measles, pneumonia, and convulsion in the Yoruba land. Incisions of this kind may be found on the back, head, arm, or the specific body part that is affected. They are also used for children born after an àbíkú to spiritually protect the child from the same fate. Facial marks can also signal membership of different Yoruba communities based on whether they are either vertical or horizontal in shape. Different Yoruba families and communities also have peculiar facial marks by which they are easily identified as belonging to a particular social group or community.

Mourning and widowhood rites

Mourning the dead in the Yoruba culture focuses on allowing the relatives of the dead to demonstrate their love for the deceased. Mourning is usually observed by the women in the family, while the men take care of the corpse and the burial ceremony. There are special processes and rituals required from either the wife or husband of the dead relative. The widower also goes through a mourning period, but unlike the widow, the process is less gruesome or elaborate as wearing a shroud and being inherited by any family member.

When a woman's husband dies, she is thrown into the process of mourning and widowhood rites and subject to many dehumanizing rites and procedures. During the mourning period, the woman is made to wear a special widow's dress for the mourning period. Her hair must be unkempt, and she must be secluded, sometimes staying indoors for as long as forty days until the end of the mourning period. She has no right to her husband's property, as her children inherit them, or if she does not have any child, the husband's property goes to his family members. In a process known as ṣíṣú l'ópó, the newly bereaved wife is handed to her late husband's brother or another close relative of the spouse. If the woman decides to remain married to the family through the husband's next of kin, everything that belonged to the husband is transferred to the new husband.[62] If she refuses, she will have to return to her parent's house to be known as dálémọṣú, a derogatory term used to discriminate against women who return to live in their parents' home after leaving their husband's house for one reason or the other.

Collectivity and communal living

The Yoruba world is organized as a collectivity, with people having a close relationship with their kin, kith, and neighbors. Individuality is considered a foreign concept as it is believed that communal living and activities ensure the stability of the community and sustain everybody in society. Farming a large piece of land or even building a house is an easy task as one only needs to make their request known, and people will assist them in clearing their lands, planting, and building their house. Afolayan notes that this value was expressed in the proverb, "It is only when the right washes the left, and the left washes the right that the two hands can be clean."[63] The traditional communal and collective life is also translated in the present by having extended members of the family living in the same building because of the belief that there is happiness in shared efforts to raise their children and build houses.

Rustic living and transparency

In the preliterate Yoruba society, people lived a simple and transparent life without expecting any kind of gratification. Everybody had their own farm with crops grown for family consumption, while other food could be bought in the market at a low price. In the Yoruba world, especially in the rural areas and villages, there are days assigned for the market, where all can buy and sell their goods, different from daily market days where household items and petty materials can be purchased. For some Yoruba communities, their market day is every five days, when farmers and sellers from the community and other surrounding villages could come and sell their wares. There is also a system of trading in the community whereby fruits, vegetables, and other food crops are placed at a junction to the farm or market in a basket, with some separated from the bunch and placed with some coins or a penny to indicate the amount each of the items is sold for. This system relies on mutual trust and transparency to sell and buy goods without people being present.

In rural areas, life is serene and peaceful as elders control any untoward behavior displayed by any member of the community. The elders are the governing bodies besides the Baálè, the head of the kinship community. The Yoruba believe that one person gives birth to a child, but the whole community raises them. As such, any elder can act in place of the parents in correcting a child for any misdemeanor or improper behavior. The elders act as society's seat of power, tradition, and wisdom, setting society's rules, principles, and customs, as well as giving direction to youths and children. They represent the voice of reason and intelligence, with their words seasoned with Yoruba proverbs and knowledge systems.

The importance of the elders' role in stabilizing the community and family is captured by the proverb that says that the elders cannot be home and the child's neck will be askew. When things go wrong in the family, community, or society, it is believed that there are no elders present because they are the pillars to stabilize the community. The elders were also responsible in preliterate Yoruba society for encoding and decoding the customs and traditions of the community by transposing these cultural values and beliefs into easy forms to remember. They communicate these values in folktales, riddles, stories, history, and lessons passed on to their children and grandchildren.

Coronation ceremony

Due to different dialects of the same language, different titles and appellations are used to describe the monarch in each Yoruba community, but when a new king or monarch is crowned in a Yoruba community, there are rituals and a series of customs that must be observed before the coronation, according to community traditions. Several activities indicate that the coronation ceremony is imminent, especially necessary because ascendancy to the throne is not usually hereditary; instead, there is a rotation system among the ruling families who choose representatives to be next in line to the throne.

Afolayan observes that Yoruba kingship was not just a natural right of the few ruling families. It was conferred through the lengthy and excruciating process of lineage selection, oracular divination, and popular acclamation. Thus, members of the families must identify the potential future rulers, then the oracle of divination identifies the family and individual. There are rituals reserved for the most highly initiated community members, and then potential kings must seek approval by the popular acclamation of the people.[64] The final ceremonial aspects of the process are open to everyone. The leader is introduced and presented to the common citizens in the marketplace,[65] and the chief priest, kingmakers, elders, and council of chiefs oversee the customs of the land demand.

The process is usually arduous and elaborate, as traditions and customs must be strictly followed to avoid any form of mistake or duplicity. When the time to unveil the king to the people comes, the oracle, through divination, appoints the designated carrier to bear the king to the market. A king's bearer only has to execute this function once throughout his lifetime, as he will never have to do it again. The carrier is armed with charms and amulets, which have spiritual importance and are believed to enhance the carrier with supernatural strength and the ability to carry the king successfully. They symbolize the harbinger of the gods and must leave the coronation after allowing the king-elect to disembark and go to a sacred grove for a week to separate and purify himself, as no person is supposed to touch the king and remain alive, according to tradition.

The selected king is adorned with beads on his neck and a white wrapper or robe at the waist, while his body is marked with white chalk. Before and after the Oba (the king), people from the royal family, chiefs, and priests must go, and the carrier brings the king into a circle made with white chalk. While the king-elect disembarks, the chiefs surround him and pay obeisance by kneeling and putting their face to the ground and declaring his majesty, "Kabiyesi, Kabiyesi, Kabiyesi."

In the Yoruba communities, kings are popularly referred to as second-in-command to the gods; their words are believed to be guided by the ancestors, so their decrees and words are law. They are revered and highly respected because of their perceived proximity to the deified ancestors and are known as the head and husbands of witches and wizards because of their superior position in the Yoruba cosmology. Each community in the Yoruba world has a specific title for its kings, sometimes representing the name of the city, town, or community.

Ẹrú ọba and the king's slaves

It is customary in the Yoruba world for a king to have slaves who live for the pleasure and service of the king. They often act as the human carpet for the king to step on when he climbs off his horse. These slaves may be procured within and/or outside the community through wars, kidnapping, gift/tribute, and pawning. In some cases, these slaves may be procured as punishment for crimes committed in the community, as projected in Akinjobi–Babatunde's work.[66] Afolayan enunciates that these slaves lived in the service of the royal households.[67] These are aspects of the Yoruba world that enhance the authority and supremacy of the king over his subjects. In the preliterate Yoruba society, the king has authority over all, and his decrees are absolute. These slaves serve him and continue to live in the palace as his servants.

Literature, the Arts, and Recreation

In the exploration of the memoir by Afolayan, some of the aspects of the Yoruba oral tradition, arts, and entertainment activities will be explicated to reveal the ingenuity of these people in fashioning their own folklore and arts. The artistic eruptions and literary exploits captured in *Fate of Our Mothers* will be discussed in this section of the chapter.

Proverbs and idioms

In the world of the Yoruba people, proverbs and wise sayings are basic linguistic tools employed as markers of maturity and wisdom. Afolayan observes that "Our people used to say, 'too numerous to count are the teeth buried in the gums of a defective jaws'."[68] This proverb means that power is useless and ineffective when it resides in an indolent person. Literally, the proverb explains the futility of counting the teeth in a faulty jaw. Proverbs mark the transition from the fledgling lexicon of a child to the seasoned and broad language of the adult. The Yoruba people's linguistic system is much more than just a way of speaking or conversing. The Yoruba world is constructed and preserved by the clever manipulation and deployment of words and proverbs. They even had a proverb about proverbs: "A proverb is the horse of words; when words are lost in transition, proverbs are the search crew for fishing them out."[69]

Proverbs become their domain of language in the Yoruba world, serving as in-group codes and ciphers synonymous with spice and condiments of speech, which Omofoyewa avers to be the main ingredients needed to drive home an elder's wise counsel or rebuke forcefully and beautifully.[70] The words are the signifiers, meaningful at the literal level of description, but the signified are the concepts recognized in the referent. At the surface level, the proverbs are meaningful in describing aspects of Yoruba life, while their metaphors and cultural understanding are the deep structure that gives more meaning at the semantic level.

These proverbs require a good understanding of their importance and relevance to an appropriate situation. Yoruba makes up its own linguistic rules and contextual meaning, and so Afolayan contextualizes these proverbs as a language that can only be understood or comprehended by living in and within the Yoruba world. These proverbs are woven into the linguistic structure of the Yoruba world that any attempt to separate it or transplant it loses the semantic symbolism, and when these proverbs are translated to other languages, their meanings and essence are lost.

Sometimes they are narrated as stories to children to give them a graphic illustration using animals and nature with anthropocentric abilities. For example, "Ẹni òjò pa tí Ṣàngó ò pa, kó máa dúpẹ́" literally means in English, "He who was drenched by the rain but not struck by the wrath of Ṣàngó should be thankful." Ṣàngó is the god of thunder and lightning in the Yoruba world, who punishes offenses by sending thunderbolts and lightning to the offender who may have committed a taboo or crime of stealing from a Ṣàngó adherent. Semiotically, the proverb translates to "Those who face trials should be grateful that they did not take his life."

Other Yoruba proverbs describe the order of Yoruba life; "Pátápátá làá f'ójú, kùmbọ̀kùmbọ̀ làá d'ẹ́tẹ̀, ojú àfọ̀ọ̀fọ́tán ìjà níí dá sí'lẹ̀" (Blindness should take away both eyes, leprosy should take away fingers and toes, half-blindness/-half-sight is a precursor to controversy),[71] which cautions that half-hearted work and effort can be dangerous or complicates things. This meaning is furthered semiotically enriched for Yoruba speakers by describing cultural values and illustrating that life is characterized by a fully lived life and efforts, without doing things in half-measures or starting a mission and not seeing it to completion. Another proverb that directly relates to the Yoruba language is "Àgbọ́ọ̀gbọ́tán ègùn, ìjà níí dá sílẹ̀," or "A language half-mastered is only good enough to get one in trouble."[72]

The Yoruba people are known to speak metaphorically and indirectly when delicate situations arise. The prosaic sentence, "The water spilled, but the calabash did not break," is a metaphorical way of tactfully referring to the death of a baby during childbirth in which the life of the mother is spared. It is not uncommon for the Yoruba to talk in this manner as they read the situation of things and determine the suitable linguistic tool or medium to express their thoughts. This skill is required in the Yoruba society, which carefully employs proverbs and idioms as effective and suitable means of communicating in a wide range of situations.

Yoruba folktales (àlọ́)

In the Yoruba society, there are about two types of folktales (àlọ́): àlọ́ àpamọ́ and àlọ́ àpagbè. The former is known as the English variant riddle and is also played as a game meant to stimulate children to think deeply and use their intellect to answer these riddles, with an elder supplying the answer when the children do not know it. Àlọ́ àpamọ̀ has no strict system of performance like that of the àpagbè, and it is usually introduced before the àpagbè, which encodes cultural lessons, values, and mores. Alo apamo is initiated like a question-and-answer forum between these children and may be supervised by an adult. This game variant seeks to initiate the children into Yoruba cosmology and may sometimes contain trivial issues such as flora and fauna of the immediate environment. Essentially, àlọ́ àpamọ̀ is not as complex in structure and context as the àlọ́ àpagbè. It can be introduced before and/or after the àlọ́ àpagbè, usually to break a tense moment or as an anticlimax to the main narrative.

Alternatively, the àlọ́ àpagbè is a lengthy tale with a formal performance system. It has an opening coda where the narrator or performer of the folktale starts with a call and response ("Àlọ́ oo: Àlọ̀") with the audience, which can be repeated about three times. When the performer—an adult woman or man—begins the performance of the folktale, the audience of young children also doubles as performers by singing along with the performer when he or she initiates a song in the folktale. Usually at the end, the performer asks the children questions about the tale and the lessons they learned, a critically important part of the performance where morals and mores of the Yoruba society are imparted and reinforced.

Folktales are features of traditional education, told to children to propagate culture, traditions, and values into the future. These tales are testimonies of a vast culture and the existence of large bodies of literature in the Yoruba preliterate world. They are sometimes elaborate, with some having the structure of epic poetry, and they have moral lessons at the core of the narratives to impress on the youth and children the values of their community. As they are easily absorbed and understood, folktales were particularly important to elders trying to impact lessons and morals to young children. Afolayan elaborates on this form of performance, which his father illustrated in the tale of the turtle and the two eagles:

Two eagles, husband and wife, were flying together, way beyond the Niger, down towards the sea. They took a break on the way under a shady tree. While snacking on bugs and pecking on palm kernels, a turtle saw them and asked where they were headed. They told him they were running away seeking respite from the drought in the desert of the north and flying south to the blue sea. They promised to be back during the rainy season when the drought would have tapered. The turtle urged them to please take him along since he too would die of the drought if he stayed in the hot desert through the season. The eagles sympathized with their new friend but said they had no way of carrying him along since he would be too heavy to mount on the back of one of them. The turtle then came up with a clever idea. He pointed to a long, strong stick, asked if each one of the eagles would hold it at each end with their claws and that he would bite into the stick in the middle; that way, they would be able to carry him along without much trouble. The eagles went along with the turtle's suggestion and actually thought it was a good idea. The eagles warned the turtle that he had to keep quiet throughout the journey so he would not lose grip of the stick and fall to his death. "Regardless of what you hear, see, or think, you must not say a word," they warned. "I promise," he said. And so the eagles started the journey with their new cargo, the turtle. They flew past the blue indigo river and flew past the red river of blood. They went beyond the land of Tapa and crossed the green woods of Gbari. As they reached the field of yams of Ibariba land, a farmer looked up and saw them. He spoke with wonderment, 'Oh my God who taught these ordinary animals to be this wise.' The turtle forgot the warning of the eagles and his oath of silence. He opened his mouth and yelled arrogantly, 'Emi Kan Yii Naa Ni!' (It's me and me alone!). By the time he remembered his promise, his mouth had opened wide and he had lost his grip. He felt miserably down and hit the ground terribly hard, shattering its shell. It would take all the potters and bricklayers of this world to reconstruct the turtle and that is why his body ever remained bumpy and patchy."

When Baba Agba finished this folktale, I knew what he would say next, and I was right. He looked at me and asked, "What is the lesson?" I quickly answered him, not to take glory for what one's group has done.[73]

This and many more tales are an indispensable method of doling out wisdom to children, and folktales remain one of the significant oral literature forms of the preliterate Yoruba people. These tales are passed from one generation to another through word of mouth and engagement with the children. Asking them to identify the morals of the stories serves as important life lessons and helps the children determine for themselves the merit or the demerit of the actions of the animate or inanimate characters.

Traditional sports and games

Before the advent of modern games and sports activities, the Yoruba people also had their form of games and sports for children, youth, and adults. Bojúbojú, the Yoruba form of hide and seek, is often played by children for entertainment, but many—such as brainteasers, riddles, narrative folktales, and silly jokes—have an oral component that helps children understand the linguistic complexity of the Yoruba world while still being entertaining. Brainteasers are meant to activate and initiate young minds into thinking and employing their brains to seek knowledge.

Following the Yoruba belief in the appropriateness of time and seasons, some of these games take place under a prescriptive schedule. Some are practiced during the daytime, while others are done in the moonlight. Ayò ọlọ́pọ́n is an example of a game played by adults and youth in the evening for relaxation and entertainment after the day's work. Dasylva avers that among Yoruba children, tongue twisters and other manners of playing with words can lead from a casual contest between two or more children to a more elaborate setting, usually in the evening. Other games include "ẹkùn mẹran" or "bojúbojú," ta ló wà nínú ọgbà náà (hide and seek), òkòtó, ten-ten, and idì or ijàkadì (wrestling) among boys.[74]

The games reflect the immersion in the cultural ethos of the community. Tongue twisters indicate the knowledge of words and usage; ayò ọlọ́pọ́n reflects the wisdom and calculated foresight of the people; the hide-and-seek game intimate the players with safe spots for hiding in the events of war or ethnic conflict; bojúbojú is a game that reflects the secrecy of the Orò cult, which admonishes people to take cover to avoid being caught peeping the secret cult. Besides the entertainment value of these games, morals, cultural values, and traditional education are assembled for the people to digest and learn from.

In addition, these games are based on location and time because some of these games, like idì or ijàkadì, are organized during festivals or community events. The games organized during the festivals are usually performed during these occasions and not as everyday sports for entertainment because of their sensitive nature. Ijàkadì (wrestling match) requires strength, valor, skills, and training, and it possesses values that are encouraged and rewarded after the tournament.

According to Layo Ogunlola, during celebrations such as the Edi festival in Ile-Ife, boys and men of the same age group compete in local wrestling.[75] This sport is done to encourage the spirit of perseverance, bravery, and sportsmanship. The game has a sociopolitical aspect of raising strong men who may be used as security agents or warriors in the community.

Ìjálá ọdẹ: The hunters' poetry

Hunting in the Yoruba society is done by skilled professionals and is associated with a host of special traditions, such as the Ìjálá ọdẹ that initiate new hunters, celebrate their exploits, and offer worship and thanks before and after the hunt. The professional cult aspect of hunting in the Yoruba world is male-oriented, and it is structured to keep the members. They perform dirges at the funeral of a dead member of the cult as one of the sociocultural functions of the guild. This cult orders the system of hunting expeditions and activities within the community as the cultural institution organized to regulate events and activities of hunters, such as the training and initiation of new members. The cult also acts as a security-cum-protection body for the members and sets rules and regulations binding on all members. The members of this cult include blacksmiths, warriors, and goldsmiths, with Ogun as their patron deity.

For a man to become a hunter, he must be initiated into the cult and profession by going through a serious and strict initiation ritual, and before he is allowed to shoot with a bow and arrow or a gun.[76] He must pass some tests during his training, including the ability to avoid shooting upwards or parallel at a game. The skill is particularly important to avoid accidentally killing or hitting people who may be within the shooting range or on a tree. He must recognize all the wood and farm ingredients necessary for making gunpowder— the charcoal of one of two very common types of wood to be mixed with some fine rocks and a well-processed and viscous cassava starch[77] and the methods to make the most lethal and effective pellets, then demonstrate that he can make both unaided. The young hunter then must go solo hunting with a borrowed gun after he has successfully completed the initial test. His prey will be a red monkey, a unique animal known for its mastery of the jungle and its ability to evade capture by hunters. If he was successful, he would be given his own gun and officially permitted to go hunting.

Ìjálá poetry, performed by hunters during festivals, social and ritual ceremonies, and hunters' gatherings, valorizes their exploits, calls for the bravery and courage required to succeed and praises Ogun, the god of iron, whom most Yoruba hunters and warriors worship.[78] The format is simple and works so that each hunter may give an individual performance, and/or there can be a collective one where all the hunters participate as performers and as the audience. Before the Ìjálá is performed, the hunters all dance in formation, usually in a circle, to the accompaniment of drums and gongs. Guns, usually loaded with only gunpowder, are fired regularly for effect.

After a few minutes of general singing, one of the hunters steps into the middle of the circle to begin his performance. He could choose to relate the exploits of his lineage as hunters of renown; chant about folklore that binds the hunters together into a guild, such as the shared importance of Ogun; or praise the strength, bravery, and courage of the hunters in general for their social role of providing security and maintaining peace in the community. Since all the other hunters are familiar with the chants, they might join in and conclude the performance with another song before another hunter chooses to step into the ring or is nominated to go by the previous performer.

After successful hunting, it is required that a hunter shows appreciation by sticking some part of the catch on a ring made from some plant leaves placed at a junction. These sacrifices to the gods after a successful kill are made to pray for future success in hunting.[79] The junction may be where the game was captured or the intersection between two or three paths. The ring made from plants is a symbol that alerts other hunters about the successful hunt. Finally, the game is secured in the hunter's bag, which is part of the hunter's costume. If the hunting expedition involves other hunters, the game is distributed and shared amongst them, with the one who delivered the killing blow or bullet taking one-quarter of the game.

The Alárìnjó and theatrical presentation

The Yoruba world had its own significant and complex theatrical inventions and performances before the invention of the Western form of drama and theater. The Alárìnjó, or itinerant performers, are a group of entertainers and actors that go to various events and gatherings to dance and perform magical tricks in different towns. These masters of illusions turned dance into a quintessential visual type of Yoruba theater. The Alárìnjó troupe is a traditional group that uses traditional entertainment instruments such as the bàtá drum but demonstrates complicated performances that include acrobats, dance, and illusions, whetting appreciation for drama and entertainment within the Yoruba world.

The Natural World

This last section of this chapter will explore the natural phenomena of the Yoruba people, as Afolayan explores in his memoir. The appraisal and discussion of the spatial and temporal characteristics of the Yoruba span the context of the memoir *Fate of Our Mothers*. The sociocultural significance and ambiance of this phenomenon to the people will be briefly explored to justify the inclusion in the text and chapter.

Orin àrùnjẹ́: The herb with àṣẹ and cleaning functions

Long before the introduction of Western education, the Yoruba people had a dental hygiene regimen and a knowledge system that added deeper importance to the regimen beyond simply cleaning the teeth and mouth. This system instilled àṣẹ, with its spiritual potency and stamp of authority, on the mouth. In the preliterate Yoruba society, branches from trees and plants are used as brushes for cleaning the mouth. These branches are believed to possess special antibodies for medicinal and traditional purposes that cleanse the mouth and clean a user's words.[80] The orin àrùnjẹ́ is a special type of branch believed to possess the magical power of àṣẹ, the sacred utterance, the power inherent in the word.[81] This particular herbal plant is commonly grown in the Southwestern part of Nigeria, where it is usually found in the forest and savannah, as shown by Olawumi et al. in their study of plants used for oral hygiene.[82]

From their surveys in states like Oyo and Ogun in Southwestern Nigeria, this herbal plant is one of the many plants for oral hygiene and treatment of other ailments. Besides the dental functions of the orin àrùnjẹ́, the branch transforms the mouth into a source of authority that makes what has been uttered irrevocable. As such, only the elders are the ones who use these tree branches to clean their mouths. The herbal plant also has a significant spiritual function to cleanse the words and utterances of adults who tap into this form of Yoruba herbal medicine. The use of this herb is purely voluntary in the Yoruba world, as misuse may attract dire effects. This stem/branch can be used by both the young and old for oral hygiene and is sold by people who sell different kinds of herbs and plants.

The sun as a time signifier

As Fayemi Kazeem observes,[83] the traditional view of time in the Yoruba world is complex and nearly impossible to grasp without understanding the full meaning of the keywords used to express this unique conception of time in Yoruba culture. The Yoruba words àkókò, ìgbà, and àsìkò often refer to time without distinction. Each of these, àkókò, ìgbà, and àsìkò can be distinguished as time around an occurrence/event, epoch or era, and season respectively, and synonymous with time; however, the context of their usage differs in the length and scope of time. Time in the Yoruba world is entrenched within their belief and philosophy regarding the cosmic organization and separation of day, night, season, era, and events of the world as they experience them and are encoded in idioms, proverbs, myths, and legends. It is the complex calculations and framing for different parts of the day and experiences at different periods in the Yoruba world. Fayemi agrees by saying the Yoruba "idea of time is strongly rooted in their communal worldview, which is transmitted through proverbs and folklore."[84]

In the Yoruba proverbial notion of time, "ìgbà ò lọ bí òréré, ayé ò lọ bí ọ̀pá ìbọn" (time does not span without limit, life is not linear like the barrel of a gun) is relative to events and experiences of the people that time are segmented into periods and epochs. Time is the frame that captures events. Fayemi further posits that environmentally, time is measured either "through celestial-cosmic cycle, the terrestrial-ecological cycle, or both. While the celestial-cosmic time mechanism is used in chronicling the day and the months, the terrestrial-ecological time consists of measuring smaller units of time, such as minutes and hours of the day." [85] In the Yoruba tradition, "the day is based on the observable cosmological facts of the sun and the moon. The sun is used in guessing the time in the mid-morning and afternoon by interpreting the length and shape of shadows."[86] In the evening and at midnight, the moon is also important in identifying the time. Other times of the day can be determined by the terrestrial-ecological element of time, which agents are used in telling time.

Furthermore, Fayemi explains that in the absence of an ecological agent, other phenomena, such as the crowing of the cock and sounds from the dove and other animals, are employed to tell what time it is. The crowing of the cock may signify dawn, while the roosting of the birds may indicate dusk. Characteristically, according to Kazeem, there are about seven time frames/periods in the Yoruba world: òru (midnight), àfèmójúmó (dawn), òwúrò (morning), iyálèta (noon), òsán (afternoon), iròlé (sunset), and alé (early night).[87] So the sun's movement becomes a signifier for both time calculations well before Western education and how the sun is represented within the Yoruba world.

The sun represents more than the time and season for the Yoruba, ordering days by signifying what should be done at a particular time.[88] Oòrùn ojó-kanrí, a time frame when the sun shines brightest, was one of the times ingeniously calculated by the Yoruba from the sun's position, estimated to be noon. The ray or heat from the sun is used to name this timeframe for the Yoruba people to indicate the time to either rest or avoid the scorch from the sunlight. At this time, farmers in the Yoruba world either choose to rest or take a break to snack on fruits or lunch. Oórún ojó-kanrí alerts them to take a break from the day's work or hasten their work/activities to avoid scorching from the sun.

Other objects in the sky, such as the moon and the galaxies, were also important in the Yoruba world. As Baba Agba told Afolayan, the falling of the stars was symbolic of somebody's death, and the size of the star would reveal how important the deceased was on the social scale of life.[89] The sun, moon, and stars unveil the glorious future of humanity as they signify the fate of individual persons in Yoruba cosmology. The cosmic is observed to determine the future turn of events and what is expected. They read the clouds as if their lives depended on them. If the clouds were deep blue and came from the east side of the village, every villager brought out their earthen vessels and pots of all sizes and left them outside their homes.[90] The observation of the atmosphere, moon, sun, and stars as a signification of time, activities to be carried out, and events to unfold is installed in the varied belief system of the Yoruba about the sun, time, and cosmic organization.

Afolayan hints that this is a common activity engaged by the villagers to gaze at the clouds and determine whether it would rain or not. Before the advent of science and technology, the Yoruba could learn about the weather forecast for the day, and it was a reliably accurate prediction based on the knowledge gained from long years of studying the clouds and observing the signs of nature. Clouds coming from the direction of oríta, the junction of the road, or from the west side of the village were often called apòrè, the harbinger of friends. They neither brought rain nor winds but on the second day of their formation, villagers believed there would be plenty of visitors from the other side of the river.[91]

Clouds were not just ordinary space to the Yoruba people, as captured by Afolayan in *Fate of Our Mothers*. They could be read and understood as bringing peace and tranquility or danger and turbulence. Afolayan observes that villagers loved yellowish-red clouds. They announced to the villagers that there would be seven days of dry and warm breezes. They were often accompanied by good and restful nights of sleep. Circling and restless clouds, no matter the direction they came from, were bad.[92] Times and seasons are observed by the careful watching and reading of the clouds, sun, moon, and stars in the Yoruba world.

Flora and fauna

These are some of the plants and animals in the Yoruba world and what they represent to them. These animals have significant meanings and attachments to the Yoruba people. Some of these animals have a metaphysical connotation, as some serve as symbols of deities and ancestral worship. In line with this, Ajibade notes that "the devotees of the deity Oya consider it a taboo to eat the buffalo. This deity is believed to be the mother of all buffalos."[93] The belief that some animals may host human spirits at the metaphysical level reveals the relationship between the Yoruba and these animals. Ọká is one of the most dangerous reptiles known to the Yoruba people, and its bite is only cured by amputating the bitten finger. Awọn, the alligator, and crocodiles, elegigun are also part of the reptilian family kept by some families in some parts of the Yoruba world and are notable for the danger they pose to humans in the village.

The Delesolu Compound in Oje, Ibadan, Oyo State, is known to be a keeper of legendary crocodiles, as opined by Ayoola.[94] These animals may be dangerous to people who do not have a familial or spiritual connection to them. Ordinarily, these wild animals are dangerous to anybody, but when connected as a symbol of ancestral worship to a family, the worshippers and members of that family are insulated from harm. This is supported by Ayoola as he states that snakes of any kind as livestock are not something anyone in Yoruba society would want to keep. However, the Ologunun (the devotees of Ogun, Yoruba god of iron, smithy, and war) among the Yoruba are considered able because they are the ones who are notorious for keeping snakes as domestic reptiles.[95]

Despite their hazards, these animals also serve as food for the people as they can be caught by hunters. There are other nonviolent animals like the akọ aláǹgbá, the male agama lizard that can be found everywhere in the house, and other reptiles such as ọmọ onílé (wall gecko) and aláñgbàdódò (monitor lizard) are also known to be cunning and believed to suck blood by merely looking at their prey. Ẹsinṣin, the housefly, is one of the most hated insects because of the havoc they can cause. Some of the Yoruba proverbs and idioms convey the dislike or abhorrence for these insects.

Ajibade opines that "among the Yoruba, there are many taboos and myths about different types of animals, representing relationships that exist between the people and the animals and the Yoruba philosophy about these particular animals."[96] The injunction to always cover one's food to avoid being affected by diseases through contact is noticeable. The Yoruba people weave nuggets to express their disdain for flies because they perch on trash, wounds, manure, and feces.

Afolayan describes trees such as the Araba, common in the Yoruba forests and bushes, and has a metaphorical meaning to the Yoruba as it represents strength and might.[97] The araba tree is one of the strongest and most enormous trees in the Yoruba rainforest, and it requires a lot of strength for it to be felled and used for different purposes. The description of the vegetation available in the Yoruba world is vast, and so, in the memoir, the author trickles it down to the common ones and then moves on to intimate the reader with the commonest occupation of the Yoruba people.

Agriculture is the main occupation of the Yoruba people to supplement the crops grown for subsistence farming, and food crops, such as cassava, are cultivated about three times a year through the stalk. And then, when it matures, it passes through a process of harvest, processing from raw crops to finished products such as garri, fufu, and amala. The cassava goes through the process of harvest from the farm to when it is peeled, cut into bits for fermentation, or ground into pulp or pellets, as the case may be. Garri is made from cassava as flakes that can be taken with cold water or made into solid form as èbà and taken with soup. Fufu is also derived from soaked and cooked cassava, and amala (èlùbọ́ láfún) is a derivative of the dry cassava pellets. The planting, harvesting, and processing of these crops may be carried out by both men and women; however, women are notable for turning this crop into edible food.

This flora and fauna make up and populate the natural habitat of the Yoruba world and, therefore, also fit into its culture. The devotion to the animals and their importance (or lack of same) inspires the rendition and composition of songs and poems. The notable ones are praised for their distinct attributes and characteristics, importance to people, and significance to humanity and nature. Ajibade states that the Yoruba create oríkì for their animals. One example is the antelope, which they call Ẹtu. The praise poem goes thus:

> Etu obeje
> Elese osun
> Aritete-gbon-on-ni
> Eranko tii le tiroo
> Eranko tii wa gonbo
> [Antelope Obeje
> The one who has legs painted red with camwood
> The one who has thighs with which to touch the dew
> The animal that put on eyelashes
> The animal that wears gọ̀nbọ̀ facial marks.][98]

The poem about the antelope eulogizes and describes the animal's appearance and attitude, as this particular animal has marks similar to the gọ̀nbọ̀ facial marks of the Yoruba people. The praise poem shows the relationship and interaction of the Yoruba with these animals.

Conclusion

In *Fate of Our Mothers*, Afolayan distills the Yoruba's sociopolitical, cultural, economic, and religious echoes. This chapter is extended to establish the meaning of the Yoruba world's traditions, space, narratives, textual and oral literature, philosophy, belief, and knowledge systems analyzing the tones, hues, and ambiances of the metaphysical, linguistic, sociolinguistic, and semantic features. The work engages the belief in the oracular Orí and àdáyébá, as the personal witness to one's choice of destiny or fate before Olodumare. Orí is the source of a person's fortune or misfortune as it is the driving force of the choices he makes on earth. The belief in predestination is closely attached to the belief in àdáyébá; predestination is a foreshadowing of the destiny and fate of a man in the psychosocial development of his future. The Yoruba world is strongly stabilized and sustained by these beliefs.

In exploring the language and the linguistic elements such as idioms, dictums, proverbs, and aphorisms of the Yoruba, it is clear that they are the beauty of the Yoruba language and people. Omofoyewa avers that since "proverbs are considered to be traditional, and originate from the observation of natural phenomena and human relations, old people are regarded as the repository of proverbs, a product of traditional intelligence, logic, and verbal wit."[99] From the oral tradition and folklore, such as folktales and proverbs, Afolayan's explorations reveal the dynamics of the Yoruba language and the wisdom inherent in the Yoruba world. The Yoruba world is highly infused with linguistic and oratorical skills to captivate and address any issue that seems to require tact, wisdom, and understanding.

In conclusion, Afolayan's *Fate of Our Mothers* presents a bundle of texts, spaces, and narratives of the Yoruba sociocultural, sociopolitical, economic, and religious knowledge. The memoir explores, narrates, and captures the different angles of the Yoruba people's cultural materials and traditional nuances installed in his education and experience as a Yoruba. The chapter posits that *Fate of Our Mothers* is a graphic illustration and expression of the Yoruba worldview, traditions, society, and religion bound intricately with the author's experience as a guiding light to the ebullient resources in the Yoruba world. The appraisal of this cultural wealth in the text is a testament to the ingenuity of the people represented by the author. The portrayal and sustenance of the Yoruba world in literature, cultural studies, archaeology, and social sciences will keep the root watered and flourishing.

Notes

1 Akinlabi Akinbiyi and Harrison Adeniyi, "The Language and Its Dialects," in *Culture and Customs of the Yoruba*, eds. Toyin Falola and Akintunde Akinyemi (Austin: Pan-African University Press, 2017), 31.

2 Michael O. Afolayan, *Fate of Our Mothers* (Austin: Pan-African University Press, 2015), 7.

3 Segun Ogungbemi, "Traditional Religious Belief System," in *Culture and Customs of the Yoruba*, eds. Toyin Falola and Akintunde Akinyemi (Austin: Pan-African University Press, 2017), 311.

4 Afolayan, *Fate of Our Mothers*, 39.

5 Afolayan, *Fate of Our Mothers*, 67–68.

6 Sola Adeyemi, "Performing Arts," in *Culture and Customs of the Yoruba*, eds. Toyin Falola and Akintunde Akinyemi (Austin: Pan-African University Press, 2017), 253.

7 Afolayan, *Fate of Our Mothers*, 9.

8 Christopher Omolewu Olatubosun, "Taboo," in *Culture and Customs of the Yoruba*, eds. Toyin Falola and Akintunde Akinyemi (Austin: Pan-African University Press, 2017), 445.

9 Olatubosun, "Taboo," 446.

10 Afolayan, *Fate of Our Mothers*, 13.

11 Afolayan, *Fate of Our Mothers*, 15.

12 Afolayan, *Fate of Our Mothers*, 63.

13 Afolayan, *Fate of Our Mothers*, 102.

14 Afolayan, *Fate of Our Mothers*, 102–103.

15 Mobolaji Oyebisi Ajibade, "Death, Mourning, Burial, and Funeral," in *Culture and Customs of the Yoruba*, eds. Toyin Falola and Akintunde Akinyemi (Austin: Pan-African University Press, 2017), 355.

16 Olusegun Oladosu, "Yoruba Indigenous Drums: An Aesthetic Symbol in Ecological Ritual of the Yoruba People," *European Scientific Journal* 11, no. 5 (2015): 216.

17 Olawole Famule, "Masks, Masque, and Masquerades," in *Culture and Customs of the Yoruba*, eds. Toyin Falola and Akintunde Akinyemi (Austin: Pan-African University Press, 2017), 392.

18 Famule, "Masks, Masque, and Masquerades," 395.

19 Segun, "Traditional Religious Belief System," 312.

20 Segun, "Traditional Religious Belief System," 151.

21 Segun, "Traditional Religious Belief System," 152.

22 Segun, "Traditional Religious Belief System," 292.

23 Segun, "Traditional Religious Belief System," 312.

24 Segun, "Traditional Religious Belief System," 313.

25 George Olusola Ajibade, "Cults, Secret Societies, and Fraternities," in *Culture and Customs of the Yoruba*, 787.

26 Okunola Rashidi Akanji and Ojo Matthias Olufemi Dada, "Oro Cult: The Traditional Ways of Political Administration, Judiciary System and Religious Cleansing among the Pre-Colonial Yoruba Natives of Nigeria," *The Journal of International Social Research* 5, no. 23 (2012): 20.

27 Akanji and Dada, "Oro Cult."

28 Afolayan, *Fate of Our Mothers*, 194.

29 Afolayan, *Fate of Our Mothers*.

30 Akanji and Dada, "Oro Cult," 21.

31 Akanji and Dada, "Oro Cult," 22.

32 Segun Soetan, "Charms and Amulets," in *Culture and Customs of the Yoruba*, eds. Toyin Falola and Akintunde Akinyemi (Austin: Pan-African University Press, 2017), 229.

33 Soetan, "Charms and Amulets."

34 Soetan, "Charms and Amulets," 229.

35 Soetan, "Charms and Amulets," 228.

36 Soetan, "Charms and Amulets," 173.

37 Afolayan, *Fate of Our Mothers*, 38.

38 Pamela J. Olubunmi Smith, " 'E ku,' Yoruba Greetings—A Protocol," in *Culture and Customs of the Yoruba*, eds. Toyin Falola and Akintunde Akinyemi (Austin: Pan-African University Press, 2017), 72.

39 Smith, "E ku," 75–76.

40 Smith, "E ku," 8.

41 Smith, "E ku," 8.

42 Enoch Olujide Gbadegesin, "Marriage and Marital Systems," in *Culture and Customs of the Yoruba*, eds. Toyin Falola and Akintunde Akinyemi (Austin: Pan-African University Press, 2017), 723.

43 Gbadegesin, "Marriage and Martial Systems," 156.

44 Gbadegesin, "Marriage and Martial Systems," 156.

45 Gbadegesin, "Marriage and Martial Systems," 87.

46 Gbadegesin, "Marriage and Martial Systems," 89.

47 Gbadegesin, "Marriage and Martial Systems," 91.

48 Gbadegesin, "Marriage and Martial Systems," 125.

49 Gbadegesin, "Marriage and Martial Systems," 19.

50 Harrison Adeniyi, "Naming, Names, and Praise Names," in *Culture and Customs of the Yoruba*, eds. Toyin Falola and Akintunde Akinyemi (Austin: Pan-African University Press, 2017), 85.

51 Adeniyi, "Naming, Names, and Praise Names," 88.

52 Adeniyi, "Naming, Names, and Praise Names," 88.

53 Adeniyi, "Naming, Names, and Praise Names," 89.

54 Afolayan, *Fate of Our Mothers*, 29.

55 Afolayan, *Fate of Our Mothers*, 30.

56 Afolayan, *Fate of Our Mothers*, 126.

57 Afolayan, *Fate of Our Mothers*, 127.
58 Afolayan, *Fate of Our Mothers*, 87–88.
59 Afolayan, *Fate of Our Mothers*, 127.
60 Afolayan, *Fate of Our Mothers*, 78.
61 Afolayan, *Fate of Our Mothers*, 75.
62 Afolayan, *Fate of Our Mothers*, 154.
63 Afolayan, *Fate of Our Mothers*, 31.
64 Afolayan, *Fate of Our Mothers*, 246.
65 Afolayan, *Fate of Our Mothers*, 248.
66 Tosin Akinjobi-Babatunde, "Pawning, Pawnship, and Slavery," in *Culture and Customs of the Yoruba*, eds. Toyin Falola and Akintunde Akinyemi (Austin: Pan-African University Press, 2017), 572.
67 Akinjobi-Babatunde, "Pawning, Pawnship, and Slavery," 253.
68 Afolayan, *Fate of Our Mothers*, 7.
69 Afolayan, *Fate of Our Mothers*, 8.
70 Kazeem Adebayo Omofoyewa, "Idioms, Proverbs, and Dictums," in *Culture and Customs of the Yoruba*, eds. Toyin Falola and Akintunde Akinyemi (Austin: Pan-African University Press, 2017), 102.
71 Omofoyewa, "Idioms, Proverbs, and Dictums," 27.
72 Omofoyewa, "Idioms, Proverbs, and Dictums," 27.
73 Afolayan, *Fate of Our Mothers*, 48–49.
74 Ademola Dasylva, "Folklore, Oral Traditions, and Oral Literature," in *Culture and Customs of the Yoruba*, eds. Toyin Falola and Akintunde Akinyemi (Austin: Pan-African University Press, 2017), 145.
75 Layo Ogunlola, "Sports, Games, Recreation, and Leisure," in *Culture and Customs of the Yoruba*, eds. Toyin Falola and Akintunde Akinyemi (Austin: Pan-African University Press, 2017), 751.
76 Afolayan, *Fate of Our Mothers*, 135.
77 Afolayan, *Fate of Our Mothers*, 135–136.
78 Adeyemi, "Performing Arts," in *Culture and Customs of the Yoruba*, 253.
79 Afolayan, *Fate of Our Mothers*, 142.
80 Afolayan, *Fate of Our Mothers*, 13.
81 Afolayan, *Fate of Our Mothers*.
82 A. T. Olawumi et al., "Inventory of Plants Utilized in Oral Hygiene in South-Western Nigeria," *African Journal of Agriculture Technology and Environment* 6, no. 1 (2017): 92.
83 Fayemi Ademola Kazeem, "Time in Yorùbá Culture," *Al-Hikmat* 36 (2016): 963.
84 Kazeem, "Time in Yorùbá Culture," 964.
85 Kazeem, "Time in Yorùbá Culture," 966.
86 Kazeem, "Time in Yorùbá Culture," 966.
87 Kazeem, "Time in Yorùbá Culture," 967.
88 Afolayan, *Fate of Our Mothers*, 14.
89 Afolayan, *Fate of Our Mothers*, 15.
90 Afolayan, *Fate of Our Mothers*, 16.
91 Afolayan, *Fate of Our Mothers*, 17.
92 Afolayan, *Fate of Our Mothers*.
93 George Olusola Ajibade, "Animals in the Traditional Worldview of the Yoruba," *Folklore: Electronic Journal of Folklore* 30 (2005): 157.
94 Ayoola Gabriel, "Livestock: Domestication and Species," in *Culture and Customs of the Yoruba*, eds. Toyin Falola and Akintunde Akinyemi (Austin: Pan-African University Press, 2017), 548.
95 Gabriel, "Livestock," in Culture and Customs of the Yoruba, 546.
96 Ajibade, "Animals in the Traditional Worldview of the Yoruba," 156.
97 Ajibade, "Animals in the Traditional Worldview of the Yoruba."
98 Ajibade, "Animals in the Traditional Worldview of the Yoruba," 161.
99 Omofoyewa, "Idioms, Proverbs, and Dictums," 105.

Chapter Six

THE INDELIBILITY OF IGBO TRADITION (HOME) IN KALU OGBAA'S *CARRYING MY FATHER'S TORCH*

Introduction

African memoirists in the diaspora are commonly known for their nostalgic evaluation of home and the many lessons and representations that come with it. This whole body of work is an essential compilation of memoirs of authors with African origins, as what has been established in previous chapters is that African memoirs are essentially and existentially different from memoirs of authors from other parts of the world. African memoirs of slave descendants are marked by forceful migration and hundreds of years of racial discrimination, social subjugation, psychological traumas, and related plights of Africans forcefully taken into the diaspora.

However, memoirs of authors who migrated out of their volition, political exile, or self-styled exile and economic reasons are different from the memoirs of generations of slave descendants. They are media explicating precarious situations for which they left their homeland: the cultural differences between their homelands and abroad, and the indelibility of their youthful days in their home countries. Despite these differences, what is common to these variants of memoirs is that they reflect on human conditions, the continuous juxtaposition of cultural differences, and the double consciousness of being of African descent yet living in a foreign land that is sociopolitically different from home. There is also the idea of home as a physical space of structures, experiences, and history, while there is also the notion of home in relation to skin color, acclimatization to their new homes (abroad), and the constant reminder to syncretize being Black and being a minority in a new country.

The foregoing is a reiteration of the characteristics of many African memoirs. The aforementioned explications are not entirely capable of characterizing the nature of African diaspora memoirs. However, they capture a big section of what African memoirs are like. What cannot be erased from the motives of Africans in diaspora writing memoirs is that they write with the intention of getting their stories told. In African history, whether as erroneously told by Europeans or as told by Africans themselves, there is a fissure created by the unavailability of a scientific mode of writing. Most of what Africans later wrote were transcribed from oral sources, arts, and motifs. Therefore, it has always caused a debate about authenticity. Without writing, one could argue that the slave trade and inhumane treatment of Africans at home and in the diaspora would be debated and subjected to scrutiny as though these things never happened. So, for Africans in the diaspora, there is intentionality in writing; there is the consciousness that by preserving their memories, struggles, and experiences in text, these struggles and experiences can be dubitable. On the same note, there is also the intentionality about getting their stories to a huge number of people.

Succinctly, African diaspora memoirs are set out for many purposes that make them unique. African memoirs are determined by regional peculiarities. Contrary to the notion of a homogenous Africa, African memoirs show that, though there is some common ground between authors' cultural backgrounds, there are still particularities in memoirs that are defined by regions of the authors. Kalu Ogbaa's *Carrying My Father's Torch* exemplifies all the aforementioned characteristics. Ogbaa's memoir captures his childhood and youthful days in Nigeria and his travails abroad. According to the author:

> I wanted to write my story while I could still recall with clarity all the important incidents in my life. Memory, as we all know, is a tricky thing; we lose some of it as we grow older. The more the incidents taking place in our lives become distant, the more our memories of them become cloudier. That was why I could no longer defer carrying out this book project, which has been on my mind for a long time.[1]

One indubitable aspect of memoirs is memory. The essence of memoirs is the recollection of memories. As Ogbaa lucidly explicates, memories are only useful when one can still remember them. He further states:

> Little did I know then that, like the soldier coming home after a long tour of duty abroad, I was going to strip myself naked so as to see the scars and wounds of my life struggles all over my metaphoric body. Writing would remind me of the pains I suffered and endured as each individual incident occurred—incidents of traumatic accidents, family struggles with poverty, and deaths. Nevertheless, I had to confront and tell of them if my story was to be truthful.[2]

As earlier suggested, the author corroborates the claim that one of the essential functions of memoirs is for readers and the world to know the truth about the stories of a writer, politician, academia, and so on.

Ogbaa's memoir is a recollection of his memories influenced by his Igbo background. His memoir demonstrates the indelible marks that sociocultural experiences leave on lives. Like any other Igbo who lived during the Nigerian Civil War, Ogbaa's life and that of his people were greatly defined by the events leading to the war, the effect of the war, and the postwar era. This is where regional peculiarities to memoirs— experiences and memories—come in. *Carrying My Father's Torch* is a metaphor for the impact Ogbaa's father had on him, but more significantly, the impact Igbo traditions had on his father, and these sociocultural realities are what Ogbaa inherited not just from his father but also from his people.

This chapter will critically examine the permanence of home in Ogbaa's life to exemplify the inability of Africans in the diaspora to forget home. Furthermore, there is often a celebration of motherhood in the African diaspora; however, Ogbaa evaluated fatherhood as much as he did with motherhood. Therefore, it is appropriate to explicate the nature of fatherhood that Ogbaa captured in his father. Also, there is a manner in which Africans in the diaspora, despite acclimatization to the new home, still adhere strictly to what has shaped their identities. In Ogbaa's case, Igbo history, customs, and traditions shaped his experiences and inherited behaviors that made him at some points and marred him at others.

This chapter will also carefully illustrate the communitarian notion of Igbo in contrast to the individualistic nature of existence in the West. In all of these, this chapter will argue that Ogbaa's life experiences are like wrestling matches, which is a common tradition among the Igbo of the eastern part of Nigeria. Wrestling is a part of the Igbo tradition that distinguishes a warrior and a man of strength. While Ogbaa's father was a renowned wrestler, Ogbaa's wrestling matches were with life and living. Summarily, this chapter aims to put into perspective the cultural, historical, and religious influences on Ogbaa and, most significantly, how all of these, in addition to the devastation and segregation of the Igbo, prepared Ogbaa for racial segregation in the United States. It is a chapter that emphasizes the inseparability of home and what it represents in the lives of Africans in the diaspora.

No Perfect Formula of Loving: The Impact of Fatherhood

The centrality of the memoir is built around the idea of fatherhood. Ogbaa's memoir would not have achieved its aim without the concept of fatherhood. Psychologically, it is believed that male children tend to love their mothers, and female children are attached to their fathers. Whatever the case may be, veneration for motherhood is evident in memoirs from Oladejo Afolayan, Cherno Njie, and Emmanuel Babatunde. In Babatunde's memoir, *Kelebogile—I Am Grateful: An African Journey through Celibate Priesthood to Married Life*, he analyzes the nature of motherhood and womanhood as seen in his mother and his wife. Consequently, he explicates that motherhood is the antithesis of witchcraft, thereby giving it an important role in the preservation of the history of a people and their continued existence.[3]

Ogbaa's sentiments are similar to Cherno Njie's in *Sweat Is Invisible in the Rain* and Oladejo Afolayan's *Fate of Our Mothers*. Succinctly, the former believes that women play complementary roles in the family and society,[4] while the latter also corroborates that motherhood is intrinsically linked to fatherhood. Afolayan clearly states, "I am convinced that in our family we cannot celebrate fatherhood without first venerating motherhood. Concealed behind the veil of our father's courage and convictions were the faces of our mothers."[5]

Afolayan's submission is an important entry point into discussing fatherhood as portrayed in Ogbaa's memoir. The reason is that the author has a close-knit affection for his father as much as he does for his mother. The memoir's title, *Carrying My Father's Torch*, does not jettison the notion of motherhood, nor does it relegate the bond between Ogbaa and his mother. As demonstrated by Ogbaa's mother, the essentiality of motherhood is scattered in the memoir, but to make a case of Ogbaa's explications of his mother's motherhood, it is pertinent to glean together instances that exemplify its pains and joys.

One of the many events in which Ogbaa explicates motherhood was an accident that Ogbaa had in his childhood. The author narrates:

One evening, however, while sleeping on my mother's bosom, I turned suddenly in her arms and slipped off the bed. My right leg landed in the log fire left smoldering to warm us during the cold harmattan nights. Despite Mother's quick reaction, picking me up from the floor near the hearth, and running to the neighbors for help, I sustained severe burns on my knee and thigh. Mother was beside herself with grief, crying "*Nna m ee, nwa m anwuale; nna m ee, nwa m anwuale; nna m ee, nwa m anwuale* [...] (Oh, my father! My baby is dead. Oh, my father! My baby is dead. Oh, my father! My baby is dead [...].)." All the while, she beat her chest, crawling and rolling on the ground until she passed out. When she came to, people had already taken me to a native healer, who assured her that I would survive the burns.[6]

The author's assessment of his mother's motherhood is best understood in the following excerpt:

Although she became sad and angry to the point of almost losing her joy of motherhood, I remained a joy to her in spite of my injuries. Thenceforward, my mother resolved never to let anything bad happen to me again.[7]

This event and many others are best characterized as the irony associated with the joys of motherhood. As a result, this particular event and the trials of Ogbaa's mother brought them together. The struggles with motherhood that Ogbaa's mother had made him call to question the relationship between his father and mother. In one instance, he reflects:

When Mother later told me the story of her losses at the hand of Father, I wondered how my father was unable to imagine the impact of what he was doing to my mother, and our family cohesion. Was he punishing her for a crime he suspected she secretly committed against him? If so, why couldn't he tell her directly about it? Mother, just as confused, said she never knew the reason. Consequently, she was often depressed, living in a state deep anguished brooding. And she appeared sadder than at any other time I had known her. So much so that I, too, became depressed, holding in a hatred for my father that was only suppressed by a deeper fear of his authority and stature. I had to love him unconditionally, and he took it for granted that all was well within his family. But not all was well.[8]

The excerpt above captures the attachment between Ogbaa and his mother and the somewhat harmony of opposites in his relationship with his father. Though the author carries his father's torch, their relationship is full of admiration dictated by fear, manliness, and stature. This is to say that despite the author's clear declaration of his father's impact on him, they are both good and bad. Furthermore, the impact of Mazi Stephen Ogbaa Ikpo, Ogbaa's father, is far greater than that of Ogonnaya Ogbaa Ikpo, Ogbaa's mother. As said earlier, this is not to relegate his mother's impact. In fact, the author explains:

In spite of what she went through, Mother learned to find contentment toward the end of her life. And her children, who always occupied a special place in her heart, count us blessed with such a sweet and kind-hearted mother. To this day, whenever I see her in photos or recall her in my memories, her spirit of compassion never ceases to amaze me. In fact, since her death in April 2004, whenever I meet those who knew my mother and closely interacted with her have continued to tell me what a wonderful, humble, and quiet human being she was. As her son, I gratefully cherished such eloquent and glowing testimonies about my mother who, even though she was orphaned early in life, and despite her tough struggles in life as well as the spousal abuse she experienced and endured from my father, ended her life's journey on such a contented note. I could not have asked for a better blessing from God who gave me the grace to experience her ever-abiding love and care all through the time she lived with me on earth. It is a love that I will always feel deeply in my heart until I cross the River to meet her in the world beyond, where we will never separate again.[9]

But evidently, the author's pattern of life is modeled after his father's teachings, figures, and actions. Four aspects of Mazi Stephen's life that greatly influenced Kalu Ogbaa are his wrestling prowess, his many roles in his community and church, his entangled relationship with Ogbaa's mother, and his sacrifices.

Wrestling is a metaphor in Ogbaa's memoir. It is pertinent for readers to know that wrestling is an essential part of Igbo culture well-represented in Igbo literature. The main character in Chinua Achebe's *Things Fall Apart*, Okonkwo, was known for his wrestling prowess. Ogbaa's father was also known for his wrestling skill. During wrestling contests, praises were always heaped on him. For young Ogbaa, he had no full grasp of why his father was revered and cherished among his clansmen. Ogbaa narrates:

I did not fully understand my father's delight watching those matches until I read Chinua Achebe's novel, *Things Fall Apart* (1958). My father's stories all came rushing back. And the more pages I read, the more the life of the novel's main character, Okonkwo Unoka, reminded me of another successful Igbo wrestler and farmer living in another rural Igbo community: Stephen Ogbaa Ikpo, my father. Reading about Okonkwo's life, including the wrestling matches he won, his involvement with Christian missionaries, his own clan's customs and beliefs that so paralleled our own Ihechiowa clan's traditional religion, customs, rituals, and ceremonies, I was struck by the sense of brotherhood shared by such honored men. I became conscious of my link to that brotherhood…[10]

Lucidly, Okonkwo from Achebe's *Things Fall Apart* and Mazi Stephen Ogbaa Ikpo in Ogbaa's memoir represent a common practice amongst the Igbo. With wrestling in both cases, the warriors bring honor and glory to their people. With this, they are revered in their community and given so many roles. Metaphorically, these wrestlers do not fight physically; for them, wrestling builds character so much so that these characteristics determine their conduct in everyday life. The sense of brotherhood among the wrestlers and clansmen of each wrestler should also not be overlooked. Though wrestling is literally fighting, it is a game that draws people together. The significance of wrestling in the Igbo tradition is ineradicable in how it taught young Ogbaa the culture of his people and gave him a sense of solidarity.

To buttress the point above, Ogbaa's first wrestling match explains the sense of brotherhood he inherited from seeing his father wrestle. Ogbaa is intimidated and challenged to a fight by Ogbonnaya Obi, a left-handed bully who cannot refuse intimidating his mates. On a fateful day, he brawls with Ogbaa, and the people gather and cheer them on. As they wrestle, Ogbaa's father strolls into the arena, and Ogbaa becomes determined not to disgrace his father. In the middle of the fight, an elder steps in and declares the two victors. This fight is pertinent to the influence of fatherhood and the type of fatherhood Ogbaa's father demonstrates. This is well captured in this excerpt:

> When I returned home, my father grinned and shook my hand. He then turned and left without saying a word about the fight. Father never said much. Only action. Some days, he would show me the greatest love a father could show to his most beloved son, but on other days, he would discipline me harshly over mistakes I had made, some of which I considered minor. On such days, I wondered if he loved me at all.[11]

Wrestling revealed the kind of parenting Ogbaa's father exercised. He was not a talker, but he was a man of action. Wrestling itself is about action rather than talking. This further influenced Ogbaa in his parenting style even when he moved far away from home. This is well explicated in another section of this chapter. The significance of Ogbaa's first wrestling match was not limited to Ogbaa's father's style of parenting. One other aspect of wrestling is how Ogbonnaya Obi and Ogbaa later become friends. The day after the first fight, Ogbonnaya Obi challenges Ogbaa again, brawling like they did the day before. During the fight, Ogbaa injures Ogbonnaya. Ogbaa taught him a sense of camaraderie and community. After treating Ogbonnaya's wound, Ogbaa's father says, "Never fight again. You are both clansmen. I will whip you both if I catch you fighting."[12] Ogbaa also believed that that event gave him a sense of brotherhood. Brotherliness is one of the indispensable aspects of African communitarianism. Ogbaa, in practical words from his experience, narrates:

> I was sad that I had hurt Ogbonnaya so badly, even though I hadn't started the fight. I quickly agreed never to fight a clansman again. Ogbonnaya, too, had learned his lesson. Indeed, we eventually became friends and allies that teamed up to fight other bullies. And whenever we fought, we always defeated all our adversaries who, while trying to avoid punches from my right hand, received dangerous blows from Ogbonnaya's left fist. I enjoyed the thrills of our collaborative effort whenever we defeated our opponents in such fights, but I never fully appreciated the lesson of the right hand working collaboratively with the left to achieve victory in all aspects of our community life until I was grown.[13]

The first lesson on creating a sense of community and belonging was taught by Ogbaa's father after his fight with Ogbonnaya. This parenting style is more actions than words, and one would see why the memoir shows that Ogbaa watched his father's actions. Overall, wrestling is a metaphor for unity despite differences, courage, and the display of customs and traditions. Importantly, wrestling is a metaphor for the struggles of life. The memoirist succinctly narrates that his father "explained how wrestling was an important metaphor for the struggles in one's life, a means of understanding various ways of dealing with life's challenges."[14] This is one of the many lessons that set up Ogbaa to stand tall against the challenges he later faced in life.

Figure 6.1 Kalu Ogbaa

Mazi Stephen Ogbaa Ikpo's influence on Ogbaa is remarkable. It is not limited to the cultures and customs he saw his father demonstrate. Also, his father's influence can be seen in the sense that Mazi Stephen was a man of many responsibilities. On the family front, fatherhood is displayed in his responsibility to his immediate family. In relation to Ogbaa, his fatherly figure reflects in his education. On the one hand, because of his father's courage and strong will, Ogbaa saw education as a means to wrestle through life, an ineffaceable trait learned from his father. On the other hand, Ogbaa's father greatly influenced his education. Ogbaa recounts how his father and brother taught him how to read and write in the evening.[15] This was the necessary foundation upon which Ogbaa's desire for knowledge and educational achievements was built. Significantly, the sacrifices Ogbaa's father made covered up the flaws he had.

As one of the many things that Igbo tradition taught Ogbaa, the impact of fatherhood cannot be overestimated. Fatherhood is an essential part of Ogbaa's memoir. His father left an indelible mark on his life, and the lack of a father is also portrayed in the story of Ogbaa's friend, James Okoro. While in Standard VI, James' father dies, and that loss brings a downward spiral in his life, so much so that he fails. In an attempt to get James back on his feet, Ogbaa asks his father to plead with James' uncle to allow him back in school.

Even whenJames re-enrolls, the vacuum of his father's loss pulls him down. Ogbaa captured the situation thus:

> My father's presence always reminded him of his own father's absence. In addition, his absence from school the whole of 1956 did not help him cope with the tedium of work in his final year of primary school education. In the end, he failed Standard VI exams again, despite all the help I gave him with his homework. I tried to help him think less often of his father so that he could concentrate on his academics, which was the only way he could succeed in getting a future job to help his widowed mother. But it was of no avail.[16]

As portrayed by Ogbaa here, the impact of fatherhood is as significant as life. It becomes glaringly clear that despite the failure of his parents' marriage, he respected his father and saw him as his hero. Not just for being alive but for being a man who taught him about responsibilities, dedication, strength, and honor. In carrying his father's torch, Ogbaa also carried his father's ghost with him. In character traits, Ogbaa is a reincarnate of his father. From the way his marriage with his first wife ended, Ogbaa believes that it is a repetition of the failures of his father's marital commitment to his mother. In fact, it is a direct replication of the failure, just in a different era. Ogbaa's father, despite his responsibilities to his community and churches, makes irredeemable mistakes towards his family; he caters to his roles, but around his father, Ogbaa walks on eggshells. Also, the brutalization of Ogbaa's mother creates a psychological mark on Ogbaa that could not be erased.[17] Ogbaa believes he struggled to break free of his father's ghost. He narrates:

> I often struggled over these years with the fear that my failed marriage was, at least at some level, plagued by the very same character flaws that had plagued my father's marriage to Mother. But all through the years, I had striven to place the family first and practice the kind of patience, compassion, and gentleness that I never received from Father. There is, however, something to be said about the difficulty of breaking the bonds of blood, and I suppose there were times when I let my guard down and allowed Father's habits and behaviors to influence my own actions and reactions as concerned familial relationships.[18]

To put the importance of the above extract clearly, it is required that "the bonds of blood" be analyzed. In the African sense, there is the notion that if a child does not take after his father, he will take after his mother. In other words, father and mother as metaphorical to a sense of home in Black diaspora studies means that Ogbaa took after his father and exhibited the same character flaws many years later. This shows how, even in the diaspora, Africans find it difficult to break free from behavioral traits they have inherited while in their homeland. In addition, the idea of home is not restricted to geography and physical space. The idea of home is as mental as it is physical. Home engages the body and the soul. Home is defined by the physical space and the psychological marks it leaves on diasporans. The potentiality of the significance of home is enormous. In Ogbaa's case, there are traits he learned from his father's impact, which mentally defined him so much that even in American society, he could not adapt to the American way of raising children. This indelibility of home is entrenched in Ogbaa's remarks:

Yes, I, Kalu Ogbaa *nwa* Ikpo the great wrestler, succeeded in teaching my children to become great students. However, I woefully failed to see that the Igbo man's control of his children and wife that I learned from my father in Nigeria, which I transplanted to America, would bring my downfall. I learned the lesson too late for me to change. Indeed, the children were ostensibly happy that their mother divorced me.[19]

In theoretical terms, in the diaspora, it became impossible for Ogbaa to alienate himself from the Igbo tradition of raising children. Therefore, it is not out of place to submit that home, though left physically by Africans in the diaspora, they still carry it in their minds.

I Have, You Must Have Too: Igbo Communitarian Sense of Life

Despite regional peculiarities, one of the most common features of African history and memoirs is the notion of communitarianism. Memoirs examined in this work place importance on the African sense of togetherness. Essentially, migration for Africans in the diaspora means they have to experience western cultures firsthand. In contrast to the rural communities in Africa, in which most authors of memoirs are raised, there is a community relationship between everyone who is against the solipsistic nature of existence in the West. The nature of existence in the West is a pragmatic display of Protagoras' notion that "Man is the measure of all things that are that they are, and of things that are not that they are not."[20] Protagoras did not say "men." With the use of "man," Protagoras establishes the notion that an individual can determine the extent of existence and morality on his own.

The African conception of existence and being is contrary to this. John Mbiti's "I am, because we are; and since we are, therefore I am."[21] Every culture in Africa has its own versions of sayings that point to the intersubjective definition of being. According to Sophie Oluwole, in the Yoruba culture, there is a saying, "Ká rìn, ká pọ̀, yíyẹ ló ń yẹni," meaning "it is harmonious and becoming to walk together in unity." They also believe that "Ẹni tó ní ẹnikan ò sí, òun fúnra rẹ̀ ni ò sí," which means "Anybody who denies the existence of others denies in the same vein his/her own existence."[22] The concept of Ubuntu preaches "Umuntu Ngumuntu Ngabantu," that is, "we admit our own existence by recognising the existence of others."[23] To corroborate, there is an Igbo adage that " 'I-am-the-one-and-only!' is a bad name."[24]

Succinctly, there is a communitarian adherence in Africa that transcends regions and histories. This is not to say that there are not people who isolate themselves, but they are a few. Communitarianism is not an over-romanticization of Africa's past. It is recognizing the cultural way of life of the people. According to Kwame Gyekye, communitarianism is a doctrine that allows the individual to see the common good of society as far important in the scheme of things. This is not at the expense of the individual but for the good of a greater amount of people.[25] Communitarianism, as defined in traditional African ethos, is utilitarian. Through the coming together of a group of people or a society, the interests of a larger number of people are served rather than the interest of a few. It is this coming together that brings connection and a sense of belonging.

From the foregoing, communitarianism is about "we" over "me." That intersubjective pronoun defines what a community is. Precious Obioha argues that:

> A community is not formed every time a group of people happens to interact with one another, true communities are bound together by the values, norms and experiences they shared among their members. The deeper and more strongly held those common values are, the stronger the sense of community is. The trade between personal freedom and community, however, does not seem obvious or necessary to many.[26]

By identifying what constitutes a good community, one defines what communitarianism aims to achieve. On what the ideal society should do, Obioha opines:

> Every society has its share of the well offs and the worse offs; the fittest and the weak elements of the society. A good human society is not the community of the well offs or the fittest alone but that of all and sundry. A good human community bespeaks of a socio-political arrangement that galvanizes these various elements of the society into a mutual and cooperative whole where the talented productivities of the well offs and the fittest are made to benefit the weak and the worse off of the society to the intent that the happiness and the flourishing of everyone is guaranteed.[27]

Categorically, Obioha's thoughts represent mutual responsibility and complementarity. A community is good based on its ability to bring individuals together no matter the social class; in fact, social class is null and void as everyone is regarded as a complementary binary. It is not surprising that Obioha conceptualizes communitarianism thus:

> Communitarianism as a socio-political arrangement sees the human person as an inherently (intrinsically) communal being, embedded in a context of social relationships and interdependence, never isolated, atomic individual. Consequently, it sees the community not as mere association of individual persons whose interests and ends are contingently congruent, but as a group of persons linked by interpersonal bonds, biological and/or nonbiological, who consider themselves primarily as members of the group and who have common interest, goals and values.[28]

In an Igbo family system, the sense of community is based on the preceding. This supposed sense of community is displayed in attributes like collaboration, generosity, care, compassion, and mutual social responsibility. Auma-Osolo and Osolo-Nasubo opine that:

> Mutual social responsibility simply means that members would be conditioned or obliged to do their very best for each other with the full knowledge and understanding that if the society prospers, its members will share in that prosperity. At the same time, it is realised that society cannot prosper without the full cooperation of its members and that exploitation, discrimination, and an elite class would not have the air to breathe.[29]

The aim is not to create the idea of any faux utopian communal existence in traditional African societies. Rather, it is to elucidate the concept of communitarianism and its pragmatism in the Igbo way of life. With this, the first sense of community can be seen in the customs, rites, and rituals performed when a wrestling match is about to occur. Wrestling matches bring people together so that both wrestlers and traditions are celebrated.

As established earlier, wrestling is a metaphor for life's struggles. Subsequently, wrestling in the context of Ogbaa's memoir connotes going through life's struggles not as an individual but as a member of a community that shares the burden of its members. When Ogbaa wrestled with Ogbonnaya Obi,[30] the life lesson they both learned is never to fight their own clansman. Also, Ogbaa claimed to have learned the lesson of how the right hand needs to work collaboratively with the left hand to achieve victory in all aspects of life. Though Ogbaa only learned this while he was six, Ogbaa's birth teaches the essence of compassion, collaboration, and interdependent existence. Ogbaa explains that his mother went into labor while working on the farm. Thankfully, she was midwifed by women in a nearby bush.

In Chinweizu's *Gender and Monotheism: The Assault by Monotheism on African Gender Diarchy*, he uses the Igbo saying that "if one thing stands, another stands by it"[31] to explain the dual nature of existence. This applies to the event that took place at Ogbaa's birth. In a community where there is no sense of togetherness and entrenched understanding of affirming one's existence through the existence of others, Ogbaa's mother and Ogbaa would have died during labor because of the lack of compassion from the women in the nearby bush. In essence, this is an apt display of the African notion that hands should be rubbed together to have clean hands. It is a suggestion that, from time to time, no one can exist in the seclusion of the other.

Communal living is a recurring trait among the Igbo people. The consistent engagement of the people in the Arochukwu community in which Ogbaa's Umuchiakwa village is situated relates with a shared interest. Despite their differences, they all sought the best interest of the community. One instance that best explains this is Ogbaa's application for a village loan to be able to proceed with his education. Communitarianism for Africans is not just a mere fantasy or a romanticization of the past but a deliberate and unswerving desire to build a community that stands for all. They transmit theories into pragmatics. Ogbaa's narration of the history of the village loan puts this point into perspective. Ogbaa recounts that:

> The history of our village loan scholarship scheme began in 1964 when Agwu Uche gained admission to study at the UNN and he needed financial assistance. Unable to pay all of his tuition and fees, he approached his mentor, Imaga Oleh, for help. Instead of giving him money, Imaga Oleh took him and his friend Amah Ola of Okpo Ihechiowa, with a small bottle of foreign gin, to the chief of the Nde Ngwo compound, Kalu Okoro, to get advice about how to approach the Eziukwu bloc about his university sponsorship. Chief Okoro sent for me to witness the meeting, as was custom whenever people discussed educational issues in our compound. When I arrived, I suggested that we discuss the matter at the home of *Eze Ezi*, the chief of the compound over our bloc…Then he sent a town crier out to summon all the male villagers in the twelve compounds for an urgent meeting in our compound hall.[32]

When the villagers arrive, Imaga Oleh, according to Ogbaa, stands up to address the villagers:

I come humbly to you all on behalf of my friend and your son, Teacher Agwu Uche, to ask for a favor that will be of great benefit to all of us in the long run. He has just gained admission to study at the University of Nigeria, Nsukka, which is the first of its kind for our people. But he doesn't have the money to pay for all of his tuition and fees and buy the stationery he needs. That is why we have come to ask for assistance from the village. I thank you all for honoring our sudden invitation.[33]

By the end of the meeting, the village decides to grant Agwu Uche a loan, and the villagers accept Ogbaa's suggestion that the village offer loans for university education to villagers in the future. Ironically, when Ogbaa applied in 1970, he was not awarded a loan. However, Ogbaa narrates:

When word got out that the village had not given me the loan, the Eziukwu bloc people were so outraged that they decided to give me some financial assistance on their own. Agwu Uche, Emmanuel Ekpesu Kalu, Kalu Ojiuko, and three others contributed £4 each to seed the loan. Then three elders took me to the village and called on all Ezukwu people to contribute as much money as they could to enable their "son" to attend the university. Their efforts yielded £165. I signed an agreement to pay it back as a loan as soon as I graduated from the university and got a job, which was a similar agreement, in spirit, to the original agreement I would have signed with the village. I was humbled and grateful for what Ezukwu people did for me. The efforts of the bloc were able to pull together what normally would have taken an entire village to do. I was more proud than ever of my community, which only spurred me to succeed at the highest level at university.[34]

In the two cases, the idea of community is reemphasized. Following the conceptual analysis of Gyekye and Obioha, the characterization of what communitarianism and community entail is better explained. In practical terms, the coming together of the villagers for Agwu Uche and Ogbaa exemplifies the essence of the interdependence relationship of the individuals. The villagers who donated money to Ogbaa and those who established the loan scholarship could have used their money on something entirely different. Like Obioha's reference made earlier, Agwu Uche and Ogbaa are the weak links in their society, and those who help them are the well offs. In the same vein, the villagers take pride in the fact that one of them is going to university. They are also aware and hopeful that the students will one day be of great impact to their community.

The two events also demonstrate the popular African saying that it takes a village to raise a child. This saying reflects the belief that parenting is not individualistic but communal. Growing up in communities where life is interdependent makes sure that family is not restricted to just immediate blood relations but also includes people with whom you coexist. In the memoir, the actions of everyone with whom Ogbaa grew up and knew in his community contribute immensely to his life and his grasp of existential quandaries. With adherence to communal living, destinies and orientations are shaped. Ogbaa admits:

I wrote the book partly to demonstrate, in practical terms, the importance of the Igbo apothegm, "It takes a village to raise a child," as it positively affected me as an individual. For me, life began with this guiding principle, passed on through the village elders, who coined and adopted it all through the ages. As shown in the discussions in all the chapters of the book, my academic and spiritual journeys, which began in my rural village of Umuchiakuma in Southeast Nigeria, were influenced greatly by the foundations of character the village laid for me. There, I acquired at a very young age its value system, the Igbo morality, worldview, and oral educational system, which have continued to influence my values, even now. To give some balance to my upbringing, my father and teachers complemented my oral Igbo values with written Christian morality, Western worldview and education, when I became a Christian and student in the church and school the Church of Scotland Mission established in my village.[35]

Overall, the place of community in the life of Ogbaa cannot be underestimated. Despite being a Christian, this understanding of community and Igbo values and mores gave him a sense of belonging.

It is pertinent to note that despite Ogbaa's migration to the United States, he still regarded the Igbo sense of brotherhood as something that made him feel welcomed and at home. After he moved to Austin, he admits, "Another warm discovery was the large number of Nigerian (indeed Igbo) families who lived in Austin and who gladly welcomed us on arrival (one of them even kindly offered us their home for two weeks until we rented our own apartment)."[36]

It is not surprising that Ogbaa seemed to look for an Igbo everywhere he stepped into the United States. This is explicable in the sense that Ogbaa relied so much on people who shared the same homeland identity with him. This is not to dismiss the fact that he is a man of two identities (the Igbo man from Umuchiakuma village and the Igbo man in the United States). It is rather to prove that the characteristics of the identity of home cannot be separated from Ogbaa. For instance, Ogbaa said, "Before moving to New Haven on August 15, 1992, I contacted Cyprian Ukah, a fellow Igbo man living in New Haven, by phone about renting a house for our family."[37]

One objection that may be raised in connection to this is that this sense of brotherhood does not alienate those with whom one does not share an ethnicity. The answer is that the brotherhood that Ogbaa inherited from the Igbo tradition does not mean he picks the humanity of his kinsmen over the humanity of others. However, the point is that the sense of the Igbo family system formed him and prepared him to understand that there is a need to connect to your own people no matter where you find yourself. To corroborate this, when Ogbaa had accommodation problems after the separation from his wife, he met Obiora, an Igbo man. He told Obiora his problems and asked for help because Obiora was a director of a student residential hall. Ogbaa sums up the situation:

I was so desperate, I was not ashamed to ask the favor from a fellow Igboman, even though I'd only known him briefly. I relied on our ethnic Igbo apothegm that had always worked for us in times of war and peace: "*Onye aghala nwanne ya* (Never neglect a brother or sister in trouble)."[38]

The lessons Ogbaa learned from the Igbo communal system of living while he was in Nigeria became an asset for him. In the case of help that Obiora rendered to

Ogbaa, one would imagine that Obiora himself learned from the Igbo saying that when the nose is affected, the eyes weep. Though it was not easy for him, he understood the idea of never neglecting a brother or sister in trouble. Overall, Ogbaa joined the pool of people who continue to give to his community. Therefore, the moral, spiritual and financial investments made by Ogbaa's community are not put to waste. When Ogbaa returned home after his doctorate program and after his employment at Imo State University, he began to look for ways to get electricity to his village. He also paid politicians visits to solicit for the development of his village. On an occasion, after Peter Kalu Ulu tells Ogbaa to join politics in order to contribute to the community, Ogbaa replies:

> I believe I can contribute to the academic and physical development of our community. In terms of human development, I give lectures to our secondary school and university students about how they should pursue their education to achieve the same success as I did. Additionally, I have privately approached the government and political leaders in the state to bring development projects like the supply of electricity and running water to our clan. God willing, you will soon see the results of my discussions with them. I think I can achieve the plans I have for our community development without living the life of a corrupt politician, which is the bane of our contemporary Nigerian society.[39]

The relationship between the community and the individual is mutual and based on both complementarity and reciprocity. When all of these are imbibed, one is informed and shaped towards communalistic leanings rather than individualistic beliefs. Interestingly, Africans in the diaspora were mostly raised in systems like the Igbo communal life. They tend to experience culture shock when they are abroad. Unsurprisingly, the lack of an Igbo family system in the United States cost him his marriage and his many attempts to reconcile with his wife.

In a small Igbo community, Ogbaa and his wife would have been called by the head of their compound, and the matter will be resolved. Ogbaa himself reminisced that "in Nigeria, we'd had our fights and misunderstandings, like other married couples. But our parents, our friends, and our church had helped us to settle them amicably."[40] The significance of this is that on this occasion, the cultural mores and marital jurisprudence of the Igbo were not available in the United States to help him out as it would have been in Nigeria. Either way, the sense of community had an impact on Ogbaa both at home and abroad.

Different Crusades: Cultural Clashes and Necessary Influences

Whether at home or in the diaspora, Africans are made up of elements of cultural clash. When two cultures meet, it is logical that they influence one another. For Babatunde Sofela:

> An encounter between cultures, no matter how mild, is apt to produce some results. These would depend upon some basic factors such as the aims behind the encounter, the personnel involved, and the duration of the encounter. And evaluation of such results may be difficult to make. The encounter between colonialism and African culture, due to the complex nature of both culture and colonialism, is such that defies clear, simple identification.[41]

Cultural clash does not entail just the contact of colonialism and culture. In the case of transatlantic slaves, it is contact between cultures caused by the inhumane and forceful migration of Blacks. With this, they are introduced to foreign languages, ethos, religion, and orientation. For Africans in the diaspora who migrated of their own choice to the United States, they are not new to cultural clash because of colonialism and the eurochristian missionary in Africa.

Ogbaa's early years took place during the colonial period. The impact of western modernity was immense on Nigeria. With both political and economic intentions, Britain provided technological advancement and a western model of modernity that enabled Nigerians to proselytize their own belief system. In the years of colonialism, some people strictly continued their traditional religions but were still participants in imperialist schemes like taxes, civil obedience, foreign education, and so on. Nonetheless, these missionaries and colonialists introduced Africans in Africa to westernization. Ogbaa narrates:

> Scottish missionaries and teachers formally introduced me to several aspects of Western civilization at the church and primary school I attended in Umuama Ihechiowa: Christianity, the English language and literature, and European history and culture.[42]

From the foregoing, Ogbaa, like many others, became westernized Africans even in their homeland. They became learned in the western way. With globalization being Western-driven at the time, the West set up standards that appeared to be the best set of models to live by. In this sense, anyone without western education was called illiterate, and anyone who was not Christian was called a pagan or heathen. Due to this dichotomy, a clash between two cultures began. The division was not only limited to Christians and heathens but also among Christians of differing denominations. Ogbaa recalls:

> The raging "crusades" in my village not only divided the villagers into Christians and heathens, or believers and non-believers, but also into Protestants and Catholics. In addition, the disagreements between the two Christian denominations were so boisterous and hateful that non-Christians called all the Christians "Nde Uka"— literally meaning "quarrelsome people"— and referred to Christians then and now as "Onye uka." Consequently, from about 1844, the beginning of missionary activities in Igboland, the sermons from the Bible are interpreted in Igbo as "Uka Chukwu" or "Okwu Chukwu" ("Word of God"), because the traditional Igbo saw the preachers as people who were always ready to engage others in impassioned debates, with or without invitation. Consequently, in the eyes of the traditional Igbo, Christianity was *not* a peaceful organized religion.[43]

The sentiments of the African traditionalists are well understood. African religions are arguably some of the most peaceful religions in the world. Their believers have never had their own version of jihad or crusade for conversion and domination. Also, these religions, unlike Christianity and Islam, do not preach about eternal damnation for those who do not believe in them. It is on this basis that Ogba reflects:

When I became educated enough to study the history of the holy wars between Christians (Crusaders) and Muslims (Jihadists), I, too, had my doubts. Like my forebears, I began to wonder whether either religion, both of which claimed Abraham as the father of their faiths, were indeed as peaceful and superior to our own traditional religions as foreign missionaries portrayed them to our people when they first came to Igboland and other West African countries.[44]

Abrahamic religions thrive on the fear of the afterlife that many are consistently obsessed with. Be a good believer and be saved from damnation in the afterlife, or do not become a believer (or be a bad one) and be sent to hellfire. Clinging to the Christian faith, for instance, affords you an enjoyable eternity, and this is something most people want to have access to. Christians believe that those who are not "saved" like them are damned, which makes them pray for people they consider pagans. Ogbaa calls into question this belief because of the case of Chief Kalu Ogoro. By citing Chief Kalu Ogoro as an example, Ogbaa self-evaluates his father's dilemma preaching that they should not let their pagan neighbors' evil ways overcome them. He methodically doubts:

> But, even in my pre-teen years, I was skeptical of such admonition coming from him because I saw nothing but goodness and love in some of them, especially my adoptive namesake, Chief Kalu Ogoro, who always gave me mouth-watering dried meat and smoked fish to eat, although Father didn't approve. I could never quite believe that a person like Chief Ogoro would be condemned to hell. I saw him feed the poor and hungry. I saw him take care of orphans and widows in our compound. I saw him make peace between villagers who fought themselves over land disputes. I saw him serve as an oral historian of our village. And, I saw him organize our people to carry out many community development projects in our compound, village, and clan. I believe that most of those roles he played could have been done in the name of Christ if he had been a Christian. Could doing all that without converting to Christianity earn him a place in hell? Because of these observations, I continued to struggle with such religious conflicts well into my adult life.[45]

This situation is one of the current religious problems afflicting the world even in the twenty-first century. Religious fanatics have taken religion to another level, which has led to terrorism. This clash of cultures in the aspect of religions also slightly causes a chasm in African societies that pride themselves on their communitarian spirit. In the early years of these cultural clashes, people still found a way to manage their differences. However, today, Muslims, Christians, and traditionalists cannot coexist.

Another aspect of the cultural clash is between Igbo traditional medicine and western medicine. When Ogbaa's father is poisoned, he is taken to traditional healers to heal and revive himself. He is only able to regain some consciousness then. No one knows exactly what is wrong with him until Ogbaa's headmaster reveals that Ogbaa's father's symptoms indicate tuberculosis. He is later rushed to an infectious disease hospital in Enugu and was cured.[46] Though traditional healers could not cure him, what was lacking, one would believe, was only a matter of prognosis. The advancement of western medicine cannot be denied, and it has become the most reliable form of medicine. Notwithstanding, Igbo traditional medicine was able to provide treatment for Ogbaa when he had an accident.[47]

Whether with medicine, parenting, education, or religion, the recommended idea is that cultures should complement one another, and ideas from different cultures should be syncretized. Ogbaa submits:

> Since my education has enabled me to think critically and objectively— I have never shied away from confronting some Western attitudes I found prejudicial to everything African. But I also agree with some Western evaluations of things African, which seem good or bad, acceptable or unacceptable, when they are measured objectively by universal standards.[48]

Similar to the analysis done above is the clash between the communalistic cultures of the Igbo and the United States. It has been established that Igbo culture is essentially communalistic, and western culture is solipsistically characterized. In addition, the cultural clash in the diaspora is also dictated by racism and years of social injustice against Africans. Therefore, it is pertinent to reiterate how cultures clash when Africans move abroad. They are not naïve in thinking that cultures will be the same everywhere; however, they profoundly contemplate forsaking home (that represents their cultures) for abroad (that represents an adoption of a new culture). Ogbaa also had this contemplation and reflection before going back to the United States the second time. Knowing the financial and status opportunities America could offer his children, he was reflective of some distinguishing attributes that America is associated with. Ogbaa reflects in this excerpt:

> In America, I would have more opportunities to grow professionally and to make more money than I did in Nigeria. Even more importantly, America could give my children the opportunity to receive a higher quality of education than they were receiving in Nigeria. On the other hand, the racist attitudes of some professors and fellow graduate students reared their ugly heads once again, albeit subtly and subliminally in most cases. Therefore, I had to ask myself some soul-searching questions, the answers to which would help me make the right decision: Would I be able to ignore or endure permanently the type of racial discrimination, deprivation, and segregation I once experienced if I decided to stay? Would not those who depended on me for both material and moral support in Nigeria consider my staying in America a betrayal of their trust? Would I be able to live the atomistic life of Westerners in my newfound land as opposed to the communal life I used to live in Nigeria? Could I, a double minority—black and foreign—endure the life of an exile in America even though it would be self-imposed?[49]

Apparently, when leaving Africa, many things are considered before embarking on that journey, not just geography but, on many occasions, a cultural switch. However, the chapters of this work indicate that despite the unpleasant attributes of the West, many Africans in the diaspora decide to migrate based on economic, political, and professional reasons. In the case of Ogbaa, it is based on the reasons of self-preservation for him and his family, along with the continued persecution of the Igbo people years after the Nigerian/Biafran civil war. Ogbaa sacrificed the communal aspect of his culture for western individualism, which affected his marriage in the long run.

Lessons from Biafra: Adjustment to Racial Segregation and Inseparability of Home

The impact of home on Ogbaa cannot be fully explicated without the Nigeria/Biafra civil war shaping and preparing him for segregation in America. In fact, it made him understand the plights of Blacks like him in America. The genesis of the war, when followed to its very roots, is a result of the amalgamation of the southern and northern protectorates by the British. The British colonialist joined together people who were culturally distinctive to make it easy for them to govern. However, the idea then and now appears to be blameworthy. Despite this, some historians and analysts of the war believe that the animosity that paved the way for the war began with the first military coup in Nigeria. Olusegun Obasanjo states that:

> The Nigerian civil war broke out on 6 July 1967 [...] the war itself was the culmination of an uneasy peace and stability that had plagued Nigeria from independence. This uneasy peace and stability had their genesis in the genesis in the geography, history and demography of Nigeria. But the immediate cause of the civil war itself may be identified as the coup and counter-coup of 1966, which altered the political equation and destroyed the fragile trust existing among the major ethnic groups.[50]

Ogbaa also agrees that the genesis of the civil war can be traced back to 1966. He narrates that:

> 1966 was the most cruel and bloody year in Nigerian national history. A group of Nigerian Army Majors plotted and carried out the first coup in Nigeria on January 15, assassinating the country's political leaders, especially those from the Northern region. Following the coup, some high military officers from the Northern region led soldiers and civilians, enraged over the insult, on a rampage destroying the lives and properties of thousands of Eastern Nigerian peoples, especially the Igbo, who were living in the Northern region. The organizers and rioters justified their actions by claiming that Igbo military officers led the coup. As evidence to support their claim, they pointed to several powerful sociopolitical, religious, and military leaders from the North whom the Nigerian Army Majors had assassinated, such as Alhaji Sir Ahmadu Bello, Premier of Northern Nigeria and the Sardauna of Sokoto; Alhaji Sir Abubakar Tafawa Balewa, the Prime Minister of Nigeria; and Brigadier Zakari Maimalari.[51]

He continues:

> Furthermore, senior military officers of Northern Nigeria then systematically carried out what they called counter-coups on May 29, July 29, and September 29, 1966, again killing thousands of Eastern military officers and civilians, especially the Igbo ethnic peoples, including women and children, publically raping women and schoolchildren, disemboweling pregnant women, and decapitating old, infirm men. Those who escaped the killings flooded back into their homeland, Eastern Nigeria, creating refugee problems too large and too complex for the government to handle with any level of practical efficiency.[52]

The excerpts above bring to the fore the foundation and early days of the looming problem. Despite the intervention of the Organization of African Unity (OAU), it was already too late because the Eastern part of Nigeria under Military Col. Chukwuemeka Odumegwu Ojukwu had declared itself, and the Nigerian government had made the resolution to stop Biafra's secession through might and force. With this, the killings of the Igbo in the North and the West began to increase. By July 6, 1967, war broke out. The war immensely destabilized the economy, along with its physical and social infrastructure. In the middle of this, Ogbaa played his own role. Though unable to join the military, he helped educate and organize the people on the importance of vigilance. Ogbaa recounts that:

> Every villager and clansman had to contribute money, food, vehicles, clothes, and other materials to support our troops on the warfronts... A group of educated men in the clan, including myself, called together our young primary school teachers, university and secondary school students, as well as civil servants to organize "Ihe Youth Association (IYA)." IYA's primary objective was to promote the secondary and university education of all sons and daughters of the clan, because Ihechiowa, the largest clan in Arochukwu District, had produced only a few university graduates compared to those produced by the smaller neighboring clans of Arochukwu and Ututu. Consequently, one of the greatest ironies of the Nigeria-Biafra War is that it drove native Ihechiowa indigenes home from other parts of the country and thus made it possible for the youth to meet regularly and have serious discussions on issues of higher education.[53]

Figure 6.2 Chukwuemeka Odumegwu-Ojukwu

Ogbaa's story is a harrowing story of a great number of Igbo who suffered immensely because of the failure of diplomacy. When the war stories are told, it is remembered as not just a war of egos between General Yakubu Gowon and Col. Ojukwu but also as genocide. In an attempt to make the Biafran troops and people surrender, the Nigerian government ensured that Biafra suffered from an economic blockade and starvation. Chinua Achebe claims that "the Biafrans paid a great humanitarian price by ceding a great deal of territory to the Nigerians and employing this war strategy. The famine worsened as the war raged, as the traditional Igbo society of farmers could not plant their crops."[54]

By the end of the war, millions of Igbo had died and were displaced. The devastation of the war was both physical and psychological. The war and how it was handled during and after left an open wound in the hearts of many Igbo about Nigeria's history and continuing existence. With what Ogbaa and the Igbo went through, he was prepared for segregation and understood it better. When he moved to America, his experience of the Nigerian civil war was compared to the racism and brutality that African-Americans faced. When a new friend Ogbaa made during his first time in America told him about racism and bigotry in America, Ogbaa claims, "I told Jocelyn I'd seen ethnic bigotry practiced in Nigeria. Some of my Igbo people were among those who perpetrated it, and consequently we as a people collectively suffered its evil effects more than we deserved during the Nigeria-Biafra War."[55]

In an altercation between Ogbaa and the department secretary, Ogbaa realized the cultural differences in the relations between the department secretary and a professor. This incident earned Ogbaa a summon from the union president of women. After they passed their judgment, Ogbaa submits that:

> After hearing the judgment on the case, and noting the total absence of blacks among the witnesses, I recalled the similar treatment Nigerians had given to my Igbo people back home— the same kind of treatment that had driven me into self-exile here in America. Thank God, I thought, the decision was not worse. Emotionally, however, the incident reminded me of other various forms of segregation and deprivation based on my race and national origin I'd experienced at American universities. But since I was determined to settle in the U.S. as a latter-day immigrant to afford my family a better life, I decided to adjust and, to this day, bear up under many American cultural mores that are alien to me.[56]

The attempted ethnic extermination of the Igbo Ogbaa experienced in Nigeria, he believes, is similar to the segregation black people experienced in America. This prompted him to always fight for equality, even in diversity. On one occasion, Ogbaa used nature and clothing to explicate the need for unity in diversity. He narrates:

> Tony, already knowing my passion for racial equality, took me early in the semester to the first Senate open forum where I made an impassioned presentation in favor of the implementation of the proposed campus-wide Human Diversity program. I asked everyone to look out the windows at the various colors in nature. Now, I told them, look at everyone around you. They're all dressed in multicolored clothes. If both nature and people enjoy such a wide variety of color, I continued, how much better would it be for our faculty to reflect such a variety of colors in the courses?[57]

Ogbaa's argument is influenced by the communalistic culture in which he was raised. It is not that people do not have their differences, but the differences were put to use for the common goal of the community and are beneficial to all. Despite Ogbaa's achievements, he found the most joy in services rendered to minority students.[58] Ogbaa claims that:

> Additionally, while working with those students, other students, from the Caribbean and Africa, drew my attention to the intra-racist attitude that some African Americans were showing toward them. I spoke against such behavior at the BSU meetings, admonishing every black student to work together as brothers and sisters for the benefit of all. But when the Caribbean students could no longer tolerate the purported intra-racism, they asked me to help them form their own separate organization. With my help, they formed the West Indian Academic Society in 1996. I served as their official academic advisor for five years. Later, the African students asked me to help them form their own separate organization. I did, and they named it African Students Organization. I also became their official academic advisor. Once the three black student organizations found their feet, I decided to visit and advise them occasionally until other faculty and staff members took over.[59]

Additionally, Ogba's engagement in forming unions for Black students is a strong indication of the lessons from home and how they have forever impacted him to never look away in cases of inequality and where minorities are being suppressed. In the diaspora, he still maintains a strong affiliation to home. In Connecticut, Ogbaa is one of the elders of the Association of Nigerians. Ogbaa claims that the aim of the association is:

> To foster healthy sociocultural interactions and cooperation among Nigerians residing in Connecticut and to disseminate information about political, economic, and social issues in Nigeria to our community that would enable us to maintain a link with our homeland. We held monthly meetings in members' homes and discussed the burning issues of the day in Nigeria, as well as America, which affected us as Nigerian Americans and permanent residents. We also used the platform to condemn people coming to the country illegally or overstaying their visits, and those who came with student visas but failed to stay in the colleges and universities where they gained admission. Collectively these activities could tarnish the image of all Nigerians as a community in America.[60]

Ogbaa further reiterates the goals and activities of the association:

> Collectively, ANC organizes annual cultural dances and fashion shows as a means of exhibiting an aspect of the Nigerian culture, which is distinct from the collective Black or Africana culture and in America...that asks the federal government of Nigeria (through its consular officials) to address current atrocities that affect the people in our homeland, including rigged elections, misuse and abuse of petrol money by the political class, and the destructive activities of the Islamic fundamentalists (known as Boko Haram), which the federal government in Abuja has not been able to stop.[61]

The purpose of these excerpts is to cite the different connections between home (and experiences gained from home) and the day-to-day existential matters of the diaspora.

Ogbaa's background and experience make it impossible for him to separate himself from the ethos, mores, and history of home. If anything, home has made it possible for him to create a "home away from home" in the diaspora. Culturally, though with failures in certain aspects of his life, Ogbaa has exceptionally exported the Igbo tradition of creating family among the people around him. As stated so far in this chapter, a community is not just about clans but also a coming together of people with similar values, norms, and experiences. Ogbaa has been able to create communities for minority students, which will help them find a sense of belonging. With the African National Congress (ANC), he has also created a community of Nigerians who want nothing but the best for Nigerians in Nigeria and Nigerians in the diaspora.

Conclusion

From the first wrestling match with Ogbonnaya Obi to his tenure in Southern, Ogbaa has exhibited that no one can exist in insolation, and more importantly, this precipitates the need for unity where he found himself. The idea of the indelibility of Igbo traditions is not solely rested on the idea of tradition, but they are also hinged on what these traditions represent, and in this case, they represent the fluid idea of home for Ogbaa. Therefore, it is imperative to restate that the concept of home is not solely physical but also mental. In other words, Ogbaa's experiences gained in his village and Nigeria have left indelible imprints on his behaviors, beliefs, mores, and values. As much as this is true for Ogbaa, it is true for most Africans in the diaspora. Despite the need for acculturation and acclimatization to the ethos of the diaspora, the identity of home remains a significant factor in what dictates the lives that many Africans in the diaspora lead. As a result, this chapter exemplifies the inseparability of the identity of home from Africans. Ogbaa's *Carrying My Father's Torch* is an expressive and overt metaphor for carrying home with you wherever you go.

Notes

1 Kalu Ogbaa, *Carrying My Father's Torch: A Memoir* (Durham: Carolina Academic, Press, 2014), 279.
2 Ogbaa, *Carrying My Father's Torch*, 279.
3 Emmanuel Babatunde, *Kelebogile—I Am Grateful: An African Journey through Celibate Priesthood to Married Life* (Maitland: Xulon Press, 2018).
4 Cherno M. Njie, *Sweat Is Invisible in the Rain* (Austin: Pan-African University Press, 2020).
5 Oladejo Afolayan, *Fate of Our Mothers: The Collected Memories of an African Village Boy* (Austin: Pan-African University Press, 2015), 18.
6 Ogbaa, *Carrying My Father's Torch*, 25.
7 Ogbaa, *Carrying My Father's Torch*, 26.
8 Ogbaa, *Carrying My Father's Torch*, 49.
9 Ogbaa, *Carrying My Father's Torch*, 28–29.
10 Ogbaa, *Carrying My Father's Torch*, 3–4.
11 Ogbaa, *Carrying My Father's Torch*, 5.
12 Ogbaa, *Carrying My Father's Torch*, 7.
13 Ogbaa, *Carrying My Father's Torch*, 7.
14 Ogbaa, *Carrying My Father's Torch*, 12.

15 Ogbaa, *Carrying My Father's Torch*, 44.
16 Ogbaa, *Carrying My Father's Torch*, 74.
17 Ogbaa, *Carrying My Father's Torch*, 25–29.
18 Ogbaa, *Carrying My Father's Torch*, 256.
19 Ogbaa, *Carrying My Father's Torch*, 254.
20 H. A. Diels and W. Krantz, *Fragments of the Pre-Socratic Philosophers* (Philadelphia: University of Pennsylvania Press, 1968).
21 John S. Mbiti, *African Religion and Philosophy* (Nairobi: East African Educational Publishers, 1969), 108.
22 Sophie B. Oluwole, *Socrates and Orunmila: Two Patron Saints of Classical Philosophy* (Lagos: Ark Publishers, 2015), 168.
23 Bola Dauda, "African Humanism and Ethics: The Cases of Ubuntu and Omolúwàbí," in *The Palgrave Handbook of African Philosophy*, eds. Toyin Falola and Adeshina Afolayan (New York: Palgrave Macmillan, 2017), 482.
24 L. Chinweizu, "Gender and Monotheism: The Assault by Monotheism on African Gender Diarchy?" in *The Essentials of African Studies*, Vol 1, ed. Sophie Oluwole (Lagos: General African Studies Unit University of Lagos, 1997), 7.
25 Kwame Gyekye, *An Essay on African Philosophical Thought: The Akan Conceptual Scheme* (New York: Cambridge University Press, 1987), 1550.
26 Uwaezuoke Precious Obioha, "Radical Communitarian Idea of the Human Person in African Philosophical Thought: A Critique," *Western Journal of Black Studies* 38, no. 1 (2014): 105.
27 Obioha, "Radical Communitarian Idea," 106.
28 Obioha, "Radical Communitarian Idea," 107.
29 A. Auma-Osolo and N. Osolo-Nasubo, "Democratic African Socialism: An Account of African Communal Philosophy," *African Studies Review* 14, no. 2 (1971): 267.
30 Ogbaa, *Carrying My Father's Torch*, 7.
31 Chinweizu, "Gender and Monotheism," 5.
32 Ogbaa, *Carrying My Father's Torch*, 105–106.
33 Ogbaa, *Carrying My Father's Torch*, 106.
34 Ogbaa, *Carrying My Father's Torch*, 109–110.
35 Ogbaa, *Carrying My Father's Torch*, 280.
36 Ogbaa, *Carrying My Father's Torch*, 159.
37 Ogbaa, *Carrying My Father's Torch*, 239.
38 Ogbaa, *Carrying My Father's Torch*, 248.
39 Ogbaa, *Carrying My Father's Torch*, 193.
40 Ogbaa, *Carrying My Father's Torch*, 254.
41 Babatunde Sofela, "Colonialism and Culture: The Egba-British Encounter," *LASU Journal of African Studies* 6 (2012): 273.
42 Ogbaa, *Carrying My Father's Torch*, 31.
43 Ogbaa, *Carrying My Father's Torch*, 32.
44 Ogbaa, *Carrying My Father's Torch*, 32.
45 Ogbaa, *Carrying My Father's Torch*, 33–34.
46 Ogbaa, *Carrying My Father's Torch*, 57–60.
47 Ogbaa, *Carrying My Father's Torch*, 25.
48 Ogbaa, *Carrying My Father's Torch*, 34.
49 Ogbaa, *Carrying My Father's Torch*, 221.
50 Olusegun Obasanjo, *My Command: An Account of the Nigerian Civil War 1967–1970* (Lagos: Kachifo, 2015), xvii.
51 Ogbaa, *Carrying My Father's Torch*, 79.
52 Ogbaa, *Carrying My Father's Torch*, 79.
53 Ogbaa, *Carrying My Father's Torch*, 85.

54 Chinua Achebe, *There Was a Country: A Personal History of Biafra* (London: Penguin, 2012), 209–210.
55 Ogbaa, *Carrying My Fathers' Torch*, 154.
56 Ogbaa, *Carrying My Father's Torch*, 243.
57 Ogbaa, *Carrying My Father's Torch*, 241.
58 Ogbaa, *Carrying My Father's Torch*, 274.
59 Ogbaa, *Carrying My Father's Torch*, 276.
60 Ogbaa, *Carrying My Father's Torch*, 276.
61 Ogbaa, *Carrying My Father's Torch*, 276.

Chapter Seven

EXPERIENCES, REFLECTIONS, AND REFRACTIONS ON THE CUSP IN A. B. ASSENSOH'S *A MATTER OF SHARING*

Introduction

This reflective-cum-refractive chapter is geared toward an examination of A.B. Assensoh's reflections on some major discourses in his memoir, *A Matter of Sharing*, in which the memoirist reflected on so many issues, as well as matters that he deemed worthy of sharing, coupled with the experiences that have shaped his life and the world around him. One of the issues he shared and reflected on is the indispensability of the mother's influence on her child. Meanwhile, this chapter will investigate the author's reflections on the memoir on different issues: his personal life story, experiences, political, and historical matters that have impacted his life and career. In Assensoh's own words:

> My travels and stay in various countries have, indeed, broadened my outlook on life generally. Also, it simply makes me shake my head when I come across the repeat performances of events, and I just sigh: "Oh, it is a replay of what I saw in Europe, Asia, America or in Africa." This part of the publication is being used to offer a distillation of some of the issues that I have discussed before, including matters about certain significant individuals.[1]

Interestingly, Assensoh's memoir reflects his thoughts on salient issues that have impacted his life, education, and career. This chapter will further explore and investigate his reminiscences on politics and history, which sometimes intersect in the memoir. Also, this chapter will interrogate and expound on the conceptualization of reflection and its implication for the thematic exercise. The chapter is divided into four intersecting categories: the personal, the historical, the political, and the literary. In it, the personal category will capture the author's reflections on his family, birth, parentage, and career. In this part of the chapter, the exploration of the author's outlook on life—as a reflection of his childhood experiences, education, and career—will be discussed. The implication of examining this aspect will connect the chapter to his view of other matters or discourses in the memoir. His education and career will be viewed as the connecting map to his reflection on salient discourses with international import.

The historic part of the chapter is yoked to the author's reflection on African politics and political growth. It examines the historical events and issues that have been carefully reflected on and pondered on by the memoirist. It reflects upon the histories of some African countries and their political exploits as narrated in the memoir, as well as the literary voyages and ponderings of the author in connection with several prominent scholars and writers from Africa. This will also include the political upheavals in some African countries and their possible effects on the development of the African continent, as seen by the memoirist.

For this chapter, the reflection will be the thoughts, writings, and ruminations about personal life experiences and contemplations on different discourses captured and explored by Assensoh in the memoir. The reflection on social-cultural matters, history, and politics will be assessed to extract the assumptions and conclusions of the memoirist on these subjects. The topics and discourses in the memoir are varied as they reflect the author's journeys, education, and experiences. Some of the topics shared in the memoir are the author's contemplations on issues that have personally affected him. Reflection refers to the author's writings, which express his ideas and thoughts on several personal, political, and historical discourses in the memoir. Here, Assensoh reveals his thoughts on historical-cum-political issues in his days in Ghana and also some that impacted his views and opinions of the individuals involved. The memoir represents a series of reflections on his growth, education, and career, as well as African politics, military interventions, killings in both Africa and the United States, and the impact of some influential leaders in the world.

The title of the memoir, *A Matter of Sharing*, is very apt and of great symbolism as Assensoh shares and dissects some issues and discourses that are carefully written and reflected on. The memoir conflates personal, public, and international issues that Assensoh, an African, journalist, and historian, shares with deep reflection.

Figure 7.1 A. B. Assensoh

The Personal Matters

In this section, the author ruminates on his journey and the events that are memorable and worthy of sharing. These issues are gleaned from his experiences as a child in his formative years, an adult maneuvering his way into the world of politics and journalism, and as a seasoned scholar who has contributed to some of the matters discussed in the memoir.

The Indispensable Role of Mothers: Women and Their Contributions

In *A Matter of Sharing*, the role of the author's mother—in his life and education—is reflected and discussed to initiate a line of thought that "everywhere in the world, mothers are known to have played wonderful roles in the lives of their children, indeed from cradle to grave."[2] This statement reflects the huge contribution the author's mother made in his life. This essentiality and importance of the mother's frame is deeply explored in the memoir as an indication of the significant roles mothers play in the lives of their child(ren). This is also juxtaposed with the roles and claims by fathers as the sire of the child(ren) in the conception and raising of the child.

While creating a celebratory frame for mothers, it is implied that fathers are nowhere to be found in the nourishment and raising roles, from the example of the author's father. Assensoh, however, creates a convincing illustration of the varied shackles around women in preliterate African society, as the less favored of the division of the genders in the marriage setting. Assensoh opines:

> It is shown in this autobiographical essay about my 93-year-old mother's marriage to my late father (when she was in her 20s, and he was in his early 50s) as well as how my dear Mother grew apathetic to polygamy and, as a result, she decided to get her freedom by seeking a divorce from her customary marriage.[3]

The foregoing is a reminiscence of Assensoh's mother's experience with polygamy in her husband's household and becomes a point of illumination for women's experiences in such a setting. One of the experiences that women endure in a polygamous setting is explored by Assensoh when he recalls his mother's experience in her husband's house. Mother Hannah, aged 22 years, took her time to explain that she could not have as much access to her husband (Nana Assensoh) as she wanted. But what she hated most was the conjugal marital or sleeping arrangements she had to endure. Assensoh narrated about his father's household:

> As a polygamous home of six wives—with my mother being the fifth wife, in line of seniority—it meant that she was at the bottom of the priority list in sleeping arrangements with her husband. At the end of the month, the oldest wife of my father (the late Mother Konko, who hailed from Agogo in the Asante Akim area of the Ashanti Region) would practically sit-in-state like an important traditional queen in Ashanti. As part of the process, she would dish out the number of days for each of the other five wives to go and sleep with our father.[4]

The arrangement discussed above is reminiscent of what is obtainable in a polygamous home. The man/husband remains the Alpha and Omega of the household and does as he wishes. The mother's decision to divorce Assensoh's father leads to a series of life-changing events in both their lives. As Assensoh says, after the marriage was dissolved, "My late father became indifferent to my mother and, later, declared: 'When I divorce a woman, I divorce the children I had with her, too'." This statement shows the role of Assensoh's father in his life, as he was disowned along with his parents' separation. However, the mother takes up the role of the father together with hers in order to give her son a better life and education. This is illustrated in the memoir when Assensoh writes that "yet, my mother did everything possible for me to have a normal life, followed by a decent education in Ghana. Later, with scholarships, I studied up to the Ph.D. degree level in some of the fine academic institutions in Europe and in the United States of America."[5]

The author's fascination and love for his mother springs from the wealth of care and sacrifices his mother made to give him a good life. Assensoh's success is credited to his mother's contribution and efforts to secure her son's future, which are extracted and shown below from the memoir:

Now, I am a History Professor Emeritus at one university (Indiana University in Bloomington, Indiana, USA) as well as a Courtesy Professor Emeritus at another (University of Oregon in Eugene, Oregon, USA), and I do credit my mother with the bulk of the obvious successes I have attained over the years.[6]

The future success of the memoir's author is hinged on the mother's subsequent role and contribution to his career. The credit to his mother and the roles mothers play is indispensable because of the acknowledgments that mothers have received from various quarters and realms of power. Assensoh, inter alia, wrote:

As I recollected the events that constitute this essay, with my mother playing a center role, I still remember the loud-echoing melodious signature tune of a Nigerian musical album (or song) that I loved to listen to in Europe, in the early 1970s, titled "Sweet Mother." I also remember a sign that a late friend (Professor Lawrence Hanks of blessed memory and of Indiana University, Bloomington, Indiana, USA) purchased for my wife's office (in her capacity as Dean of Indiana University). It read: "Be kind to women because they make half of the world's population, and they are also the mothers of the other half." I found the axiomatic statement to be great, hence, forever, I will say: "Thank you, sweet Mother."[7]

Another discourse connected to this issue is the role of women in the lives of their husbands. On this, Assensoh captures the efforts and roles of two women: Mrs. Christine Achebe and Mrs. Coretta Scott King. These two women are described as "indomitable" in the memoir because of their dedication to their husbands, dead or alive. In their different spaces, these women have promoted the successes and business of their spouses and have ensured its progress after the men's deaths. Assensoh notes how Mrs. King had approved his appointment to the King Center from Stanford University, and her office also arranged his affiliation with Emory University.[8] Assensoh, in the same vein, describes

Mrs. Achebe's role as a supportive spouse to her husband, the late Professor Chinua Achebe: "Lady Christie Achebe, Professor in the Psychology Department of Bard College, was by Professor Chinua Achebe's side through thick and thin, and especially since his 1991 sad auto accident in Nigeria, which left him paralyzed from the waist down."[9]

Assensoh makes comparisons between these two women and their contributions and similarities, which are captured in the memoir with glowing admiration. These two represent women and their unmatched resilience and support for their families. They exude the strong and supportive characteristics resident in this gender; women possess indomitable spirits, which are celebrated in the memoir in the following words:

> For both black women to have withstood the test of time and their circumstances with dignity means a lot for the black race. In spite of their crushing circumstances, both women remained on the sides of their men to the bitter end. Mrs. King said it best on April 8, 1968 in Memphis city Tennessee about four days after her husband was brutally murdered by an assassin's bullet when she spoke to a large gathering of sympathizers and supporters at the Memphis City Hall. Mrs. King, among other moving details, said: "I came here today because I was impelled to come. During my husband's lifetime, I have always been at his side when I felt that he needed me, and needed me most." […] Yet, like Lady Christie, as already underscored was, Coretta King was perpetually by her husband's side because he was confined to a wheelchair due to his 1990 auto crash that paralyzed him.[10]

Assensoh uses these women's narratives and efforts to signify the importance of women, especially Black women, in the world. Through their contributions to the family unit, these women are examples of the roles of women and mothers in society and as agents of sociocultural progress.

The Impact of Divorce and Remarriage on the Child

From the memoir, a thread of the impact of divorce/remarriage on the child(ren) runs in the text. Assensoh reminisces on the effect of his parents' divorce on his life and education, which has a two-edged blade of positive and negative consequences. Assensoh notes that:

> After my mother married Opanin Boateng, my father heard about it. Therefore, he stopped sending maintenance money for my upkeep. However, I started school at Kasaam Methodist Primary School until I was in fifth grade (or Standard two). Later, my father demanded that I should leave my mother's place to go and stay with him at Dunkwa-on–Offin to continue my education. That request was a blessing in disguise because it helped me attain decent metropolitan education within the educational unit of the Roman Catholic Church of Ghana.[11]

From the illustration of the author's experience in the memoir, divorce places the child(ren) in a vulnerable position, whereby they may suffer a lack of care or attention from either of their parents. In this case, because of the absence of his mother's love and fatherly care, the author only gets a reprieve from staying in school. In like manner, he observes that:

> For the next four years, I stayed with my father and his many wives, each of whom had to be called "mother" i.e., Mother (Maame) Konko, who was the oldest wife and, therefore, the head wife. I was unhappy at the time. Therefore, I spent most of my free time helping at the Catholic Church's Mission House, sometimes working at the bookstore.[12]

Divorce hugely impacts the lives of children, and it impresses on their accomplishments in life. Assensoh's experience, as reflected in his memoir, is a simple yet significant indication of the effects of divorce:

> At about 14 years old, in middle school (or junior high school by American educational standards), I used some of my earned tennis club house funds to buy a train ticket—without my father's permission—to leave town to return to stay with my mother. That was an escape from Dunkwa-on-Offin to live with my kinfolks at Kasaam, near Kumasi. My father was not pleased with that decision. Therefore, it did give him a reason to "disown" me once more. From that time on, it was my mother's responsibility to do everything for me.[13]

That was a particularly hard time for a child to experience: the separation alone causes the child to lose the affection and care of both parents at the same time. The trauma of living without the mother in a house where every woman had her children to care for is a huge burden for the child. This also shows that Assensoh's father shirks his responsibility towards his son, who had to escape from his father's "claws" into his mother's embrace. This part of the memoir reaffirms the unparalleled affection and role of the mother in the life of her child. Meanwhile, Assensoh shares how moving back to his mother's home reflects on the decision of his father to "disown" him, which also culminated in his refusal to help when his son had financial problems. Assensoh reflects that "I needed financial help to go and start my studies at the school. My maternal uncles said that they had their own children to take care of, including some nephews whose parents could not afford for them to have an education. My father refused to assist me to enter Opoku Ware Secondary School."[14] The father's decision not to support his son in his admittance into secondary school made Assensoh go through a difficult but rewarding life journey toward his dreams.

Assensoh reiterates his mother's efforts to have a better chance at life and a good education when his father could have easily helped him but chose not to. Assensoh discloses how his mother, with no formal education, worked hard to support him, adding:

> Sometimes, she had to cook local dishes like kenkey, fried or boiled yams or rice and stew as well as a typical indigenous meal called akankyie, made from corn dough and ripe plantain mixed together. On some occasions, my mother contracted to weed a farm belonging to a richer neighbor in order raise funds for my lorry fare to travel back to the college at Somanya, where we also received about ten dollars a month in allowances. I often used part of my allowance to order course and examination materials from Wosley Hall, Oxford, Bennet College and Rapid Results College (RRC), all of which were correspondence schools in the United Kingdom. My mother often sent money to help with the fees of the correspondence courses.[15]

It is further gathered from the author's musings and remembrances of his childhood that the divorce and his mother's subsequent remarriage take a huge toll on him, as in the refusal to send child support and finance for his education. The impact of divorce on a child is mostly adverse and can negatively impact the child's future. Assensoh's reflection on his past and childhood reveals that he succeeded and became a distinguished Professor Emeritus against all odds and the unfavorable conditions surrounding his growth.

Literary Matter

In this chapter, the reflections of the memoirist on the lives, works, and achievements of some West African writers are explored. Assensoh's contemplations on the issue of the Nobel Literature Prize and the politics it plays are also discussed. In his recollections, Assensoh shares his meeting with some West African intellectuals, who had impressed on him some memorable matters. These scholars are of the West African geopolitical expression and have been successful in their various fields. Their impacts were felt on the continent as contributors and influencers who created a space for their works to thrive and receive international recognition. One such person, whom Assensoh reflects on, is Professor Chinua Achebe, who never received the Nobel Literature Prize till his death in 2013. Assensoh observes that the failure of the literary icon to receive the coveted prize is linked to his view on the African literature conference for writers:

> During this time, in the late 1960s, Professor Achebe had a strong voice as a distinguished writer and also as one of the leaders handling the Heinemann African Writers Series of London. Apart from the claim that Professor Achebe and another African writer were vehemently opposed to the conference being held in Sweden in 1967, Mr. Berglof also introduced me to a couple of Swedish writers, who repeated the same allegation against Professor Achebe, who was among the top writers from Africa that we were campaigning to be considered for the Nobel Literature Prize.[16]

Assensoh's memoir captures the nuances of the Nobel Prize organizers in Sweden as prejudiced, and they could not handle a divergent or controversial argument at the conference venue. Whether the allegation was true or not, the thread of diversity of views was not tolerated by the organizers of the conference, who should have embraced diversity as a value for a progressive world of scholars. In the memoir, Assensoh intimates that his conversation with Professor Achebe seems to veer towards confirming the allegation. However, whether Prof. Achebe deserves the prize is not in doubt because of his scholarly works and contributions to the literary world. Assensoh adds:

> [...] Professor Achebe invited me to his hotel room where he was to ready himself for some scheduled interview with the Dutch press. While with him, I asked him about the Swedish allegations. He explained briefly that whatever he said was in concert with what most of the leading African writers wanted. As a man of proverbs, he added, "Brother Assensoh, our people say that if you want to kill a dog, you give it a bad name."[17]

The foregoing words confirm the argument that the Nobel Literature Prize was being politicized as a way of denying the Nigerian author, Prof. Achebe, what others saw as a much-deserved prize. This sad event points to the fact that this scholar, and probably many others, may lose the chance to be recognized and given merit for their works if they have a controversial stance not accepted by those giving such prizes. Assensoh reflects on how this impacted him:

> In my private but sad world, I reminisced about the painful fact that, as things stood, Professor Achebe was going to continue to miss his turn in receiving the coveted Nobel Literature Prize, irrespective of the fact that he was a productive writer, and that his early book, *Things Fall Apart*, had sold over 10 million copies and also been translated into over 50 international languages.[18]

Again, Assensoh connects Professor Achebe's story with his colleague and fellow literary giant from Nigeria, Professor Wole Soyinka. The connection between the duo, Achebe and Soyinka, is made plain in the memoir, as they both were running for the prize. Assensoh explores his meeting with the literary icon, who received him warmly:

> Sometimes in early 1973, Professor Wole Soyinka came to Stockholm for a cultural and literary festival organized by some Africans and Swedish nationals. I went to see him, and he received me warmly in his hotel room, treating me like a younger brother. In fact, I sat on the chair by the only table in the room, while Professor Soyinka sat on the tip of his bed.[19]

The literary-cum-cultural scholar exudes the spirit of brotherhood by receiving his fellow brother from the neighboring country of Ghana. This action, as well as the one displayed by his counterpart, Achebe, demonstrates the love and communal fellowship that permeates the African continent. According to Assensoh, Professor Soyinka proved, as written in the memoir, that his literary outputs were not based on the platform of recognition for awards but on their utility in the African milieu. This reaction was prompted by the literary scholar when Assensoh tried to make a discussion of the fact that African intellectuals and students in Stockholm were advancing the case of African writers to be recognized and considered for the Nobel Literature Prize. Assensoh further explains that this African writer was unperturbed by the campaign for the prize, and he did not care for the prize. Assensoh notes:

> To my surprise, Professor Soyinka got up from where he was sitting on the bed, and raising his voice and pointing his index right finger, he cautioned my African friends and me to stop the Nobel campaign, adding that he did not write for prizes, per se: 'If I write, and I am given any prize, fine, but I do not make it my business to write because I want a particular accolade, and I am sure Chinua is also like the way I feel.'[20]

Assensoh reflects on his meeting with these West African scholars, among whom was Buchi Emecheta, a Nigerian writer who had also come to the PEN annual conference in 1989. Also, there were other writers from West Africa, such as the late eminent Ghanaian literary intellectual Professor Kofi Awoonor. Assensoh notes that, at the time, Dr. Awoonor had been in New York as Ghana's UN Ambassador for about three of the four years (1990–94) that he was to spend as a diplomat. Assensoh writes: "I did not ask the question I had on my mind about the prize because Ambassador Awoonor, who was present, was also a writer, and it would not have been polite not to make him privy to the discussion."[21] The writer-cum-ambassador was an icon who represented the African continent well in the literary world.

In the memoir, it is apparent that the death and life of the Ghanaian literary icon was felt by many as the cause of his death was tragic and unfortunate:

> Many Africans, from all walks of life, including political leaders, scholars and students, have mourned the senseless murder of Professor Kofi Awoonor in faraway Kenya. Among compatriots expressing condolences as well as shock was Ghanaian President John D. Mahama, who on his way to New York, paused to describe, as a sad twist of fate, the death of Professor Kofi Awoonor, especially his presence at the Nairobi Mall, where terrorists killed shoppers, including Ghana's former Chairman of the prestigious Council of State.[22]

Assensoh's memoir conflates the achievements, histories, works, and deaths of some of these literary icons and how they will be forever and fondly remembered. The death of this literary and political icon was a shock to many, especially the memoirist, who expressed his anguish and sorrow at the tragic loss to Ghana and the African continent. Assensoh says that with a lot of affection and respect for Professor Awoonor, who had met his tragic and, indeed, untimely death at the Westgate Mall in Kenya. He added: "Many of his friends – including myself – did not want to believe that he was really dead."[23] The death of this writer, who had been contributing to the literary world, was captured when Assensoh underscored that it was also disclosed that the late Professor was in Kenya to promote his forthcoming book, which happened to be his last literary work, and was posthumously published, and titled, *The Promise of Hope*. Apart from the Nairobi festival in which he had already participated, the new autobiographical book was a principal reason for Professor Awoonor's presence in Kenya.[24]

The memories of the African writers, the Nobel Prize, and the deaths of Achebe and Awoonor captured by Assensoh in the memoir reflect the great impact these African scholars have had on the author, Africa, and the world. Their works have been etched on the sands of time, and their memories will continually resonate in the minds of generations of scholars in the world.

History and Politics

This part of the chapter examines the author's reflection on political and historical events and discourses he experienced as an adult. In this section, the political upheavals and historical records of memorable events in Africa are explored. The memoir captures Ghana's political intrigues with connections to other African countries.

Intermarriage in Africa: A Tool for Unity and Peace

Intermarriage is a form of marriage that involves people of different states, ethnic groups, religions, classes, nationalities, and races. Jeroen Smits opines that intermarriages reduce the "probability of violent conflict among social groups."[25] Intermarriage also plays a sociopolitical function in society, which is why Assensoh examines this interethnic marriage as a subdivision of intermarriage and its implication for Africa. One interesting subject that Assensoh reflects on in his memoir is the interethnic marriage among prominent African leaders. This discussion relates to the Pan-Africanist ideologies of the African leaders in fostering unity and cooperation amongst countries in the African continent. This topic shows the extent of the movement for unity circulated at the time. However, it is debatable that interethnic and inter-race marriages were for political reasons. Assensoh's recollection of his discussion with friends on the issue of marriage across borders and a book on the subject makes it noteworthy:

> I then remembered an interesting book I read, authored by Mr. James Mickson, one of Ghana's prolific writers in the 1970s. Titled *When the Heart Decides*, the book underscored how love between men and women in many places on the African continent could cut across ethnic lines. It was even an interesting phenomenon when well-educated men like Ghanaian lawyer Joe Appiah (popularly nicknamed "Uncle Joe" in Ghana), Sir Sereste Khama of Botswana and others return to their countries, then under British colonial rule, with British women as their wives.[26]

Assensoh reflects on the impact of interethnic marriages and intermarriages in his memoir and how these are tools for nationalism and unity, which are harnessed by leaders to promote peace and unity amongst several states and countries. Assensoh notes this in his discussion with his friends on the subject and its effects on the nation and continent. Assensoh also observes that as pressmen who had the opportunity to travel far and wide, they were also aware that the Senegalese President, Leopold Sedar Senghor's wife was from France and, as a result, Senegal's First Lady was a French woman. He added: "Then, with a lot of attractive women around in Ghana, the late President Kwame Nkrumah went to Egypt to pick a wife, who subsequently became Ghana's beautiful and worthy First Lady."[27] These marriages were some of the intermarriages that Assensoh highlights with political leaders who were against colonial oppression but could not also deny their affection for these women.

It can be argued that this phenomenon achieves multiple purposes of fostering unity among the nations involved and satisfying the people's desires. Intermarriages, Assensoh adds, were among the tools for social cohesion in many multiethnic societies and countries in Africa. His reflection on this discourse shows that this is not a new idea but a sociocultural and political phenomenon that contributes to the unity of the different ethnic groups, races, classes, and religious groups and divisions of nations and continents.

As captured by Assensoh in the memoir, these African leaders created links for the unification of the African continent and the rest of the world. The reduction of international conflicts among nations is again one of the benefits of this marriage system. Intermarriages unite people of diverse cultures, backgrounds, castes, and faiths with the potential to create a global world of peace and harmony. This system enhances the spirit of nationalism and cultural integration in society. The implication of these intermarriages for the African continent is rooted in the Pan-African ideologies of creating a homogenous state and structure for all Blacks in the world. However, these marriages also transcend the Pan-Africanist ideals to initiate the integration of all cultures, races, and peoples of the world.

Ritual Murders and African Juju in the Twentieth Century

Juju, an object with magical ability or mythic power itself, is a feature of the belief in the traditional power in Africa. The popular assumption is that juju is used for malevolent purposes. However, this aspect of African culture is used for varied reasons, many of which are positive and constructive, such as healing, curing ailments and sicknesses, protection, and security. According to Ibo Cbanga:

> Juju operates on the principle of spiritual contagious contact based on physical contact. The underlying belief is that two entities that have been in close contact have similar properties even after being separated. It then becomes possible to manipulate one in order to reach the other. Thus, in that context, a person's hair, fingernails, a piece of clothing, a shoe, a sock, or a piece of jewel worn by them are all perfect candidates for juju because they are believed to retain the spiritual aura of their owner.[28]

Juju is a sub-strand of the African traditional religion (ATR), which operates by manipulating spiritual resources in the African tradition and belief system. However, as captured and depicted, this belief system "nurtures the negative stereotype often ascribed to ATR reflecting belief systems rooted in fear of destructive spiritual forces within a perverted cosmology."[29] The conceptualization of juju as evil and destructive is a misconception that juxtaposes this indigenous belief system with the importation of foreign religions such as Islam and Christianity. This implies the denial and rejection of value in this aspect of ATR and the projection of the imported beliefs culled from foreign religions. Ritual is an aspect of the ATR, which is a means of propitiation and offering sacrifices to the deities or gods. Ritual is a religious performance that signifies the invocation of powerful spiritual or mythical forces to accomplish a beneficial outcome.

In the case of ritual murders, this involves the removal of different body parts from a person while alive or dead. The purpose is to harvest "the body parts for use as traditional medicine."[30] One of the reasons for ritual murder is that it is fueled by the belief that it effectively makes the ritualist wealthy. Therefore, a good number of convinced persons in many societies across Africa engage in this activity to ensure speedy wealth, among other reasons. This activity shocked Assensoh upon realizing that such a thing is happening in a country that professes to be predominantly Christian. Assensoh says: "I was shocked to realize that several top Liberian governmental and ruling True Whig Party officials were known to be, allegedly, involved in ritual murders, whereby the limbs, tongues, and even private parts of victims were mutilated and used for all forms of rituals, including what as 'African medicine or juju'."[31] This is a common occurrence in African societies where human parts are cut off to use as part of the source materials of the "juju" to gain riches or wealth. This event is a testament to the belief in traditional medicine and power, which is alleged to be effective. According to Assensoh:

> Liberia's senseless killings of the 1970s, meant for ritual murders, reached a personal or intimate crescendo when a fellow Ghanaian was brutally murdered. That was why I did not have sympathies for the former Liberian Maryland County Superintendent Anderson, when he was arrested with several others for ritualistic murder of Moses Tweh in March 1977 and, after exhaustive court trials, they were sentenced to death by hanging.[32]

Assensoh reflects on this issue which has claimed many lives, among whom is the fellow from Ghana. The memoir shows that this aspect of the African culture is yet to be annulled. The implication of this practice is dire for the nation and retrogressive for the development of the continent, as many promising lives have been cut short. The representation of this aspect of ATR in the memoir typifies the significance of this African cultural aspect in the modern age. However, Assensoh condemns this practice in Liberia, where incessant killings have terminated many lives that would have been beneficial to the country and continent. This ritual murder is not a reflection of the purpose of ritual in ATR but a manipulation of the spiritual and mythical resources in the African belief system, which some have manipulated for their gratification.

The Politicization of Public Execution and Killings in Africa

In the memoir, Assensoh discusses and explores incidences peculiar to the African milieu, such as ritual murders and the public execution of offenders on the continent. Public executions are used as political weapons by regimes and governments to instill fear and dread into the opposition and the citizens. He debates the justice of the public execution of a Nigerian scholar, Dr. Obi, who was accused of committing murder. Assensoh ponders on the public display of executions in Africa and whether this is a justifiable means of justice. He adds:

> The hanging was a sorrowful and the most barbaric scene to watch. As a journalist—indeed the Editor-in-Chief of our three newspapers owned by the Dennis family of Liberia—I was given an official tag, like several other Journalists, by the Liberian Department of Information for us to be able to go closer to watch the hanging spectacle.[33]

Public execution of convicted criminals is a common practice in the African milieu as a sign to other opposition groups of the fierceness and intolerance level of the ruling regime. Assensoh shows his disdain for this act which he "considered to be a barbaric extra-judiciary killing." This act is intended to create a spectacle and instill fear in the citizenry rather than to validate the essence of justice in the country. In his reminiscence, Assensoh recalls the event of the day and how this sentence was carried out: "On the fateful Friday morning of the hanging in November 1971, a newspaper Editor by the name of Mr. Rufus Darpoh of the Liberian Star telephoned to alert me to the exact time of the hanging, which was being kept a secret to prevent a possible revolt by Catholic nuns and anti-death penalty adherents."[34] The public execution was more of a travesty than a demonstration of justice as it was organized in a manner befitting public entertainment for the crowd.

Assensoh claims that this experience of the gruesome execution of a man he is acquainted with is a repulsive demonstration and a mockery of the claim of democracy and civilization. The inhumanity of the public display of killings only fuels bitterness and sorrow/agony. He states:

> Many of us, seeing a public hanging for the first time, wondered how Dr. Obi would hang on the tree, as expected by his jailers and official executioner. About thirty minutes later, the platform for the hanging was cleared, and Dr. Obi was standing by himself with the noose around his neck, and still hand-cuffed. A whistle was blown as if a soccer match or a sporting event was about to start. Simultaneously, some persons under the erected platform removed the wood beneath Dr. Obi, and we saw him hanging.[35]

This part of the memoir reveals the politics in the judicial system and the backhand justice of sentencing the man to public execution by hanging. The politicization of the whole justice system in many African countries is a matter of deep contemplation and disappointment to the author. It is as if the author is saying that there is no justice in the hushed and subsequent hasty conviction of the accused. This poses a question about how a continent on the edge of civilization and development encourages and condones this mafia-like sentence and reveals the rot in the justice system in these countries and the political undertone involved in the sentence.

Assensoh makes a connection with the new government's decision and its agenda to dictate the mode of operation in the state. He says:

> Upon becoming the President of Liberia, Dr. Tolbert decides to carry out death sentences in Liberia, unlike how his predecessor had allowed condemned murders to languish in jail. The rumor was that the new President (Tolbert) wanted to show Liberians that he would not spare anybody who committed crimes, including treason, and had been sentenced to die by hanging. He would carry out the death sentences. That, indeed, was why Dr. Obi became a victim of the new order of business in Liberia.[36]

According to Assensoh, the death sentence passed on Dr. Obi had a ripple effect on the citizenry and the nation. The thin line between justice and injustice was crossed, as there were divided opinions about the convicted man. This public execution reflects the political move and tactics of the ruling government to seek satisfaction on behalf of the families of the murdered. Assensoh concludes that the public executions were more political than a demonstration of justice.

Africa and Its Political Struggle: The Impact of the Military Coups

This is probably one of the major issues/matters for reflection and discussion in Assensoh's memoir. The memoir chronicles the author's experiences within the political climate and intrigues of the continent as he is embroiled in them. On the brink of new acclaimed independence from colonial rule, Africa was unstable and tumultuous due to leadership and mismanagement of the continent's wealth and resources. However, the author claims that in the case of Ghana, under the leadership of President Kwame Nkrumah, his administration faced both home and foreign opposition that led to the toppling of the government. He illustrates this in the memoir:

> In my earlier published 1978 work, titled *Kwame Nkrumah: Six Years in Exile, 1966–1972*, I very briefly detailed some aspects of the treachery that went on during the rule of the 1966 military junta of the NLC, although that publication—produced as part of my research during my Scholar-in-Residence position in Pennsylvania, was not actually earmarked to expose as much information about the treachery as I am doing here for the first time.[37]

Assensoh does not only cast aspersions and reveal the extent of the betrayals of the deposed president; he goes further to say that President Nkrumah would have been successful in returning to power; however, these elaborate and strenuous efforts were woefully sabotaged by many of the president's disciples (known as Nkrumaist), who had previously enjoyed life in positions of substance and trust, under his leadership back in Ghana before the 1966 coup.[38] In a particular dissonant tone, Assensoh blames the failure of the deposed president to regain political power on his close aides and members of his government, even though the subject himself had a human hubris of being blind to sycophants in his government and close circle. Assensoh highlights this when he notes:

> I wrote, inter alia: "it is a great disappointment and sorrow that I often reiterated, that if Nkrumah's top political associates in Ghana had not sold their consciences for bread and butter, the ex-president would have regained power in less than a year after his overthrow." The foregoing words were part of my published selective recollections of events about the military coup d'état of February 24, 1966 and how several top political operatives of the late President were, for financial and other reasons, selling their consciences to the very military and police leaders that overthrown their Convention People Party (CPP) government.[39]

Assensoh was a living witness to the various intrigues and coups that rippled the continent at that time in history. He explores the coups staged in his home country and the removal of former Ghanaian president, Kwame Nkrumah, and captures the historical period and military revolution in Ghana and the implication for the exiled president. He notes that:

> Between 1966 and 1969, the city of Accra—the capital of Dr. Nkrumah's beloved Ghana— served as the headquarters of the ruling National Liberation Council (NLC), which was made up of the military-cum-police officers, who forcibly overthrew the Convention People's Party (CPP) government of President Nkrumah, a party which was firmly entrenched in the republic. As a journalist, I was involved in both sides of this intriguing political experience. I played a role in Nkrumah's very strenuous and expensive, but fruitless, efforts to regain political power from his exile base in Conakry, capital of Guinea and, in the process, return to political power in Ghana.[40]

Like the axiomatic saying that charity begins at home, the memoirist begins his reflection on the political intrigues in Africa from his home country, Ghana, and the roles he played as a journalist and a citizen of the country. In the multiple coups that followed, Assensoh reflects on the intrigues around the deposed Ghanaian president, who had been on a visit to China at the time of the revolution, and the roles he played in the political saga in Ghana during the period of the coups. He notes that: "Consequently, efforts were made by two sections of the 1966–69 security services in Ghana—namely the Special Branch of the Police Force and the Military Intelligence of the Ghana Armed Forces—to recruit me as a double agent."[41] The author claims to have played a key role in Nkrumah's efforts and plans to return and seize control of the toppled government. In the memoir, Assensoh notes that this was a common phase in the African continent as many African countries were experiencing this peculiar phase of revolution and coups from the military arm of the states' security apparatuses.

Consequently, other African countries such as Cote d'Ivoire, Liberia, Nigeria, and Egypt were not left out in the history of military coups in Africa. Assensoh notes that in Cote d'Ivoire, in 1999, General Robert Guei staged a coup to topple Bedie's government before Bedie fled from Ivory Coast into exile. Bedie later made it known that part of the instability his government faced came from the Islamic north and its ambitious leader, Alassane Ouattara, whose parents were not born in Ivory Coast.[42] The violence and coup in these countries are significant for the instability and underdevelopment of the continent. In the case of Nigerian coups, Assensoh notes that in January 1966, Nigeria witnessed its first successful coup d'état, which prompted then Ghanaian President Nkrumah to make a broadcast in which he castigated some Nigerian leaders instead of simply registering his sorrow at the fact that Nigeria had lost several prominent persons in the military upheaval.[43] Assensoh makes a comparison between the political struggles in Ghana and Nigeria, where these countries were experiencing similar activities such as coups and instability. He reflects:

> In Africa, military interventions in politics come in many forms. They include mainstream or an outright coup d'état and political assassinations, whereby an unwanted leader or a regime is eliminated through murder and, sometimes, a palace coup, whereby a collective military leadership decides to remove an unpopular colleague as a leader of a military government. Egypt has since January 25, 2011 seen two outright coups d'état that have been described as being part of the Middle East's Arab Spring exercises.[44]

Assensoh also uses Egypt to exemplify how political instability and coups have shaped the political life of the African continent. In the case of Egypt's coups, military intervention led to civilian elections that installed the government of Mohamed Morsi. However, this installation was short-lived as it was interrupted by another coup spearheaded by the military elite of Egypt.[45] This latter coup was to protest against the ruling sect in the country, especially the Muslim Brotherhood. Assensoh observes that, similarly, the Egyptian Army, on July 3, 2013, dealt a swift military blow to the first Muslim Brotherhood government in Egypt in a full-fledged coup d'état.[46] According to Assensoh, what is happening in Egypt has shown that although the country is often seen in Middle Eastern terms, it remains in the ambit of African politics, in which coups d'état are regular and popular occurrences.[47]

Unequivocally, Assensoh explored the historical-cum-political coups in Africa, especially in West Africa, as the major problem the continent was experiencing at the time. These African countries' military involvements and takeovers were significant to the troubled years and were causative agents of the African political struggle. From the example of Ghana, Nigeria, Liberia, Cote d'Ivoire, and Egypt, Assensoh clearly links the failure in political growth and government to the several military interventions in these nations with repercussions for the continent as a whole. While Assensoh blames these military agents for the turbulence suffered in the continent, he also identifies the excesses of the political leaders and their policies that have impacted the lives of the citizens in their countries. Assensoh combines his personal knowledge and education to explore these historical-cum-political events and discusses them in the memoir.

Political Instability, Killings, and Terrorism: The Bane of Africa's Development

The constant and significant thread running through Assensoh's memoir is political instability, crisis, killings, and terrorism, which are the bane of the African continent. Assensoh reflects on the death of some colleagues and friends who have been unfortunate victims of the political instability, killings, and coups in their countries. Assensoh started with the political instability in his home country, Ghana, while also briefly exploring similar cases in other African countries. Many of the countries in Africa have witnessed one or several incidences of political instability, revolution, terrorism, and coups which have been detrimental to the growth and development of these nations and the continent as a whole.

In the memoir, *A Matter of Sharing*, Assensoh explores the removal of the democratically elected president, and the coups and countercoups staged in Ghana. This led to several killings of people who may have been opposed to the military regime at the time. The author uses the quintessential example of the coup that led to the exile of Ghana's former President Nkrumah and his subsequent death to trace the level of political instability in his country. Nkrumah remains one of the foremost leaders and activists of Pan-Africanism and its propagation in Africa. This is particularly captured in the memoir when Assensoh reflects on the 100th anniversary of the birth of Ghana's first president, Kwame Nkrumah, in the contexts of African political history, Pan-Africanist ideals, and international affairs:

Again, with a sense of continental and black diasporic history, the late Prime Minister Kwame Nkrumah, who was becoming the first elected indigenous leader of Ghana, made a very historic and reverberating statement on the night of the fateful March 6th, which in essence was this, and we quote it here for the benefit of the Young students, who might not have heard it before. Dr. Nkrumah, told his huge audience, part of the new Ghanaian citizenry as well as foreign guests and dignitaries, including then Vice-President Richard Nixon of the United States: Quote: "The independence of Ghana will be meaningless unless it is linked up with the total liberation of Africa." Indeed, by Africa, the new Ghanaian leader meant continental Africa, diasporic Blacks of the United States of America, the Caribbean Islands and Southeast Asia, where we have blacks mining immigrants called Irian Jayans in Indonesia, Malaysia and other places of the world.[48]

From the excerpt above, the Pan-Africanist leader, Kwame Nkrumah, was a great leader who espoused the liberation message, the crusade for Black independence, and the unification of all Blacks in the world. The unfortunate seizure of political power in Ghana while Nkrumah was away enunciated the bane of the development of the African continent. The political instability in Ghana, which culminated in the years Nkrumah spent in exile in Guinea and in his death, slowed the progress of the nation and truncated the vision of the Pan-Africanist leader. Assensoh elucidates the importance of this great leader thus: "Ghana's late President Nkrumah was a great motivator of and influencer of many black leaders in and outside Africa, hence today it is important for meaningful black scholars and leaders ... to honor the birth, life and times of this greatest African, who lived in the 20th century."[49] The representation of Nkrumah in the memoir sparks a paradoxical feeling of sorrow and happiness. His removal from power and subsequent death in exile provokes sadness at the loss of such a great leader on the continent.

Again, Assensoh captures the peril of murders and killings in Liberia, which claimed the lives of eminent scholars and leaders. In the exploration of the military coup d'état in West Africa and Africa in general, Liberia had its own share of these turbulent times in the history of political instability and killings that had contributed to the underdevelopment of the African continent. Assensoh reflects on the death of a prominent politician in Liberia, Foreign Minister C. Cecil Dennis, Jnr., who was executed by the Master-Sergeant Samuel K. Doe-led military coup d'état.[50] The murder of several promising African intellectuals for rituals, such as the Ghanaian-born Obarima Sarfo, whom Assensoh describes as a United Kingdom-trained nautical engineer, was barbaric and counterproductive to the nation and the continent. This, and a long list of kangaroo trials and executions, have robbed the nation and continent of intellectuals and leaders who would have shot their nation and continent to global reckoning.

Furthermore, the assassinations, public hangings, and terrorist attacks in the continent, which saw the killings of a political-cum-literary icon amongst other youths, have proven that the continent is being pulled down the drain by its own people and citizens. Political instability has led to multiple changes of government and policies, which affect the economic and political growth of these African countries. Assensoh gives instances of the several revolutions and military coups in different African countries, such as Ghana, Nigeria, Liberia, and Egypt, in the following words:

> Indeed, it is a fact that most coups retard the economic progress of the affected countries. That has been demonstrated in many countries in Africa. Whenever a coup took place, potential investors were said to play wait-and-see tactics. It simply meant that they did not want to enter the affected nation to invest their funds or capital, a situation which often crippled African countries.[51]

Political instability is a malaise detrimental to the economic and political development of the African continent, as enunciated by Assensoh above. Sociopolitical instability leads to a reduction in investments, as it impacts the physical and human capital of the affected economies. Ari Aisen and Francisco Veiga also support this argument that political instability reduces GDP growth rates significantly.[52] The recorded political instability, terrorism, and military coups have impacted the African countries where these have been recorded, and the implication for the growth of the continent is huge because of the negative effects of these issues.

Kwame Nkrumah: A Pan-Africanist

Pan-Africanism is a political and cultural philosophy and movement that espouses the unification of peoples of African descent. Pan-Africanist intellectuals, such as W. E. B. Du Bois, in the United States, have been captured in the memoir by Assensoh to be instrumental to the growth and spread of this movement in America and Africa, among other places. However, Assensoh focuses on the former Ghanaian President's role and legacy in terms of African political history and Pan-Africanism. In harnessing the growth and spread of Pan-African ideals and ideologies among his fellow African leaders like Jomo Kenyatta, Julius Nyerere, and other world leaders, Nkrumah's contribution to the political movement of Pan-Africanism is explored in Assensoh's *A Matter of Sharing*. Assensoh notes in the memoir that:

> Interestingly, Kwame Nkrumah [...] had never forgotten his black comrades and former classmates with whom he consulted and often corresponded, hence he invited the late Rev. Dr. Martin Luther King and Mrs. Coretta Scott King of blessed memory as well as Dr. W.E.B DuBois [...] who helped in organizing the 1945 Pan-African Congress in Manchester, UK.[53]

Nkrumah's impact in bringing together these leaders in the United States is adequately explored to reveal his undisputable efforts in the unification of all Blacks in the world. Assensoh's explorations of the Ghanaian leader's Pan-Africanist activities are explicitly captured to affirm the great leader's influence on other black leaders of the world:

> There are many black leaders in Africa, the Caribbean nations, in the US diaspora and Southeast Asia, who have played formidable and yeoman's roles in advancing the black race. Yet, it is still a truism that Ghana's late president Nkrumah had a concerted plan to see to it that his beloved Africa became free of colonialism, neo-colonialism and, indeed was united. He also felt seriously that all black men and women, world-wide, should have a place in liberated Africa.[54]

Pan-Africanist ideal is one of the recurring themes in Assensoh's *A Matter of Sharing*, which eloquently captures one of the proponents of the movement. The efforts and plans of the Ghanaian president, Nkrumah, in ensuring and proclaiming the liberation of all Blacks in the world are generously explored in the memoir. The Pan-Africanist ideologies, which call for the unification of all Blacks in the world and Africa, rubbed off on the Guinean President, Sekou Toure, who declared Nkrumah his co-president during his exilic days in Guinea. In the memoir, Assensoh avers that Nkrumah, the Ghanaian leader, encouraged the return of African-Americans to Ghana. Part of the orchestrated plan prompted Dr. Nkrumah to write a letter of favorable attestation (styled "To whom

It May Concern") on his official letter-headed paper (as the then Leader of Government Business) for Richard Wright, a leading African American author of notable books.[55]

One of the efforts of the Pan-Africanist leader in uniting all Blacks in the world is captured when Assensoh enunciates that:

> Dr. Nkrumah made a solemn appeal to African Americans (then called Negroes). In his Lincoln University commencement address, he invited African Americans or Negroes of the United States to return to the future Ghana to help the country's developmental growth [...] As a result of Dr. Nkrumah's 1951 clarion call, many African American leaders from the Unites States packed their bag and baggage to return to their post-independent ancestral country of Gold Coast in West Africa, which had been re-named Ghana on March 6, 1957. Among the top black leaders who heeded Dr. Nkrumah's call were Dr. W.E.B DuBois; George Padmore of the Caribbeans; Maya Angelo, the poet; St. Claire-Drake; and many others.[56]

Assensoh ascribes the presence of these prominent intellectuals in Africa to the efforts of Nkrumah in bringing the Black peoples of the world together. Assensoh further claims that Dr. King and Vice President Richard Nixon's meeting in Ghana during the Independence event in 1957 led to the collaborative efforts to have the Eisenhower Administration initiate several landmark civil rights legislation that later became prominent under the late Presidents John F. Kennedy and Lyndon B. Johnson.[57] To ensure the stability and comfort of the invited African America leaders in Ghana, Assensoh opines that they were granted the rights of Ghanaian citizenship. For example, after DuBois moved to Ghana, he celebrated his 95th birthday in the Ghanaian capital, Accra, in February 1963. On that important occasion, President Nkrumah and his Egyptian wife, Madam Fathia, visited Dr. DuBois and his wife, Mrs. Shirley Graham Dubois, during which the president reportedly presented Dr. DuBois with his Ghanaian citizenship documentation, including a Ghanaian diplomatic passport.[58]

Nkrumah remained instrumental in the movement for the emancipation of his people in the former Gold Coast (Ghana) and all Blacks in the world. His efforts to eradicate colonialism and neocolonialism are explored briefly in the memoir, *A Matter of Sharing*. However, Assensoh notes that, in elucidating the efforts of this great Pan-Africanist leader in the thematic context of "Ghana in Africa and the World," one may briefly look at the sad fact that the late President's lofty and lifelong plan of uniting Africa and bringing to their ancestral continent many of the Blacks of the world, including those in the United States, was interrupted in the coup d'état of February 24, 1966, which ended his leadership of Ghana.[59] Indeed, the representation of Nkrumah as a great leader and influencer for his country, Ghana, the African continent, and all Blacks in the world is aptly captured and discussed in Assensoh's memoir.

African Leaders and Leadership: A Prototype of Lincoln's Influence/Effect

Expressly stated in the memoir and pondered on by the author is the "Lincolnian" influence and effect on African leaders and government. In this memoir, Assensoh reflects on the impact of Abraham Lincoln's government and policies on African leaders and their government policies. He adds that:

> [...] in many countries of the geopolitical expression known as Third World, political leaders have often relied on varied forms of statements and axioms by former President Abraham Lincoln to discuss leadership as well as governance issues [...] Many leaders of the developing world saw a ray of hope in [President Abraham] Lincoln's leadership for they considered it exemplary because his desire for the emancipation of enslaved persons dated back to the mid-1800s.[60]

From the above, Assensoh links the historical-cum-political influence the former US president had on developing nations, especially the African countries grappling with the realities of independence in their different nation-states. The influence of the US president transcends the quotation of words and statements to shaping the system of government in these nations. It can be argued that the structures and policies of the governance of these African leaders were built on the ideologies of Abraham Lincoln on matters such as administration, politics, and women's inclusion in these governments. The adoption of the political ideologies of Lincoln in Africa is exemplified by the instance of Nkrumah's policy on women's participation in politics. Assensoh notes that, indeed, similar to the Lincolnian way of expressing equality, Nkrumah, for example, underscored the following about the dictum for women in politics in Africa: "To the men I say, assist the women to take an active part in the political life of the country; for remember, no country can be truly democratic in which women do not have equality with men."[61]

Abraham Lincoln's policy on equality in America plays as a significant background and launchpad for the development and inclusion of women in politics, as described by Nkrumah's statement and policy. The equality ideology for all American citizens and the freedom of the enslaved, which erupted from Lincoln's political ideologies, gave impetus to the African leaders' efforts toward equality for all. Assensoh affirms this in his memoir when he opines that:

> This desire for equality led the late African philosopher, Dr. Emmanuel Kwegyir Aggrey, to espouse this philosophy in the education of women. Dr. Aggrey, who was educated in the United States of America at Livingston College and Hood Theological Seminary in North Carolina, as well as at Columbia University, New York, was the mentor of Nkrumah at the famous British-established Achimota College. Very often, he said in church sermons that whenever a man was educated in preference to women, it meant giving education to an individual. However, giving formal or mainstream "school" education to a woman was like educating an entire family, because the woman, upon producing children, would always impart part of that education to them.[62]

To further validate this argument/discussion of the influence of Lincoln's ideologies on African leaders, Assensoh notes in the memoir that the former South African President Nelson Mandela's commission, named the "Truth Commission," was fashioned in the manner of Lincoln's second inaugural address of 1865, with the title "With Malice towards None." Lincoln's speech bore a great influence in fostering the spirit of forgiveness, reconciliation, and unity in Mandela's commission and country, as Assensoh expresses:

> Several other leaders and nations in Africa have followed the shining example of former President Mandela, who built on and extended Lincoln's example in tangible ways. Ghana's President John A. Kufuor established his own presidential commission of very distinguished Ghanaian leaders, which was called the National Reconciliation Commission (NRC), and tailored to the work of the South African commission.[63]

Abraham Lincoln's political ideologies and government became a significant frame for these African leaders to project their policies and governance. From the democratic system of government to the inclusion of gender equality policies, Lincoln's ideas were carried to the shores of Africa and beyond. Assensoh concluded that it was evident that Lincoln's impact extended positively beyond American shores to touch the pulse of politics, governance, citizen participation, and yearnings for democracy on the African continent as well. As African nations and their leaders continue to work out the complications of democratic governance and also try to reap the benefits of democracy itself, they owe a debt of gratitude to America's 16th and Civil War President, Mr. Lincoln, who paved the way for the emancipation of their kith and kin on the African continent.[64] The leadership and government of Lincoln remain a pedestal for these African leaders and government to build and sustain democratic societies where equality thrives.

Conclusion

This chapter begins with an introductory note on reflection, and there is also a division of the chapter into the categories for discussions. It then defines reflection as the writings, thoughts, and contemplation on specific issues or discourses in the past. The chapter discusses the memoir and the reflections of the author contained in the text. The memoir is replete with political issues in Africa and the interconnection of history in the periods concerned. This chapter discusses the personal matter of the author of the memoir and explores the interplay of the author's personal, political, and historical experiences in the memoir. In exploring the author's reflection on the impact of the mother versus the father on the children, the chapter captures the elevation of the mother above the father figure as the essential ingredient in the life of a child. The absence of the father figure in the life of a child is barely felt, as captured in the memoir through Assensoh's personal experience. The mother becomes a frame that envelops and protects the child and its future, while the father's contribution is minimal or nonexistent.

The chapter further discusses the importance of the mother figure in the life of her child(ren), which is a tentacle that binds the future of the child. In this author's personal reflection, he attributes his success to his mother and the sacrifices that she made to see that he had a great future. The chapter then glides to the impact of divorce on the child(ren) as a subtle but important discussion of the hardship that characterizes the life of the author of the memoir. The author's childhood experiences, when he was rejected by his father due to his parents' divorce, unambiguously express the impact of divorce on the child.

Above all, this reflective chapter also explored the political-cum-historical issues that the memoir reflected upon. The chapter dwells on the political intrigues in Ghana, where the author originates from, and the different coups that were staged to remove the leaders. One of the major coups was the removal of President Kwame Nkrumah, and the chapter covered his exilic struggles to reclaim power. Assensoh reflects on the efforts of this leader to retake power from his exilic home in Guinea, including the failed and fruitless efforts due to the betrayal of the president's close aides and friends. The chapter also explores the author's contribution to helping the deposed president regain power in Ghana and the unfortunate incident of his detention. The detention and danger to his life spurred the author to flee for his life because of the network of efforts to make him a double agent and use him in toppling the efforts of the deposed president.

The chapter goes on to link the political instability in different African countries to the slow growth and underdevelopment of the continent. Assensoh records several countries that have experienced political instability, killings, terrorism, and military coups d'état that have claimed innocent lives and prominent individuals on the continent. In this vein, the chapter touches on the politicization of public executions in Liberia and the implications of the killings and assassinations of prominent political leaders who were part of the opposition to the ruling regime/administration.

Assensoh uses the opportunity to reflect on his meetings with some West African scholars and the politics at play in the award of the Nobel Literature Prize. He inadvertently implies that some writers who deserved the award and international prize were denied based on some internal politicking against them. In this part of the chapter, Assensoh highlights how the likes of Chinua Achebe and Wole Soyinka were embroiled in the Nobel Prize skirmish. It also espouses the contribution of these writers, especially from West Africa to world literature. The impacts of these writers were expressed in the memoir through the author's personal encounters with them as he celebrated and captured his direct relationship with them.

Additionally, the chapter shows that African writers, scholars, and intellectuals are significant in world history. It also discusses the author's reflection on the Pan-Africanist leader, Kwame Nkrumah, and his Pan-Africanist ideals. In this chapter, the activities of Pan-Africanist leaders and proponents in disseminating Pan-Africanism ideologies and spreading the movement in Africa and the world are explored. The chapter captures Assensoh's representations of Nkrumah and other Pan-Africanists in the memoir. The most significant African leader and proponent adequately explored in the chapter is Nkrumah and how his efforts have been recognized in the memoir and by the world.

In conclusion, this chapter has explored the historical, political, and personal reflections in *A Matter of Sharing*. It is a testament to the interlinked and interconnected issues on politics, history, and literature, which is reminiscent of life itself. Above all, the chapter embraces the nuances of African politics, histories, lives, and existences as explored and captured in Assensoh's very interesting memoir.

Notes

1 A. B. Assensoh, *A Matter of Sharing: My Memoir* (Austin: Pan-African University Press, 2016), 145.
2 Assensoh, *A Matter of Sharing*, 3.
3 Assensoh, *A Matter of Sharing*.
4 Assensoh, *A Matter of Sharing*, 5.
5 Assensoh, *A Matter of Sharing*, 3.
6 Assensoh, *A Matter of Sharing*.
7 Assensoh, *A Matter of Sharing*, 4.
8 Assensoh, *A Matter of Sharing*, 127.
9 Assensoh, *A Matter of Sharing*.
10 Assensoh, *A Matter of Sharing*, 128.
11 Assensoh, *A Matter of Sharing*, 6.
12 Assensoh, *A Matter of Sharing*.
13 Assensoh, *A Matter of Sharing*, 7.
14 Assensoh, *A Matter of Sharing*.
15 Assensoh, *A Matter of Sharing*, 8.
16 Assensoh, *A Matter of Sharing*, 59.
17 Assensoh, *A Matter of Sharing*, 60.
18 Assensoh, *A Matter of Sharing*, 61.
19 Assensoh, *A Matter of Sharing*, 58.
20 Assensoh, *A Matter of Sharing*.
21 Assensoh, *A Matter of Sharing*, 60.
22 Assensoh, *A Matter of Sharing*, 69.
23 Assensoh, *A Matter of Sharing*, 71.
24 Assensoh, *A Matter of Sharing*, 72.
25 Jeroen Smits, "Ethnic Intermarriage and Social Cohesion: What Can We Learn from Yugoslavia?" *Social Indicators Research* 96, no. 3 (2010): 417–432.
26 Assensoh, *A Matter of Sharing*, 49.
27 Assensoh, *A Matter of Sharing*.
28 Ibo Cbanga, "Juju," *Encyclopaedia Britannica*, n.d., https://www.britannica.com/topic/juju-magic.
29 May Ikeora, "The Role of African Traditional Religion and 'Juju' in Human Trafficking: Implications for Anti-trafficking," *Journal of International Women's Studies* 17, no. 1 (2016): 1–18.
30 Mogomme Alpheus Masoga and Temba Rugwiji, "A Reflection on Ritual Murders in the Biblical Text from an African Perspective," *Scriptura* 117 (2018): 6.
31 Assensoh, *A Matter of Sharing*, 49.
32 Assensoh, *A Matter of Sharing*, 50.
33 Assensoh, *A Matter of Sharing*, 41.
34 Assensoh, *A Matter of Sharing*, 42.
35 Assensoh, *A Matter of Sharing*, 43.
36 Assensoh, *A Matter of Sharing*, 47.
37 Assensoh, *A Matter of Sharing*, 15.
38 Assensoh, *A Matter of Sharing*, 17.
39 Assensoh, *A Matter of Sharing*, 19.
40 Assensoh, *A Matter of Sharing*, 13.
41 Assensoh, *A Matter of Sharing*.
42 Assensoh, *A Matter of Sharing*, 91.
43 Assensoh, *A Matter of Sharing*, 93.
44 Assensoh, *A Matter of Sharing*, 98.
45 Assensoh, *A Matter of Sharing*, 99.
46 Assensoh, *A Matter of Sharing*.
47 Assensoh, *A Matter of Sharing*, 101.

48 Assensoh, *A Matter of Sharing*, 74.
49 Assensoh, *A Matter of Sharing*, 76.
50 Assensoh, *A Matter of Sharing*, 51.
51 Assensoh, *A Matter of Sharing*, 146.
52 Ari Aisen and Francisco Jose Veiga, "How Does Political Instability Affect Economic Growth?" *International Monetary Fund*, IMF Working Paper 11/12 (2011), 4.
53 Assensoh, *A Matter of Sharing*, 74–75.
54 Assensoh, *A Matter of Sharing*, 78.
55 Assensoh, *A Matter of Sharing*.
56 Assensoh, *A Matter of Sharing*, 76.
57 Assensoh, *A Matter of Sharing*, 77.
58 Assensoh, *A Matter of Sharing*, 78.
59 Assensoh, *A Matter of Sharing*, 79.
60 Assensoh, *A Matter of Sharing*, 110.
61 Assensoh, *A Matter of Sharing*, 112. (quoting Kwame Nkrumah, 1967, 100)
62 Assensoh, *A Matter of Sharing*.
63 Assensoh, *A Matter of Sharing*, 113.
64 Assensoh, *A Matter of Sharing*, 116.

Chapter Eight

TOWARD A SPATIAL AND IDENTITY SYNTHESIS: REGIONAL PECULIARITIES IN AFRICAN MEMOIRS

Introduction

I deliberately chose to end this study with an overview of the nuances that dictate the texts produced by African memoirs, especially from other regions of the continent not given attention in the preceding chapters. I opened with a broader Africa-wide orientation of the memoirs, and I want to close with some peculiarities that I have framed as "regional." As a mode of writing, the memoir—which can be categorized under the (auto)biography genre—has received much attention in recent times. It has been classified as a form of fiction with dashes of believability and a semblance of truth. Critics like James Olney[1] and Paul John Eakin[2] have noted the autobiography/biography bifurcation and the interpenetration of the two forms. Autobiographers become biographers when they focus on parents, siblings, and significant other persons in their lives.

Conversely, one who injects personal details into a narrative of another life ends up producing an autobiography. To adapt James Olney's idea of the open-endedness of autobiography, an autobiography half emerges in the act of living and writing about others. People can write their lives' stories obliquely by writing the life of another, a status Eakin calls crypto-autobiography. Commenting on her own life and work, Bretell says, "as a book by a daughter about a mother who was a writer, this text involves a blending of voice, by extension, a blurring of genre … it is both a biography and an autobiography, not only because the lives of a mother and a daughter are inextricably intertwined."[3] This is natural because people do not live in isolation. The lives of people in society interpenetrate, and people define themselves in terms of the mutual inter-influencing of their lives and those of the people around them. Thus, a life is given significance by the social milieu, the culture in which it is found.

As an important mode of the narrative genre, the functions of a memoir are numerous. Even though it is a writing about the life of a singular individual, it can be viewed to perform the role of preservation, documentation, and, most importantly, offering representations of behavioral patterns to be followed and imbibed by readers. Not every person gets to live a life eventful and prominent enough to sustain the writing of full-length memoirs, so the usual subjects of memoirs tend to be persons whose lives are considered significant enough to arouse and sustain public interest.

In contrast to autobiography, the memoir is epiphanic, as it evokes different senses of emotions and overwhelming thoughts in the minds of the reader because of its effective, detailed, and often chronological narration of everyday life. Notably, the memoir has clusters of thematic preoccupations, which can be greatly attributed to the phenomenon of displacement and migration of memoirists as they navigate different spaces and carry with them various stories of universal and particular significance. Thus, it is a genre that is important in contemporary literature.

Memoirs are connected to the past; therefore, a memoir serves as a historical source, reference, and personal reflection. Memoirs are about memories, and they tend to maintain an inseparable relationship with historical facts. Over time, literary critics and observers have described the memoir as a loaded package filled with memorial arguments. Yet, what distinguishes it as a kind of literature is the clear sense of a story, as well as the presence of the storyteller in it. It narrates events that happened in the past by recalling them in the present. The actions of the storyteller, who partakes in its enactment, have the power to present real facts or exaggerate. However, the story is of the utmost importance in the memoir as readers are concerned with the personal interests, bias, and manipulation of the story and its empathetic nodes.

The function of the memoir is overbearing as it shows a proclivity to society. African fiction and memoirs, an offshoot of African literature, explore the sociopolitical, historical, and cultural experiences and identifiers of African people. It is pertinent to note that African writers are adept at talking or writing about the past. They are totally involved in the narration of the past as opposed to the present because, more often than not, to easily navigate the unknown future, we have to be deeply rooted in the dwellings and vivid narration of the past. However, it is important to note that different African regions and nations have their peculiarities, belief systems, and even worldviews about African stories that carry the essence of determining their reliability in coping with various challenges of present and future engagements. The sociopolitical phases, especially the colonial and postcolonial, which have influenced novels-memoirs in Africa, are of varied sources and orientations, but the focus in this chapter is on regional peculiarities.

Imperialism has made Africa a productive continent. It is a common thread that runs through the continent's broad geographical landscape—from the North to the South and East to West. One of the indelible and relatively innocuous consequences of imperialism is increased literacy across the continent. The thematic preoccupation of African memoirs differs from region to region. While West African fiction dealt more with orality (the inculcation of West African myths, legends, folklore, and oral traditions peculiar to the region), francophone African fiction focused on the colonial policy of assimilation, in which the francophone West Africans became citizens of France, and this policy influenced most of the fictional works from this region.

East African authors delved into the oral traditions alongside the fight for independence and then postcolonial realities and disillusionment. North African fiction was influenced by Arabic norms and features of the Islamic religion because of its early contact with the Arabs, while the majority of the women's writings were categorized with themes of freedom and rebellion against patriarchy. This shows that writings from these regions painted pictures of a multicultural continent. The experience in the southern region of Africa is also distinct, particularly in South Africa, where the writings were focused more on the apartheid system. Violence, protest, and the fight for freedom are common themes in South African writings. Recently though, the focus has shifted to reconciliation issues and the coexistence of Blacks and whites in the country.

Oral Tradition in West Africa

The West African memoir takes its roots from the oral tradition of its people. The stories, themes, language, and plot of most of the prose fiction from the region are from oral traditions. Some critics have referred to African prose fiction as pioneers or pioneering texts because they are rich in oral heritage and synchronize with the traditions of the people in the region. Orality and oral tradition were revived in African literature by early novelists such as D. O. Fagunwa, Amos Tutuola, Elechi Amadi, Chinua Achebe, and Wole Soyinka.

Also, in *Ake, Years of Childhood*, Soyinka presents himself as a narrator haunted by a sense of the past with the dilemma of struggling between history and witnessing traditions that sought to shape him. By watching himself in the narration as an alienated character and much of a stranger in a world he created (but which is still not his), he presents a simultaneous struggle and ultimately seeks to be a gatekeeper and essential narrator of continued stories in traditions and traditions in stories. One of the totems painted in memoirs is the presentation of home. The narrator believes in helping to build a place to feel at home and connected to, which is a common narrative totem in memoirs as the spatial outlook of the home is described vividly. This landmark serves as a motif for readers and creates a semblance of truth and what readers can connect to.

As a historical source, the impact of colonialism and Christianity can be seen in African memoirs. Soyinka was born during the colonial period, and it influenced his childhood. The mode of presentation of the town, Ake, was a town of two civilizations. In the same vein, Christianity provided education, and the writer benefitted from it with conflict arising from the towering of the ancestral spirits. Upon a closer look at the memoir, the readers note the various observations in relation to Soyinka's childhood observations:

- His ability to reason and sense of perception (p. 43)
- Soyinka's remarkable powers of observation (p. 228)
- Communal reflections and spatial comparisons (p. 134)
- Coping with stages of maturity (p. 230)

The context of assimilation comes in regarding the peculiarity of Francophone memoirs. Oyekan Owomoyela defines assimilation as "a system designed to transform her (France's) African subjects into Black French men and women."[4] The French assimilation policy was camouflaged to be that which would bring equality. According to Oyeniyi Okunoye, "the policy succeeded in alienating the average educated man from his own culture, people and cultural environment, offering him instead, a false sense of acceptance into the French society."[5] To Martin Lewis, assimilation encompasses the assimilation of the natives, as well as political and administrative assimilation.[6]

The idea was that African cultures should be left to coexist alongside the French without being necessarily integrated. However, in practice, it only resulted in the traditional authorities being used at the lowest cadre of the administration. Hence, it still implied that whites were superior to Blacks. In the long run, the positive-turned-negative effects of the policy on the colonized could no longer be tolerated, resulting in reactions against the policy in a movement known as Negritude. It is important to recall that the sociopolitical phases, especially the colonial and postcolonial, which have influenced novels and memoirs (prose fiction in Africa), are of varied sources and orientations.

Notably, Francophone African writers, specifically fiction writers, contested the colonial ideology. They published books focused on cultural restoration and emphasized the richness and value of African culture. For instance, in Camara Laye's *The African Child*, the author accentuates the importance of communal love, compassion, and respect, concentrating on the communal nature of African societies to show European readers how different African societies are from Europe's individualistic society.[7] As previously stated, literary works of art are analyzed in terms of their creativity and value. This is more of an aesthetic appreciation of the writings, which comes when a work of art meets or exceeds the expectation of the reader or audience.

Islamic and Arabic, and Patriarchy and Institutional Corruption in the North African Memoir

The presence of the Arabs in North Africa as early as AD 622 led to the introduction of Islam in some parts of the continent. This had a significant impact on the Muslim authors' inculcation of Koranic verses into their writings, which has remained a standard reference for modern African fiction of Arab origin, as represented by North African novelists such as Nawal El Saadawi, Naguib Mahfouz, Tayeb Salih, and others. For instance, the North is characterized by its engagement with Arab political, sociocultural, and religious experiences that shape their language, mores, ethos, and worldview.

Aside from religion, gender and identity relations also influence fictional literary works in North Africa. For example, Tayeb Salih's *Season of Migration to the North* dwells on misogynistic tendencies/attitudes. In the novel, the dialogues, quotes, narrative voice, and even selected events are prioritized and dominant for male characters, whereas they are paraphrased for female characters and subordinate in nature, as shown in Hosna's character as compared to Sa'eed's. Another example is *Woman at Point Zero* by Nawal El Saadawi, a biographical narrative written in the form of a journal or diary. This work of fiction is an intertextuality of the real story of Firdaus and the hidden face of Eiel, with a focus on the predicament of women in an Islamic society. The novel illustrates the life of a woman in a patriarchal society. In this prose work, Firdaus, a female character, takes the reader on a voyage through the story of her life. She is subjected to different traumatic experiences, such as her father beating her mother, yet she will cook his food. Firdaus grows up to know about the deep-seated inequalities in her society and how a female child is considered a misfortune.[8]

El Saadawi's *Woman at Point Zero* also explores how a man abuses a woman to the point of death. Apart from Firdaus, the major character and a historical persona, the author, El Saadawi, also faced threats from the Egyptian government after the publication of her book titled *Women and Sex*. Like Firdaus, she suffered and experienced many derogatory reactions from men in her country because she stood against female enslavement. Firdaus is treated as a weaker sex, as someone who cannot and must not compete with men. She is enslaved by the persistent encounter of oppression perpetrated by men.

Narrating Firdaus's life, El Saadawi writes: "However, all the men I did get to know, every single man of them, has filled me with but one desire: to lift my hand and bring it smashing down on his face. But because I am a woman, I never had the courage to lift my hand."[9] This portrays the intense fear that fills Firdaus's heart. Every man she meets leaves her with deep hurt. She remembers the lovers that never fulfill their promises, the men who pretend to love her but betray her trust. This says a lot about Firdaus's character and her inability to attain her desired joy. One example is her forced betrothal to an older man who tortures and maltreats her. She suffers immensely and runs away from home into the streets.

Furthermore, Firdaus was subjected to genital mutilation as a child. She laments profusely about her inability to rise beyond her gender, beyond what the world considers her limits, and beyond her blurry life. She also witnesses the persistent rancor between her parents. El Saadawi writes about Firdaus:

Figure 8.1 Nawal El Saadawi

My father, a poor peasant farmer, who could neither read, nor write, knew very few things in life. How to grow crops, how to sell a buffalo poisoned by his enemy before it died, how to exchange his virgin daughter for a dowry when there was still time, how to be quicker than his neighbour in stealing from the fields once the crop was ripe. How to bend over the headman's hand and pretend to kiss it, how to beat his wife and make her bite the dust each night.[10]

As the story progresses, Firdaus craves to be educated. She tells her uncle about her passion for school, but he scorns and abandons her instead of encouraging her. This also shows how hard it is for a female child to get educated in a male-dominated society, which makes her sad and discouraged. Most times, women are relegated to the kitchen and denied the chance to lead, act, and contribute to the development of their countries. This has caused a lot of indifference and disdain on the part of women who are suppressed and subjugated by men. El Saadawi narrates:

'What will you do in Cairo, Firdaus?'
And I would reply: 'I will go to El-Azhar and study like you.'
Then he would laugh and explain that El-Azhar was only for men. And I would cry, and hold on to his hand as the train started to move. But he would pull it away with a force and suddenness that made me fall on my face.[11]

Firdaus faces the world and strives despite the mammoth challenges that waylay her. She moves from one place to another, searching for survival. She later succumbs to the pressure of her society and becomes an object to men. Her troubled life leads her to Bayoumi, who trades her body with his friends. Firdaus recollects this in distress:

He took to locking me in the flat before going out. I now slept on the floor in [the] other room. He would come back in the middle of the night, pull the cover away from me, slap my face, and then bear down on me with all his weight. I kept my eyes closed and abandoned my body. It lay there under him without movement, emptied of all desire, or pleasure, or even pain, feeling nothing.[12]

Bayoumi strips her of her innocence, her pride, and dignity as a woman. He uses her like a whore and then dumps her, after which she takes to the streets for survival.

All the while, there is silence denser than darkness in her life. Firdaus has passed through a lot, especially from the beginning of her life. Her first sexual experience happened in a field. There are moments when she feels the desire to die, the zeal to break away from the world, and the courage to be alone, bereft of men. There are moments when she feels the whole world is against her, moments when she desires something that she will never possess because she is a woman, an invisible being in a patriarchal society.

Like in many African societies, Firdaus's life is tethered to the fact that she cannot become whatever she wants to be until she has a man by her side and acknowledges that he is the most important being since the creation of the world. Firdaus struggles all her life in a severe and unfriendly society where she encounters severe discrimination and harshness. She turns to prostitution but does it in a classy way. Firdaus is not interested in every man, nor does she consider every man her mate or someone who can take advantage of her body. She sets an incomparable standard for herself, which helps her find temporary freedom. But this ends when she stabs an influential pimp. She says, as narrated by El Saadawi:

> I might not kill a mosquito, but I can kill a man. He stared at me once again, but this time only very quickly, then said, 'I do not believe it', how can I convince you that what I say is true? 'I do not really know how you can do that; so I lifted my hand high up and landed it violently upon his face.[13]

Firdaus is eventually arrested and sentenced to death by hanging. Her story reveals how inhumanity and gender oppression thrive and how every woman is a metaphor for death. Firdaus does not deserve to die, but in this book, readers learn about what life means to be a woman and what it means to be a Firdaus in society:

> Now I am waiting for them. After a while they will come to take me away. Tomorrow morning I shall no longer be here. I will be in a place which no one knows. This journey to an unknown destination, to a place unknown to all those who live on this earth, be they king or princes, or ruler fills me with pride. All my life I was looking for something that would fill me with pride, something that would make me hold my head high, higher than the heads of everyone else, especially kings, princes and rulers.[14]

Her life ends mysteriously. She is hanged because she fights and protests the persistent oppression she faces from men. Firdaus symbolizes women who have tried their best to proclaim their liberty but have been tamed and quelled from doing this, and are thus forced to fight for their freedom in a hard way.

The Paradoxical Home: Interrogating Cultural Purity and "(Un)homeliness" in the East African Memoir

It is important to recall that the phases and changes of African prose fiction are connected to African historical experiences. During the colonial and neocolonial periods, prose works in East Africa became more prominent and radical. Besides the struggle for independence and other sociocultural problems, the question of land ownership distinguished or characterized this area, particularly in Uganda and Kenya. There is also a continual item for conflict, which is represented in the region's literature. According to Diaw Djiby:

> At this stage the bulk of African literary productions is about the disastrous situation which has prevailed in Africa in the first years of independence. More than the protest, the literary productions at this stage aimed also at awakening ignorant people, that is to say African masses. This sort of literature aimed at inviting the Africans to resist against black leaders who were carrying on white domination and to partake in the reconstruction of Africa which was ruined by imperialism.[15]

In his memoir, *One Day I Will Write About This Place*, Binyavanga Wainaina makes a profound statement concerning cosmopolitanism that sums up the Afropolitan creed.

He advocates for permissiveness and broad-mindedness in the world.[16] It should be noted that, although he writes about Africa, he does not focus on war and pestilence or the political instability and economic retrogression that plague postindependence African countries. Wainaina realizes that tolerance and liberalism are of great significance in the postmodern world where borders, which may be approximated to home, are flexible. He becomes conscious of the fact that the appreciation of cultural contamination, not purity, will afford every individual a sense of being at home across spaces in the world.

Wainaina emphasizes the need for tolerance. He remarks, "We avert conflict every day with the smallest of things. If there is no law, no order, what keeps us together? Faith in the future? Not really, but we have to build a common body language of a sort. We have to be extra considerate to each other."[17] The writer also avers that the flexibility of the postmodern world comes with diverse opportunities, and it takes a cosmopolitan mind to explore its profitability. He stresses the need for individuals to be flexible enough to find their place in the world and endorses cosmopolitanism and mobility when he refers to the fact that a passport can bring limitless opportunities.

> Which face do you pick to meet chaos? The one built from the ground up, baring all your past, all your scars? Or the adopted one, wired to a certain manner that you have discovered will open doors to the scholarshipped, résuméd […] and the piece of stamped paper that promises that you will inherit the earth.[18]

Figure 8.2 Binyavanga Wainaina

Wainaina's memoir chronicles the recollections of his experiences in several parts of Africa, from childhood to maturation. The expression, "this place," which signifies his home, Africa—Kenya in particular—divulges the intrinsically enigmatic nature of the concept "home." Wainaina reveals the realities in postindependence Africa by recalling his sojourn through different parts of Africa, like Kenya, South Africa, Togo, Nigeria, and Ghana. Like other Afropolitans, Wainaina does not dwell on issues revolving around Afro-pessimism. Rather, he reveals that Africa is bedeviled and burdened by a sense of difference and a lack of cultural tolerance. He maintains that progress in Africa is stampeded by a lack of psychical cosmopolitanism, which has made the continent everything but home to its inhabitants.

The story revolves around the protagonist, Wainaina, who takes the reader through his journey in life. The memoir starts with a child-like narration, with a playful and unaffected tone. This changes as maturation begins, and the protagonist discovers shocking events that make his environs repulsive. The protagonist struggles to find a place in society. His restless search for self-definition and a home puts him on constant mobility. Despite his sharp intellect, he migrates between African countries, trying futilely to get a university education and discover his purpose. He ends up fueling his passion as a writer and settling in the United States.

Wainaina's account of his formative experiences and maturation in Africa forms the nub of his memoir. The author subtly undermines Afro-pessimistic codes such as poverty, corruption, and war. He foregrounds the truth that "difference" and "otherness" are the major banes of development in Africa. Like the Afropolitans, he advocates for "cultural contamination."[19] The protagonist manages and survives all the demerits of the continent but is unable to comprehend the division and segregation, which is a product of ethnic and cultural differences.

Migration and cosmopolitanism are integral parts of Afropolitanism. For instance, Achille Mbembe, in his essay on Afropolitanism, outlines the necessity for mobility and intermingling of people within the continent. He opposes the consciousness of diversity that breeds "nativism."[20] *One Day I Will Write About This Place* is centered on intracontinental migration and the experiences of the migrants in their new spaces. Wainaina dwells on how postcolonial Africa is characterized by intracontinental and intercontinental migrations. He also reveals the postindependent travails of autocratic leadership, corruption, nepotism, and wars, among others. He references families and individuals dispersed abroad because of the restrictions imposed by their natal homes. However, the protagonist and author, Wainaina, displays some sense of cosmopolitan orientation in presenting the characters in his memoirs:

> Mary is from Buganda. She ran away to Kenya from Idi Amin. Many people are running to Kenya from Amin. We are Kenyans. Mum was born in Uganda, but she is now a Kenyan. Baba is Kenyan. Kenya is a peace-loving nation. Kenya is not Uganda.[21]

With the impassive tone that accompanies child narration, Wainaina stresses his subject matter. The character, Mary, extricates herself from Uganda under Idi Amin's reign because the nation lacks the warmth and fondness a home should embody. Despite her national ties in Uganda, the protagonist's mother is barred from accessing the war-torn country because its borders are sealed. Wainaina realizes the fluidity and arbitrariness of home, and he infers that his mother, who is at home in Kenya, is no longer a Ugandan. His supposition accentuates that individuals in the diaspora can lay claim to more than one home and possibly prefer the non-natal space.

Wainaina grows up being frightful of his mother's home country. He says, "I grew up with her myths and legends and horrors, narrated with an intensity that only exiles can muster."[22] His mother's connection with Uganda is maligned because of the harsh experiences and sad memories Uganda embodies. Wainaina demonstrates the mutability and arbitrariness of home in diverse ways. In his movement across spaces and places, he meets characters with different dispositions to home. He says, "Ghana has no politics."[23] For Hubert, Ghana is home. He meets another character, Yves, whose natal home, Ivory Coast, is bedeviled by war. He remarks, "Who can survive there? There is war. I live in South London. And in Chad. I also live in Accra sometimes." Yves' rituals and relationships are most unlikely to be tied to Ivory Coast.[24] This represents and reconstructs the popular notion that migrants are often nostalgic and better off in their country of origin. Wainaina creates a twist, and possible subversion, in his memoir.

For Taiye Selasi, one's country of origin is not essentially one's home. She identifies restrictions like national policies and civil wars as factors that can create boundaries and borders within one's home.[25] While it is easy to assume that the economic conditions and sociopolitical instability in Third World countries, particularly African countries, will make citizens of such countries feel at home in developed countries, Wainaina suggests that different factors can make one decide where "home" is. The term "home" is slippery, and it escapes a definite description. Wainaina, who sees a great sense of insecurity in Kenya, coins out the word "Nairobbery" from the country's capital, Nairobi. This suggests that insecurity puts a restriction on the protagonist in his home country.

In Wainaina's sojourn to the suburbs in Kenya, he meets a European who has a bar. His wife says, "he is Swiss but he only speaks French and Kamba [Kenyan dialect] … You know Europeans always have strange ideas. He is Kamba now; he doesn't want anything to do with Europe."[26] The Swiss immigrant, for reasons undisclosed, is more at home in Kenya than in his country of origin. Correspondingly, Wainaina is excited to leave his home country for South Africa. He sees the urban setting he has always fantasized about, and this creates the idea of a home and the feeling that Kenya is not worthy of being termed a "home":

> I know now I am on a highway to everywhere. I can get on an escalator with no jostling, no moving, and let machines carry me all the way into the world I want: where there are no gaps in me. There are no background noises here, no whispers in many languages in this airport […] Fuck Kenya.[27]

Wainaina reveals that home is arbitrary; hence, defining or trying to understand an individual by narrow constructs like nationality and race is impracticable. Wainaina foregrounds that, like the home, identity is ever-changing and unstable in the postmodern world. Indices of identity like passport, language, and experiences are largely dependent on home. His maternal family, who are originally Ugandans, have their homes in different parts of the world because their natal home is unreceptive and hostile. These people are conditioned to feel at home in places other than Uganda:

> Although they are very close, they haven't been together since 1961. Visas, wars, closed borders, and a thousand triumphs of chaos have kept them apart. [...] In two days, we feel like a family. In French, Swahili, English, Gikuyu, Kinyarwanda, Kiganda, and Ndebele we sing one song, a multitude of passports in our luggage.[28]

Afropolitans maintain that the notion of having a singular conventional home is almost unobtainable in the postmodern world, where migration is an integral part of the social world order. The dissolution of borders and promotion of mobility has subtly displaced the stereotyped meaning of home. Restrictions in one's "home" inspire migration, especially westward migration. Migration opens grounds for multiculturalism and "multilocality," which exposes migrants and cultural hybrids to diverse homes. Wainaina states, "We are children of the Cold War ... we watched our countries crumple like paper. Rwandese, Kenyans and others are pouring into Congo, Tanzania, Kenya. Then, Kenya shook and those who stood are pouring into South Africa."[29]

This multiplicity of experiences and exposure to diverse cultures that result from migration have effects on the perception and definition of home. Selasi argues that a country, which is home in this context, is fictitious because countries are just sovereign states created around 400 years ago. They can be destroyed and remade; hence, they should not have an overbearing presence or a degree of permanence in determining a person's home and identity.[30] Wainaina expresses this thought in *One Day I Will Write About This Place* when he observes the instability that different countries in Africa have undergone over the years. He avers that a country that may be home today may, for some reasons, cease to offer the warmth of a home in another season.

Wainaina reveals that Kenya deteriorates and stumbles under the weight of political tussle while Uganda rises and advances toward stability. This reality will presumably have effects on a citizen's perception of both countries. It poses another demerit of a singular home and the primacy of home in identity configuration:

> And brewing inside this space, from fifty or so ethnic history and angles, is Kenya-a thing still unclear, picking here, marrying across, choosing there; stealing here, and there- disemboweling that which came before, remaking it [...] on the whims of our imperial presidents, Kenyatta and Moi. [...] Uganda is different, this is a country that has not only reached the bottom of the hole countries sometimes fall into, it has scratched through that bottom [...] now it has rebuilt itself [...] gives me hope that this continent is not, finally, incontinent [...] Uganda was my childhood bogeyman, and now Kenya teeters, and Ugandans everywhere are asking me what is wrong with us.[31]

Wainaina lays a resounding emphasis on the notion that a cosmopolitan mindset will help immigrants feel at home across spaces in the world. Since migration is almost inevitable in the postmodern world, a renewed orientation toward inclusion is pertinent. Stephanie Santana remarks on how Wainaina describes cosmopolitanism in Africa, where urbanites speak five languages.[32] Cosmopolitanism is accompanied by inquisitiveness, deep interest, and a quest to understand other cultures and people. Wainaina observes how his parents are proficient in many languages. His Ugandan-Kenyan mother speaks Kinyarwanda, Bufumbira Luganda, English, and Kiswahili, while his father speaks Gikuyu, Kiswahili, and English.[33] The protagonist's parents, in this light, demonstrate a sort of acknowledgment and interest in the cultures of the language they speak. This instance privileges open-mindedness and cultural contamination as against nativism and difference.

Furthermore, Wainaina's memoir endorses cultural contamination, as he is the product of such a family. His central characters are of mixed African heritage. He also acknowledges the existence of mixed races like Kenyan Indians and Kenyan Asians. He once came across a "Togolese Nigerian super striker, Sheyi Emmanuel Adebayor," who plays football for Togo and not Nigeria.[34] Such encounters come with various little stories that, most likely, will end in the fact that Togo is more of a home than Nigeria to the player. Wainaina reveals that, in the postmodern and cosmopolitan world, the connection between identity and home and the individual is typically arbitrary and not based on social conventions or the status quo.

According to Ato Quayson, "some versions of postmodernism emphasize the inherent instability and playfulness of identity."[35] Little Wainaina is aware of the fact that his name is Ugandan. He adopts a preferred identity and affiliation by insisting that the name has ceased to be Ugandan and has become a Gikuyu. He also identifies his family as one lacking cultural purity: "I am Binyavanga, after my mother's father, and so on. So Binyavanga becomes a Gikuyu name. We are mixed-up people. We have mixed-up ways of naming too: the Anglo colonial way, the old Gikuyu way ..."[36]

The Wainainas, in *One Day I Will Write About This Place*, also share the Afropolitan trait of erudition. The principal character, although often troubled, demonstrates intelligence. Wainaina derives pleasure from reading and studying anything that crosses his path. He and his sister, Ciru, lead their classes in their various schools. When he meets his cousins in Uganda, he realizes that "All the Binyavanga children do very well in school. Many of them go to the top schools; in Buganda ... Kamanzi and Henry are always top of their class at St. Mary's Kisubi. Eventually they move to South Africa, they teach at Universities there."[37] He comments on his family's intellectual traits and how they end up migrating to other parts of Africa. It can be deduced and extended that the Binyavanga are scholars who eventually become cultural hybrids, as many of them move out of their home to take up professional positions in other spaces. Wainaina, at the end of the novel, ends up leaving Kenya for the United States.

Although critical in their assessment of Africa, Afropolitans do not sever ties and relationships with the continent. Instead, they contend that individuals should not be understood only in terms of their nationality. In like manner, Wainaina ridicules people's attempts to "Europeanize" themselves and deny their connection to the continent. He scorns the exaggerated mannerisms of some returnees. Wainaina makes an example of a Kenyan woman who claims to be more German than the Nazis until she gets drunk and loses control over her false embellishments:

They exist only to be measured against the wrong-looking Hollywood powder now visible on her face. But rightness and coolness cannot be faked [...] the curtain of face powder has opened, and there they are; three small dark tribal marks [...] three deliberate, immovable lines on her face.[38]

The playfulness and fluidity of identity are traceable to cultural impurity and contamination. Individuals, who have interacted with multiple cultures, particularly across spaces, may eschew laying claims to a singular identity. Wainaina, in this memoir, endorses cultural contamination and plurality. His protagonist, Binyavanga, conjures up images of a culturally cosmopolitan personage, Wambui, a Gikuyu-Scottish prostitute. This fictional heroine is adventurous in an unbridled way, and she has multiple personalities. This character, in his imagination, is cosmopolitan; she retains multiethnic affiliations. Wainaina subtly infers that cultural multiplicity is integral to a meaningful existence in the postmodern age:

Wambui is broken English, slangy Kiswahili, Gikuyu inflections. She is Millie Jackson. A Malloon Commaddo. She is a market woman [...] Wambui is Gikuyu by fear, or Kenyatta title deed, or school registration, or because her maternal uncle paid her father's fees or because they chose a Gikuyu name to get into a cooperative scheme in the seventies.[39]

As Wainaina matures, he realizes that his home country placed some limitations on him. Although a son of the soil and part of the continent, he feels a sense of rejection and alienation in Kenya. He is distraught by the constraints caused by corruption, unfavorable government policies, tribalism, unemployment, lack of serenity, and much more. He visits Nairobi with his father and senses a lack of opportunity and aborted dreams, and he is triggered to crave a better place:

[...] ten thousand languages all shouting, ten thousand specialists of ten thousand metals arranged into ten thousand loud permutations to fix cars, tractors [...] many people have certificates. Marketing. Carpentry, [...] Electrical technology. This is the dump site for certificates that did not send you anywhere [...] I rubbed my hand along my jacket's shoulder pads, thrilled at its padded promises in this clanging world. I am different. I am different [...][40]

One Day I Will Write About This Place explores the dynamics of intracontinental migrations. It reveals how the feeling of alienation and nostalgia is not a product of a hostile reception but of the strain of a psychical repositioning of the mind, which is required to negotiate new social constructs. Sydoine Moudouma remarks, "The process of migrating from a familiar place transforms the individual who has to negotiate new social formations."[41] Wainaina gets nostalgic and becomes a recluse in South Africa because it is fraught with sexism and sexual abuse, racism, violence, intermittent liberation struggle, radical political activism, "gangsterism," and juvenile delinquency. On two occasions, he forfeits his academic pursuits because he is not at home in South Africa:

I am desperate to go home. But I do not know what I will do there without a degree, with no money [...] I am now an illegal immigrant [...] I have failed to let myself disappear into the patterns of a school where there is no punishment, no bell [...] for I am not at home, and don't much care for the approval of people here [...]⁴²

The memoir is a representation of a space bereft of cosmopolitanism. Afropolitans deconstruct the perception that color and racial bias are some of the major causes of "unbelongingness" in diasporic spaces. Wainaina's memoir foregrounds the fact that ethnic and cultural segregation make people alienated within their own continent. Sameness of race is undermined by prejudiced clichés, as well as ethnic, cultural, and religious differences, which make the natal home unreceptive. Chielozona Eze advocates for "the enunciation of conviviality, cultural contamination, and hyperculturality, among other postmodern terms, that disrupt essentialist and oppositional notions of African identity."⁴³ Wainaina portrays the clamor for cultural purity and ethnic differentiation as restrictive factors within the African continent.

While racism is a buzzword in intercontinental migrant writings, xenophobia can be approximated to racism on an intracontinental scale. Despite the sameness of race, some host countries within Africa display hostility to migrants in ways that ridicule ideologies such as Afrocentrism, Black Nationalism, and Pan-Africanism. The protagonist relates how their gardener, Cleophas, a Kenyan, always was a victim of incessant arrests during Kenyatta's regime because he looks like a Ugandan. This factor can make Cleophas desire a better space and place outside his country of origin. During his stay in South Africa, Wainaina laments, "Three Mozambicans have been thrown off a train in Johannesburg. It is in the news. Black immigrants are being beaten daily now in Johannesburg."⁴⁴ The prejudiced maltreatment and abuse of black immigrants undermine claims of African solidarity.

Furthermore, the "they/us" binary opposition that is often ascribed to the West and the Centre in earlier discourses is narrowed down in Wainaina's memoir as segregation and difference, which create a polarity between immigrants and the citizens of their host countries within the continent. George, another black immigrant, tells Wainaina, "They don't like us because we remind them that they are still slaves."⁴⁵ Wainaina portrays the xenophobic tendencies among blacks in different parts of Africa as immigrants are received with hostility by citizens and indigenes of the host countries. Wainaina's mother, a Ugandan, who migrated to Nakuru, Kenya, encounters diverse difficulties and endures discrimination. She is openly humiliated and bullied in her shop by a Kenyan woman:

I am tired of this. Tired! You Ugandans spoiled your country—why do you want to come here and spoil ours? [...] [I]t is as if Kenya is over there, with the crowd, and behind us are the wedding women who have sided with Uganda [...] the wedding women have been shamed to silence.⁴⁶

Wainaina fully explores the diverse manifestations of tribalism in his memoir. He debunks stereotyped assumptions, especially in earlier migrant writings, that Blacks are often subjugated by white hosts because of the pigment of their skin.

One Day I Will Write About This Place focuses on intracontinental migration and opens up new discussions on the migrants' experience in diasporic spaces. During his stay in

South Africa, Wainaina comments on the existence of "reverse racism." He observes the maltreatment of white South Africans by black South Africans who still feel the sting of apartheid. This leads to an uproar from white kids who feel restricted by the unjust social structure. Wainaina comments, "This country has all its defenses up. Everybody is screaming and jostling for space … young white kids shrilling, 'Emigrate, we are emigrating to Australia because of affirmative action, which is, racism in reverse.'"[47] This circumstance also highlights that racism is multidimensional and essentially a manifestation of narrow-mindedness, insularity, and exclusion-complex, and not always about color. Wainaina undermines color in issues of inclusion and exclusion, and he gives primacy to the cosmopolitan trait of broad-mindedness and nonjudgmental mentality when he makes an example of white South Africans who express great love for Brenda Fassie's local numbers.

In recent times, on South Africa, Gabeba Baderoon writes, "the reality of contemporary South Africa is tough and expensive, often violent, and sexually predatory, often fatally xenophobic. South African literature deals directly with these realities."[48] Also, Allan Kolski Horwitz notes that "… the immediate post-apartheid period has also been characterized by: mass unemployment, coarse materialism, widespread sexual and criminal violence, large-scale corporate and state corruption and deadly epidemics of HIV/AIDS and tuberculosis."[49]

The struggle for the eradication of the South African apartheid regime came into manifestation in 1994, but, contrary to expectations wound around the supposed "new era" (the post-apartheid South African period), the attainment of the desired freedom and equality as at the end of the apartheid only marked a transition to extended apartheid. Thus, the eradication of the apartheid system turned out sour—a grand disillusionment—and the citizens and the agitators for the emancipation struggle were faced with a new struggle: internal strife.

In light of the new era, there is a change of thematic preoccupation from freedom agitation prevalent during the apartheid regime to one reflective of hope. Trevor Noah's memoir, *Born a Crime*, vividly presents the themes of communitarianism as an ideal way of life in post-apartheid South Africa. As mentioned earlier, the memoir has been greatly informed by the plethora of themes and fascinating stories it holds due to the navigation of different spaces by contemporary memoirists. Noah fits into this category as he is closer to his natal home and an immigrant in the United States too. Through his memoir, which is more of his childhood experiences in South Africa, he points to the emergence of a space that is resistant in nature in a bid to predict and present a South African future that will have the capacity to transform how citizens will navigate such space socially.

Throughout his memoir, Noah employs totems of postmodernism and reconstructive terms to aptly suggest that the social spaces of Apartheid tend to produce dynamic possibilities. Noah seeks to dwell on the transformative capacity of the audacious combination of the particularistic and universalistic balance on the notion of place in South Africa, which can be situated in a postcolonial setting. In finding and maintaining the peculiarity of the South African region, he emphasizes the presentation of the self and community inferences, as it is viewed from the lens of the apartheid and post-apartheid regime, to offer a reading that has implications globally in postcolonial contexts, which is often a fluid model promoted by many South African writers.

Conclusion

Notably, African writers are committed to making society a better place, regardless of the traditional perceptions portrayed in memoirs. They not only display aesthetic sensibilities in their art, but they also extend their creativity toward the state of social affairs. It is also observed that, despite regional peculiarities, there are connecting factors between the four regions of the North, South, East, and West that all give the memoir the designation of African Literature, which are the traditions, the culture of the people, and the similarity of beliefs and sociopolitical experiences.

In the narrative theory, every narration adds to a network of conversations about life. Narrated autobiographical memory adds to these conversations, enhances social interaction, and allows individuals to better understand others and empathize with them. Identity delineation and problem-solving are goals in self-writing. A self-writer encourages a positive reassessment of the self by others to facilitate new relationships. In real life, people constantly reinvent themselves in a narrative to ensure their continued relevance and maintain their sense of importance based on their relationships with other people. In his essay "Autobiography and Historical Consciousness," Karl Weintraub notes that self-identification is bound to the identification of the dominant bloodline. The quality of a man depends on the quality of his descent and consciousness.[50]

Thus, African prose fiction or faction are functional within their geographical space because they ensure that the sociocultural concepts dear to the people of the continent are not truncated despite recent history and discouraging neocolonial experiences. Therefore, African prose fiction and faction are significant in contemporary society and the world in general. Memoirs are simply about memories, and memories maintain an inseparable relationship with historical facts.

Notes

1 James Olney, *Autobiography: Essays Theoretical and Critical* (Princeton: Princeton University Press, 1980).
2 John Eakin, *Living Autobiography: How We Create Identity in Narrative* (Ithaca: Cornell University Press, 2008).
3 Caroline Bretell, *Blurred Genres and Blended Voices: Life History, Biography, Autobiography and the Auto/Ethnography of Women's Lives* (Oxford: Berg, 1997), 228.
4 Oyekan Owomoyela, "The Question of Language in African Literatures," in *A History of Twentieth Century African Literature*, ed. O. Owomoyela (Lincoln: University of Nebraska Press, 1993), 349.
5 Oyeniyi Okunoye, "Francophone West African (Negritude) Poetry," in *Studies in Poetry*, eds. A. O. DaSylva and O. B. Jegede (Ibadan: Stirling-Horden Publishers, 2005), 125.
6 Martin Lewis, "One Hundred Million Frenchmen: The 'Assimilation' Theory in French Colonial Policy," *Comparative Studies in Society and History* 4, no. 2 (1962): 129–153.
7 Camara Laye, *The African Child* (Paris: Plon, 1953).
8 Nawal El Saadawi, *Woman at Point Zero* (London: Zed Books Print, 1975).
9 El Saadawi, *Woman at Point Zero*, 11.
10 El Saadawi, *Woman at Point Zero*, 12

11 El Saadawi, *Woman at Point Zero*, 16.

12 El Saadawi, *Woman at Point Zero*, 50.

13 El Saadawi, *Woman at Point Zero*, 99.

14 El Saadawi, *Woman at Point Zero*, 101.

15 Diaw Djiby, "Elitism in Ngugi Wa Thiong'o's Devil on the Cross and Petals of Blood" (Unpublished Thesis, Gaston Berger University, 2005).

16 Stephanie Santana, "Exorcizing Afropolitanism: Binyavanga Wainaina Explains Why 'I Am a Pan-Africanist, not an Afropolitan' at ASAUK 2012," *Africa in Words*, February 8, 2013, https://africainwords.com/2013/02/08/exorcizing-afropolitanism-binyavanga-wainaina-explains-why-i-am-a-pan-africanist-not-an-afropolitan-at-asauk-2012/.

17 Santana, "Exorcizing Afropolitanism"; Gemma Solés, "Wainaina on Afropolitanism," *UrbanAfrica. net*, April 4, 2014, https://www.urbanafrica.net/urban-voices/wainaina-afropolitanism/.

18 Binyavanga Wainaina, *One Day I Will Write About This Place* (Lagos: Farafina, 2013), 228.

19 Chielozona Eze, "Rethinking African Culture and Identity: The Afropolitan Model," *Journal of African Cultural Studies* 26, no. 2 (2014): 234–247.

20 Achille Mbembe, "Afropolitanism," in *Africa Remix: Contemporary Art of a Continent*, eds. Simon Njami and Lucy Durán (Johannesburg: Johannesburg Art Gallery, 2007), 26–30.

21 Wainaina, *One Day I Will Write About This Place*, 16.

22 Wainaina, *One Day I Will Write About This Place*, 186.

23 Wainaina, *One Day I Will Write About This Place*, 263.

24 Wainaina, *One Day I Will Write About This Place*, 264.

25 Taiye Selasi, "Bye Bye Babar," *Callaloo* 36, no. 3 (2013): 528–530.

26 Wainaina, *One Day I Will Write About This Place*, 167.

27 Wainaina, *One Day I Will Write About This Place*, 115.

28 Wainaina, *One Day I Will Write About This Place*, 198–199.

29 Wainaina, *One Day I Will Write About This Place*, 128–129.

30 Selasi, "Bye Bye Babar."

31 Wainaina, *One Day I Will Write About This Place*, 188.

32 Santana, "Exorcizing Afropolitanism," 4.

33 Wainaina, *One Day I Will Write About This Place*, 15.

34 Wainaina, *One Day I Will Write About This Place*.

35 Ato Quayson, Postcolonialism: Theory, Practice or Process? (Cambridge: Polity, 2000), 593.

36 Wainaina, *One Day I Will Write About This Place*, 26.

37 Wainaina, *One Day I Will Write About This Place*, 217.

38 Wainaina, *One Day I Will Write About This Place*, 113.

39 Wainaina, *One Day I Will Write About This Place*, 60.

40 Wainaina, *One Day I Will Write About This Place*, 92–93.

41 Sydoine Moudouma, "Intra and Inter-Continental Migration and Diaspora and Contemporary African Fiction" (PhD thesis, University of Stellenbosch, 2000), iii.

42 Wainaina, *One Day I Will Write About This Place*, 130.

43 Eze, "Rethinking African Culture," 234.

44 Wainaina, Wainaina, *One Day I Will Write About This Place*, 128.

45 Wainaina, *One Day I Will Write About This Place*, 141.

46 Wainaina, *One Day I Will Write About This Place*, 22–23.

47 Wainaina, *One Day I Will Write About This Place*, 213.

48 Gabeba Baderoon, "Beauty in the Harsh Lines," *Interview with Amatoritsero Ede*, Sentinel Poetry (Online), no. 37, 3rd Anniversary Issue (2005), https://www.sentinelpoetry.org.uk/1205/interview.htm.

49 Allan Horwitz, "Is There 'New' Poetry in Post-Apartheid South Africa," in *Bootsoto: An Anthology of Contemporary South African Poetry*, eds. A. K. Horwitz and Ken Edwards (Hastings: Reality Street, 2009), 7.

50 Karl Weintraub, "Autobiography and Historical Consciousness," *Critical Inquiry* 1, no. 4 (1975): 825.

BIBLIOGRAPHY

Abimbola, Wande. *The Sixteen Great Poems of Ifa*. Ibadan: The University Press, 2014.

Abouzeid, Leila. *Return to Childhood*. Austin: Center for Middle Eastern Studies, The University of Texas, 1998.

Abraham, Roger. *African Folktales*. New York: Pantheon Books, 1995.

Achebe, Chinua. *There Was a Country: A Personal History of Biafra*. New York: The Penguin Press, 2012.

Adebayo, Aduke. "Tearing the Veil of Invisibility: The Roles of West African Female Writers in Contemporary Times." In *New Visions of Creation: Feminist Innovations in Literary Theory*, edited by María Elena de Valdés and Margaret R. Higonnet, 37–56. Tokyo: University of Tokyo Press, 1993.

Adeniyi, Harrison. "Naming, Names, and Praise Names." In *Culture and Customs of the Yoruba*, edited by Toyin Falola and Akintunde Akinyemi, 85–97. Austin: Pan-African University Press, 2017.

Adeyemi, Sola. "Performing Arts." In *Culture and Customs of the Yoruba*, edited by Toyin Falola and Akintunde Akinyemi, 249–267. Austin: Pan-African University Press, 2017.

Afisi, Oseni. "Power and Womanhood in Africa: An Introductory Evaluation." *The Journal of Pan African Studies* 3, no. 6 (2010): 229–238.

Afolayan, Michael O. *Fate of Our Mothers*. Austin: Pan-African University Press, 2015.

Aisen, Ari, and Francisco Jose Veiga. "How Does Political Instability Affect Economic Growth?" *IMF Working Paper*, no. 11/12 (2011): 1–29.

Ajibade, George Olusola. "Animals in the Traditional Worldview of the Yoruba." *Folklore: Electronic Journal of Folklore* 30 (2005): 155–172.

_____. "Cults, Secret Societies, and Fraternities." In *Culture and Customs of the Yoruba*, edited by Toyin Falola and Akintunde Akinyemi, 787–795. Austin: Pan-African University Press, 2017.

Ajibade, Mobolaji Oyebisi. "Death, Mourning, Burial, and Funeral." In *Culture and Customs of the Yoruba*, edited by Toyin Falola and Akintunde Akinyemi, 355–360. Austin: Pan-African University Press, 2017.

Akanji, Okunola Rashidi, and Ojo Matthias Olufemi Dada. "Oro Cult: The Traditional Ways of Political Administration, Judiciary System and Religious Cleansing Among the Pre-Colonial Yoruba Natives of Nigeria." *The Journal of International Social Research* 5, no. 23 (2012): 19–26.

Akinbiyi, Akinlabi, and Harrison Adeniyi. "The Language and Its Dialects." In *Culture and Customs of the Yoruba*, edited by Toyin Falola and Akintunde Akinyemi, 31–46. Austin: Pan-African University Press, 2017.

Akinjobi-Babatunde, Tosin. "Pawning, Pawnship, and Slavery." In *Culture and Customs of the Yoruba*, edited by Toyin Falola and Akintunde Akinyemi, 567–575. Austin: Pan-African University Press, 2017.

Al Jazeera. "Why Are Coups Common in Africa?" *Al Jazeera*, September 18, 2015. https://www.aljazeera.com/programmes/insidestory/2015/09/coups-common-africa-150917161949909.

Allen, Chris. "Understanding African Politics." *Review of African Political Economy* 22, no. 65 (1995): 301–320.

Anuolam, Charles. "Igbo Culture and Care for Life." PhD Dissertation, Universidad de Navarra, 1993.

Anyiam-Osigwe, E. O. "Man, the State and a Better World Order." In *Proceedings of the Fifth Session of the Emmanuel Onyechere Osigwe Anyiam-Osigwe Lecture Series*. Lagos: Osigwe Anyiam-Osigwe Foundation, 2003.

Assensoh, A. B. *A Matter of Sharing: My Memoir.* Austin: Pan African University Press, 2016.

Auma-Osolo, A., and N. Osolo-Nasubo. "Democratic African Socialism: An Account of African Communal Philosophy." *African Studies Review* 14, no. 2 (1971): 265–272.

Awolalu, Joseph O. "What Is African Traditional Religion." *Studies in Comparative Religion* 10, no. 2 (1976): 1–10.

Ayoola, Gabriel. "Livestock: Domestication and Species." In *Culture and Customs of the Yoruba*, edited by Toyin Falola and Akintunde Akinyemi, 537–550. Austin: Pan-African University Press, 2017.

Azania, Malaika Wa. *Memoirs of a Born Free: Reflections on the Rainbow Nation.* Johannesburg: Jacana Media, 2014.

Azeez, Ademola. "Ethnicity, Party Politics and Democracy in Nigeria: Peoples Democratic Party (PDP) as Agent of Consolidation?" *Studies of Tribes and Tribals* 7, no. 1 (2009): 1–9.

Babalola, S. A. *The Content and Form of Yoruba Ijala.* Oxford: Clarendon Press, 1966.

Babatunde, Emmanuel. *Kelebogile—I Am Grateful: An African Journey through Celibate Priesthood to Married Life.* Maitland: Xulon Press, 2018.

Baderoon, Gabeba. "Beauty in the Harsh Lines," *Interview with Amatoritsero Ede*, Sentinel Poetry (Online), no. 37, 3rd Anniversary Issue (2005), https://www.sentinelpoetry.org.uk/1205/interview.htm.

———. "This Is Our Speech: Voice, Body and Poetic Form in Recent South African Writing." *Social Dynamics* 37, no. 2 (2011): 213–227.

Bascom, William. "Folklore and Anthropology." *The Journal of American Folklore* 66, no. 262 (1953): 283–290.

Bayart, Jean Francois. *The State in Africa: The Politics of the Belly.* London and New York: Longman, 1993.

Beah, Ishmael. *A Long Way Gone: Memoirs of a Boy Soldier.* New York: Sarah Crichton Books, 2007.

Boulukos, George E. "Olaudah Equiano and the Eighteenth-Century Debate on Africa." *Eighteenth-Century Studies* 40, no. 2 (2007): 241–255.

Bourdieu, Pierre. "Social Space and Symbolic Power." *Sociological Theory* 7, no. 1 (1989): 14–25.

Bretell, Caroline. *Blurred Genres and Blended Voices: Life History, Biography, Autobiography and the Auto/Ethnography of Women's Lives.* Oxford: Berg, 1997.

Cbanga, Ibo. "Juju." *Encyclopaedia Britannica.* https://www.britannica.com/topic/juju-magic.

Chazan, Naomi, Peter Lewis, Robert Mortimer, Donald Rothchild, and John Ravenhill. *Politics and Society in Contemporary Africa.* Boulder: Lynne Rienner Publishers, Inc., 1992.

Chinweizu, L. "Gender and Monotheism: The Assault by Monotheism on African Gender Diarchy?" In *The Essentials of African Studies*, edited by Sophie Oluwole, 1–10. Vol. 1. Lagos: General African Studies Unit University of Lagos, 1997.

Daouda, Sekou. "34 Years After the Execution of Mohamed Sorie Fornah and 14 Others." *The Patriotic Vanguard*, July 21, 2009. http://www.thepatrioticvanguard.com/34-years-after-the-execution-of-mohamed-sorie-fornah-and-14-others.

Dasylva, Ademola. "Folklore, Oral Traditions, and Oral Literature." In *Culture and Customs of the Yoruba*, edited by Toyin Falola and Akintunde Akinyemi, 139–158. Austin, Texas: Pan-African University Press, 2017.

Dauda, Bola. "African Humanism and Ethics: The Cases of Ubuntu and Omolúwàbí." In *The Palgrave Handbook of African Philosophy*, edited by Toyin Falola and Adeshina Afolayan, 475–491. New York: Palgrave Macmillan, 2017.

De Beauvoir, Simone. *The Second Sex.* New York: Knopf, 1953.

De Certeau, Michel. *The Practice of Everyday Life.* Translated by Steven Rendall. Berkeley: University of California Press, 1984.

Derpanopoulos, George, Erica Frantz, Barbara Geddes, and Joseph Wright. "Are Coups Good for Democracy?" *Research & Politics* (2016): 1–7.

Descartes, R. *Meditations on First Philosophy.* Translated and edited by John Cottingham. Cambridge: Cambridge University Press, 2013.

Djiby, Diaw. "Elitism in Ngugi Wa Thiong'O' s Devil on the Cross and Petals of Blood." Unpublished Thesis, Gaston Berger University, 2005.

Diels, H. A., and W. Krantz. *Fragments of the Pre-Socratic Philosophers*. Philadelphia: University of Pennsylvania Press, 1968.

Doorenspleet, Renske, and Lia Nijzink, eds. *One Party Dominance in African Democracies*. Boulder: Lynne Rienner Publishers, 2013.

Eakin, John. *Living Autobiography: How We Create Identity in Narrative*. Ithaca: Cornell University Press, 2008.

El Saadawi, Nawal. *Woman at Point Zero*. London: Zed Books Print, 1975.

Emecheta, Buchi. *Head above Water*. London and Nigeria: Ogwugwu Afor, 2018.

Epicfehlreader. "Review: A Month & A Day by Ken Saro-Wiwa." *Epicfehlreader*, December 19, 2016. http://epicfehlreader.booklikes.com/post/1506168/a-month-a-day-a-detention-diary-memoir-by-ken-saro-wiwa.

Eze, Chielozona. "Rethinking African Culture and Identity: The Afropolitan Model." *Journal of African Cultural Studies* 26, no. 2 (2014): 234–247.

Falola, Toyin. *A Mouth Sweeter than Salt: An African Memoir*. Ann Arbor: University of Michigan Press, 2004.

_____, and Akintunde Akinyemi, eds. *Culture and Customs of the Yoruba*. Austin: Pan-African University Press, 2017.

Famule, Olawole. "Masks, Masque, and Masquerades." In *Culture and Customs of the Yoruba*, edited by Toyin Falola and Akintunde Akinyemi, 389–405. Austin: Pan-African University Press, 2017.

Forna, Aminatta. *The Devil That Danced on the Water: A Daughter's Quest*. New York: Grove Press, 2002.

Gbadegesin, Enoch Olujide. "Marriage and Marital Systems." In *Culture and Customs of the Yoruba*, edited by Toyin Falola and Akintunde Akinyemi, 721–730. Austin: Pan-African University Press, 2017.

Gbadegesin, S. *African Philosophy: Traditional Yoruba Philosophy and Contemporary African Realities*. New York: Peter Lang, 1991.

Gyeke, Kwame. *An Essay on African Philosophical Thought: The Akan Conceptual Scheme*. New York: Cambridge University Press, 1987.

Hoover, Dwight W. "The New Historicism." *The History Teacher* 25, no. 3 (1992): 355–366.

Horwitz, A. K. "Is There 'New' Poetry in Post-Apartheid South Africa?" In *Bootsotso: An Anthology of Contemporary South African Poetry*, edited by A. K. Horwitz and Ken Edwards. Hastings: Reality Street, 2009.

Ikeora, May. "The Role of African Traditional Religion and 'Juju' in Human Trafficking: Implications for Anti-Trafficking." *Journal of International Women's Studies* 17, no. 1 (2016): 1–18.

Ingham, Kenneth. *Politics in Modern Africa: The Uneven Tribal Dimension*. London: Taylor and Francis, 1990.

Kalu, Kenneth, Olajumoke Yacob-Haliso, and Toyin Falola, eds. *Africa's Big Men: Predatory State-Society Relations in Africa*. London: Routledge, 2018.

Kazeem, Fayemi Ademola. "Time in Yorùbá Culture." *Al-Hikmat* 36 (2016).

Kehinde, Ayo. "Story-Telling in the Service of Society: Exploring the Utilitarian Values of Nigerian Folktales." *Lumina* 21, no. 2 (2010): 1–17.

Kura, Sulaiman B. "African Ruling Political Parties and the Making of 'Authoritarian' Democracies: Extending the Frontiers of Social Justice in Nigeria." *African Journal on Conflict Resolution* 8, no. 2 (2008): 63–101.

Laye, Camara. *The African Child*. Paris: Plon, 1953.

Lewis, Martin. "One Hundred Million Frenchmen: The 'Assimilation' Theory in French Colonial Policy." *Comparative Studies in Society and History* 4, no. 2 (1962): 129–153.

Liberty Writers Africa. "France Collects Over $500 Billion from Former African Colonies Yearly as Colonial Tax." *Liberty Writers Africa*, October 10, 2019. https://libertywritersafrica.com/france-collects-over-500-billion-from-former-african-colonies-yearly-as-colonial-tax-outrageous/.

Madubuike, Okechukwu. "Party Dominance and Democracy in Nigeria: A Study of the Peoples' Democratic Party (1999–2007)." Thesis, University of Nigeria, Nsukka, 2007.

Mandela, Nelson. *Long Walk to Freedom: The Autobiography of Nelson Mandela*. Randburg: Macdonald Purnell, 1994.

Masoga, Mogomme Alpheus, and Temba Rugwiji. "A Reflection on Ritual Murders in the Biblical Text from an African Perspective." *Scriptura* 117 (2018): 1–13.

Masolo, Dismas A. *Self and Community in a Changing World*. Bloomington: Indiana University Press, 2010.

Mbembe, Achille. "Afropolitanism." In *Africa Remix: Contemporary Art of a Continent*, edited by Simon Njami and Lucy Durán. Johannesburg: Johannesburg Art Gallery, 2007.

Mbiti, J. S. *African Religion and Philosophy*. Nairobi: East African Educational Publishers, 1969.

Menkiti, Ifeanyi. "Community, Communism, Communitarianism: An African Intervention." In *The Palgrave Handbook of African Philosophy*, edited by A. Afolayan and T. Falola, 461–473. New York: Macmillan, 2017.

Moudouma, Sydoine "Intra and Inter-continental Migration and Diaspora and Contemporary African Fiction." PhD Thesis, University of Stellenbosch, 2000.

Mphahlele, Ezekiel. *The African Image*. Uppsala: Faber and Faber, 1962.

Myers, David Gersham. "The New Historicism in Literary Studies." *Academic Questions* 2, no. 1 (1989): 27–36.

Nagel, Thomas. "What it Is Like to Be a Bat." *The Philosophical Review* 83, no. 4 (1974): 435–450.

Njie, Cherno M. *Sweat Is Invisible in the Rain*. Austin: Pan-African University Press, 2020.

Noah, Trevor. *Born a Crime*. London: Spiegel and Grau, 2016.

Nthunya, Mpho. *Singing Away the Hunger: The Autobiography of an African Woman*. Bloomington: Indiana University Press, 1997.

Nwapa, Flora. *Efuru*. London: Heinemann, 1966.

Nyang, Sulayman S. "Politics in Post-Independence Gambia." *A Current Bibliography on African Affairs* 8, no. 2 (1975): 113–126.

Obasanjo, Olusegun. *My Command: An Account of the Nigerian Civil War 1967–1970*. Lagos: Kachifo, 2015.

Obiechina, Emmanuel. *Culture, Tradition and Society in the West African Novel*. Cambridge: Cambridge University Press, 1975.

Obioha, Uwaezuoke Precious. "Radical Communitarian Idea of the Human Person in African Philosophical Thought: A Critique." *Western Journal of Black Studies* 38, no. 1 (2014).

Ogbaa, Kalu. *Carrying My Father's Torch: A Memoir*. Durham: Carolina Academic, Press, 2014.

Ogungbemi, Segun. "Traditional Religious Belief System." In *Culture and Customs of the Yoruba*, edited by Toyin Falola and Akintunde Akinyemi, 309–319. Austin: Pan-African University Press, 2017.

Ogunlola, Layo. "Sports, Games, Recreation, and Leisure." In *Culture and Customs of the Yoruba*, edited by Toyin Falola and Akintunde Akinyemi, 745–755. Austin: Pan-African University Press, 2017.

Ojaide, Tanuri. *At Home, Away from Home: A Memoir*. Milwaukee: Cissus World Press, 2017.

Okrah, Kwadwo "The Dynamics of Gender Roles and Cultural Determinants of African Women's Desire to Participate in Modern Politics." *Journal of Global Engagement and Transformation* 2, no. 1 (2018): 1–15.

Okunoye, Oyeniyi. "Francophone West African (Negritude) Poetry." In *Studies in Poetry*, edited by A. O. Dasylva and O. B. Jegede. Ibadan: Stirling-Horden Publishers, 2005.

Oladosu, Olusegun. "Yoruba Indigenous Drums: An Aesthetic Symbol in Ecological Ritual of the Yoruba People." *European Scientific Journal* 11, no. 5 (2015): 214–230.

Olatubosun, Christopher Omolewu. "Taboo." In *Culture and Customs of the Yoruba*, edited by Toyin Falola and Akintunde Akinyemi, 445–455. Austin: Pan-African University Press, 2017.

Olawumi, A. T., S. A. Oluwalana, S. Momoh, and A. M. Aduraola. "Inventory of Plants Utilized in Oral Hygiene in South-Western Nigeria." *African Journal of Agriculture Technology and Environment* 6, no. 1 (2017): 89–105.

Olney, James. *Autobiography: Essays Theoretical and Critical*. Princeton: Princeton University Press, 1980.

Oluleye, James. *Architecturing a Destiny: An Autobiography*. Ibadan: Spectrum Books Limited, 2001.

Oluwole, Sophie B. *Socrates and Orunmila: Two Patron Saints of Classical Philosophy*. Lagos: Ark Publishers, 2015.

Omofoyewa, Kazeem Adebayo. "Idioms, Proverbs, and Dictums." In *Culture and Customs of the Yoruba*, edited by Toyin Falola and Akintunde Akinyemi, 99–111. Austin: Pan-African University Press, 2017.

Osaghae, Eghosa E. "The Study of Political Transitions in Africa." *Review of African Political Economy* 22, no. 64 (1995): 183–197.

Owolabi, K. "Edmund Husserl's Rehabilitation of Cartesian Foundationalism: A Critical Analysis." *Indian Philosophical Quarterly* 22, no. 1 (1995): 13–24.

Owomoyela, O. "The Question of Language in African Literatures." In *A History of Twentieth Century African Literature*, edited by O. Owomoyela. Lincoln: University of Nebraska Press, 1993.

Paris, Peter J. *The Spirituality of African Peoples. The Search for a Common Moral Discourse*. Minneapolis: Fortress Press, 1995.

Quayson, Ato. *Postcolonialism: Theory, Practice or Process?* Cambridge: Polity, 2000.

Raab, Diana. "Creative Transcendence: Memoir Writing for Transformation and Empowerment." *The Journal of Transpersonal Psychology* 46, no. 2 (2014): 1–21.

Rakotsoane, Francis C. L., and Antone A. Van Niekerk. "Human Life Invaluableness: An Emerging African Bioethical Principle." *Southern African Journal of Philosophy* 36, no. 2 (2017): 252–262.

Rodney, W. *How Europe Underdeveloped Africa*. London: Verso Books, 2018.

Stephanie Santana. "Exorcizing Afropolitanism: Binyavanga Wainaina Explains Why 'I Am a Pan-Africanist, Not an Afropolitan' at ASAUK 2012." *Africa in Words*, February 8, 2013. https://africainwords.com/2013/02/08/exorcizing-afropolitanism-binyavanga-wainaina-explains-why-i-am-a-pan-africanist-not-an-afropolitan-at-asauk-2012/.

Santana, Stephanie Bosch. "Exorcizing the Future: Afropolitanism's Spectral Origins." *Journal of African Cultural Studies* 28, no. 1 (2016): 120–126.

Saraci, Marinela. "An Exploration of Different Conceptions of Love and Friendship in 'An Ideal Husband.'" *Journal of Interdisciplinary Studies* 2, no. 4 (2013): 239–242.

Sardoc, Mitja. "The Anatomy of Patriotism." *Anthropological Notebook* 23, no. 1 (2017): 43–55.

Saro-Wiwa, Ken. *A Month and a Day: A Detention Diary*. London: Penguin Books, 1996.

Saro-Wiwa, Ken Jr. "Memoir: The Day My Father Was Killed." *The Cable*, October 18, 2016. https://www.thecable.ng/memoir-father-ken-saro-wiwa-jnr/amp.

Sartre, J. P. *Being and Nothingness: An Essay in Phenomenological Ontology*. Translated by Sarah Richmond. Abingdon: Routledge, 2018.

_____. *Existentialism Is a Humanism*. New Haven: Yale University Press, 2007.

Selasi, Taiye. "Bye Bye Babar." *Callaloo* 36, no. 3 (2005): 528–530.

Shaw, George Bernard. *Pygmalion*. London: Penguin Books, 1906.

Shmoop. "Study Guide: A Long Way Gone, Memoirs of a Boy Solider." *Shmoop*. https://www.shmoop.com/study-guides/literature/a-long-way-gone/summary#chapter-20-summary.

Simutanyi, Neo, and N. Mate. "One-Party Dominance and Democracy in Zambia." Paper, Framework of the Friedrich Ebert Stiftung Mozambique Regional Study on Dominant Parties and Southern Africa, 2006.

Smith, Pamela J. Olubunmi. "'E ku': Yoruba Greetings—A Protocol." In *Culture and Customs of the Yoruba*, edited by Toyin Falola and Akintunde Akinyemi, 69–83. Austin: Pan-African University Press, 2017.

Smits, Jeroen. "Ethnic Intermarriage and Social Cohesion. What Can We Learn from Yugoslavia?" *Social Indicators Research* 96, no. 3 (2010): 417–432.

Soetan, Segun. "Charms and Amulets." In *Culture and Customs of the Yoruba*, edited by Toyin Falola and Akintunde Akinyemi, 227–235. Austin: Pan-African University Press, 2017.

Sofela, Babatunde. "Colonialism and Culture: The Egba-British Encounter." *LASU Journal of African Studies* 6 (2012): 273–295.

Solés, Gemma. "Wainaina on Afropolitanism," *UrbanAfrica.net*. April 4, 2014. https://www.urbanafrica.net/urban-voices/wainaina-afropolitanism/.

Soyinka, Wole. *Ibadan: The "Penkelemes" Years—A Memoir: 1946–1965*. Ibadan: Spectrum Books, 1994.

———. "Neo-Tarzanism: The Poetics of Pseudo-Tradition." In *Art, Dialogue and Outrage: Essays on Literature and Culture*. London: Methuen, 1993.

———. *You Must Set Forth at Dawn*. New York: Random House, 2007.

Stets, J., and P. Burke. "Identity Theory and Social Identity Theory." *Social Psychology Quarterly* 63, no. 3 (2000): 224–237.

Thiong'o, Ngugi wa. *Wrestling with the Devil*. New York: The New Press, 2018.

Thyne, Clayton L., and Jonathan M. Powell. "Coup d'etat or Coup d'Autocracy? How Coups Impact Democratization, 1950–2008." *Foreign Policy Analysis* 12, no. 2 (2016): 192–213.

Tordoff, William. *Government and Politics in Africa*. 2nd ed. Basingstoke: Macmillan International Higher Education, 1993.

Tutu, Desmond. *God Has a Dream: A Vision of Hope for Our Time*. New York: Doubleday, 2004.

———. *God Is Not a Christian: Speaking Truth in Times of Crisis*. London: Rider Books, 2011.

Wainaina, Binyavanga. *One Day I Will Write About This Place*. Minneapolis: Graywolf Press, 2012.

Weintraub, Karl. "Autobiography and Historical Consciousness." *Critical Inquiry* 1, no. 4 (1975): 821–848.

White, Hayden. "New Historicism: A Comment." In *The New Historicism*, edited by Harold Veeser, 309–318. New York: Routledge, 2013.

INDEX